PRINCETON SEMINARY BULLETIN

VOLUME 29 | 2008

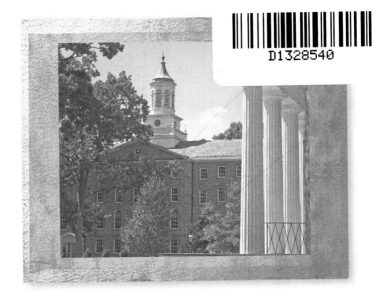

Stephen D. Crocco, Editor

Carol G. Carlson, Managing Editor

Mary M. Astarita, Editorial Adviser

PRINCETON
THEOLOGICAL SEMINARY

PRINCETON THEOLOGICAL SEMINARY

Iain R. Torrance, President

PRINCETON THEOLOGICAL SEMINARY

The Faculty, 2008–2009

Kenneth G. Appold
Charles L. Bartow
Shane Berg
C. Clifton Black II
John R. Bowlin
Michael A. Brothers
Sally A. Brown
Donald E. Capps
James H. Charlesworth
Ellen T. Charry
Stephen D. Crocco
Kenda Creasy Dean
James C. Deming
Frederick W. Dobbs-Allsopp
Nancy J. Duff
Robert C. Dykstra
Abigail Rian Evans
Richard K. Fenn
Beverly Roberts Gaventa
L. Gordon Graham
Nancy Lammers Gross
Darrell L. Guder
Geddes W. Hanson
Deborah van Deusen Hunsinger
George Hunsinger
Jeremy M. Hutton
W. Stacy Johnson
James F. Kay
Jacqueline E. Lapsley
Cleophus J. LaRue
Bo Karen Lee
Eunny Patricia Lee
Sang Hyun Lee
Bruce L. McCormack
Elsie Anne McKee
Kathleen E. McVey
Daniel L. Migliore
Gordon S. Mikoski
James H. Moorhead
Dennis T. Olson
Richard R. Osmer
George L. Parsenios
Yolanda Pierce
Luke A. Powery
Paul E. Rorem
Katherine Doob Sakenfeld
Choon-Leong Seow
Mark L. Taylor
Martin Tel
J. Wentzel van Huysteen
J. Ross Wagner
Richard Fox Young

Emeriti/ae

Diogenes Allen
James F. Armstrong
Richard S. Armstrong
William Brower
Jane Dempsey Douglass
Elizabeth G. Edwards
Karlfried Froelich
Freda A. Gardner
Thomas W. Gillespie
Scott H. Hendrix
James N. Lapsley Jr.
Conrad H. Massa
Ulrich W. Mauser
Paul W. Meyer
Patrick D. Miller
Samuel Hugh Moffett
Peter J. Paris
Luis N. Rivera-Pagán
J. J. M. Roberts
Charles A. Ryerson III
Max L. Stackhouse
John W. Stewart
Charles C. West
E. David Willis

Contents

The *Princeton Seminary Bulletin* is published twice a year by Princeton Theological Seminary, Princeton, New Jersey.

Each issue is mailed free of charge to all alumni/ae and, by agreement, to various institutions. Back issues are available online at: www.ptsem.edu/seminarybulletin/.

All correspondence should be addressed to Stephen D. Crocco, Editor, Princeton Seminary Bulletin, P.O. Box 821, Princeton, NJ 08542-0803; email: seminary.bulletin@ptsem.edu.

The *Princeton Seminary Bulletin* publishes lectures and sermons by Princeton Theological Seminary faculty and administrators and presentations by guests on the Seminary campus. Therefore, we do not accept unsolicited material.

This periodical is indexed in the *ATLA Religion Database*, published by the American Theological Library Association, 250 S. Wacker Dr., 16th Flr., Chicago, IL 60606; email: atla@atla.com; Internet: http://www.atla/com/; ISSN: 1937-8386; ISBN: 978-0-9644891-2-7.

Cover photo by Beckey White Newgren.

Editor's Note

After a long hiatus, the *Princeton Seminary Bulletin* is coming back to life, though with a different format. Faithful readers will recall that the last issue of the *Bulletin* was November 2007. In the months leading up to and following 2007, when the *Princeton Seminary Bulletin* reached its 100-year anniversary, the Seminary did a lot of soul searching about the future of the journal. The first question on everyone's mind was whether the *Bulletin* should continue. One hundred years is a good long run, and nothing lasts forever. The second question was, if it were to continue, should it continue in a paper format? I know some of you expected me to announce that the *Bulletin* would become an exclusively electronic journal. For now, the *Bulletin* will be published in electronic format, with the option to purchase a hard copy.

To make a long story short, I am delighted that the 2008 issue of the *Bulletin*—single volume—is now being published electronically and with a paper option. The electronic copy will be freely accessible. It will be prepared in a PDF format so that it can be printed. Readers who prefer a bound journal volume can order one and do so at a very reasonable price. Details for ordering will be available through the online version. The 2009 volume will soon be available and the 2010 volume is under preparation. We hope that this electronic edition will increase access to the *Bulletin*, while the paper option will serve readers and institutions that prefer a paper format. Regardless of format, the quality of the materials in the *Bulletin* remains high.

Not only does the *Princeton Seminary Bulletin* have a new format, it also has a new cover and schedule. Each year there will be one issue of approximately 200–300 pages. The *Bulletin* will continue to serve as the Seminary's "journal of record," with its primary purpose being to document the intellectual life of the Seminary by publishing the lectures, addresses, and sermons delivered on campus. However, that purpose is being broadened to include occasional special features originating a little farther beyond the usual Seminary orbit.

DOI: 10.3754/1937–8386.2008.29.1.1

This issue, for example, includes an excerpt from a new book on John Calvin by Pittsburgh Theological Seminary Professor Charles Partee, who earned his Ph.D. at Princeton Seminary in 1971. Partee's book is the fruit of his lifelong labors on John Calvin, and I am including an excerpt here to celebrate in 2009 the 500th anniversary of Calvin's birth. This issue also includes an address by Professor Jeffrey Stout of the Department of Religion at Princeton University. In 2007, Stout, a longtime friend of the Seminary, delivered the presidential address at the American Academy of Religion meeting in San Diego. An hour before Stout gave his address, and just down the hall, in the San Diego Convention Center, Professor Katharine Sakenfeld gave the presidential address at the Society of Biblical Literature. Delivered together and now published together, these addresses mark a proud moment for Princeton.

This issue of the *Bulletin* contains the usual rich fare of addresses, lectures, and sermons. Two things deserve special comment. The first is the address by Hans J. Hillerbrand commemorating the dedication of the papers of Wilhelm and Marion Pauck. Historians and theologians will recognize the Pauck name. A leading Reformation church historian in the liberal tradition, Pauck spent his career at Union Theological Seminary in New York, the University of Chicago, Vanderbilt Divinity School, and Stanford University. How did the Pauck papers end up at Princeton Seminary? A few years ago, when Marion Pauck was using our Paul Lehmann collection, she met the Special Collections staff and had the chance to see our facilities for processing, preserving, and storing manuscript collections. She was impressed and made provisions for the papers to be transferred to Princeton. Wilhelm and Marion may be best known for their biography of Paul Tillich. But as you might recall, they published only volume one of that biography. The material for the second volume—notes, drafts, interviews, etc.—is in the Pauck papers now awaiting examination by researchers.

The second piece deserving special comment is a spirited exchange between philosopher Brand Blanshard and theologian Thomas F. Torrance on the reception of Karl Barth in Scotland. This exchange, from the early 1950s, shows a high-level academic debate cast in the form of letters to the editor of *The Scotsman* in Edinburgh. Morag and Iain Torrance edited the letters.

As always, I welcome your responses, concerns, and suggestions.

STEPHEN D. CROCCO
EDITOR

Lectures

What Friends We Have in Jesus: The Leavening Effect of Transnational Mission Partnerships

by Marian McClure

Dr. Marian McClure gave this Frederick Neumann Memorial Lecture at Princeton Theological Seminary on February 11, 2008. Dr. McClure served as director of the Worldwide Ministries Division of the Presbyterian Church (USA) from 1997 through 2006. She holds a doctorate in political science from Harvard University and has written for various publications, including a foreword for A History of Presbyterian Missions: 1944–2004, *by Scott Sunquist and Caroline N. Becker (2008).*

When he stepped up to speak at the 1910 World Missionary Conference in Edinburgh, Scotland, nearly 100 years ago, the man who would later become the first Anglican bishop from India looked out at a room filled with 1,200 delegates. As he scanned their faces, Vedanayagam Samuel Azariah could not help but note that he was one of only seventeen delegates of color in Edinburgh for the historic mission conference he was about to address. Judging from the speech he gave, he must have been asking himself how he could move the senders of missionaries to improve the modes of cooperation with Christians in each mission location, especially in the context of colonialism. And he probably also wondered how he could convey the conviction that would later put him at odds with Mahatma Gandhi—the conviction that the transnational church of Jesus Christ is more powerful and effective for good than is nationalism.

Given this unique opportunity to communicate with the influential assembly, the bishop chose to deliver a speech titled "The Problem of Co-operation between Foreign and Native Workers." In his words, "Co-operation is assured when the personal, official and spiritual relationships are right, and is hindered when these relationships are wrong." His speech explained that personal relationships are right when modeled on Jesus being a friend to his disciples,

DOI: 10.3754/1937–8386.2008.29.1.3

coming alongside them. He said official relationships are right when one party is neither paymaster nor employer to the other and instead shows joy when one party decreases so that the other can increase. And he said that spiritual relationships are right when the foreign workers cultivate the forms of spirituality that are natural in a place, which in the case of India was mysticism. Concluding with now famous words, he said, "You have given your goods to feed the poor. You have given your bodies to be burned. We also ask for love. Give us friends!"[1]

Almost a century has passed. At the centenary celebration, "Edinburgh 2010," speakers will look out at a very different crowd of delegates. Instead of a gathering of Protestants only, they will see Protestant, Catholic, Orthodox, and Pentecostal Christians. Instead of a small, hand-picked group of people representing churches in the early stages of their establishment by mission efforts from the West, speakers will note that at least half the delegates are from areas other than Western Europe and North America, and they will see people from churches founded by Christians from the global South.

For all the dramatic changes in the course of a century, the importance of this topic of cooperation, of giving friends, of right relationships in mission, remains central for us and demands both a review and a look forward. The topic's relevance endures for a number of reasons.

Theologically, we confess that in Christ, God brings all people and all creation into right relationships, into reconciliation. The Church in mission serves as an exemplar of such relationships. The sent-ness of the church into the whole world makes the challenge of being exemplars of right relationship extremely dynamic and challenging. Change for all parties is the norm, not the exception. This dynamism is captured dramatically and concisely in Jesus's parable in Matthew 13:33: "The kingdom of heaven is like yeast that a woman took and mixed in with three measures of flour until all of it was leavened." There is an inescapable link between the results of God's reign at one level, the level of the loaf, and the chemistry, so to speak, of what is in the individual's heart and relationships. That is why the grand and cosmic vision of the church's place in salvation history in the first chapters of Ephesians ends with a prayer for specific individuals to be "rooted and grounded" in the love of Christ.

The continuing theological relevance of Bishop Azariah's focus on relationships in mission is joined by the continuing context of unequal distribution of power and wealth. In 1910 colonialism was deeply entrenched and colonial rulers

---

[1] Michael Kinnamon and Brian E. Cope, eds., *The Ecumenical Movement: An Anthology of Key Texts and Voices* (Grand Rapids: Eerdmans, 1997), 327–30.

seemed all-powerful. Sporadic resistance to oppression had not yet become massive movements for liberation. The geopolitics of planet Earth has changed since 1910, but today we face what most experts agree is an even greater maldistribution of resources and power.

To speak of love and friendship across the sharply drawn lines of power and wealth was and is remarkable. After all, friendship is rare in part because it is undermined by differences of social status and complicated by differences of language. And yet, Bishop Azariah's assertion about right relationships, his vision of global church friendships, *assumes* the existence of significant social and cultural differences. He was talking to people who had greater means at their disposal and was telling them how to have friendship in situations of inequality. His view of how to be friends in Jesus is a concise and practical summary of biblical marks of friendship, with especially deep echoes in the Gospel of John—"come alongside," "build up even when that involves self-sacrifice," and "be changed by the other" as one enters into the other's spirituality.[2]

As theologically apt as it was for the bishop to focus on right relationships in transnational mission, and as visionary as it was for him to call for such relationships to abound even in a context of significant worldly differences, what strikes me as most unusual is the notion that his audience could "give friends." Note that he did not say "send friends." He assumed the function of sending, but he saw something larger than that. Perhaps he saw that there is little that is random about who knows whom in this world. There are systems at work that generate and shape the opportunities people have to get acquainted and form bonds of friendship, and he was talking to some of the people in charge of those systems.

I have been privileged to be such a person. As I survey the literature on mission, I find that it looks closely at what happens when people encounter each other and the gospel message across every sort of boundary humans can invent. But the literature seems to give little attention to the systems in place for generating those encounters and guiding their content and longevity. In searching the titles of nearly 6,000 mission-related doctoral dissertations, I found only two dozen that contained related key words such as "friendship," "partnership," and "relationship" in the senses that I am exploring them here. There are, nevertheless, people who dedicate their vocational lives to "giving friends" for the life of the church, and I will describe them and the large structures that help them practice their very influential vocation.

---

[2] See especially John 3:28–30 and John 15:12–17.

There is no better time than now, in this era of globalization and conflict along religious or "civilization" lines, to assess the art and craft of giving friends. A short list of what is at stake in this matter of systems for giving friends would include how millions of people come to terms with the otherness of fellow human beings, what it means in practice to act like one body as Christians, how people receive and filter news of world events, and whether the fault lines between religions and cultures are reinforced or bridged.

Systems for Giving Friends

Today, there are three principal models for generating the opportunities to form transnational Christian friendships. These three models are so influential that they shape the destinations, purposes, and longevity of mission involvements of individuals who are not even aware of them.

The Nomadic Model

Some people, perhaps an increasing number, place themselves somewhere of their own choosing and pursue their call to mission. They do not wait for an agency to send them or for a certain amount of money to be raised. They may become tentmakers or entrepreneurs, but they seek to live the gospel in one place, or in multiple places, where they feel the Spirit wishes them to be. Samuel Escobar described this phenomenon in 1994 in relation to the larger debate about the new world order and with some hope that this pattern of self-placement would prove to be one of the ways evangelicals would continue turning away from imperial modes of mission.[3]

The Mapping Model

This large-scale system for forming transnational relationships works by efforts based on lists and maps and involves a belief that to reach unreached people, one must find and pass through previously unknown doors and windows. This model is mostly associated with the "frontier mission" movement. Those using this system to mobilize and place persons in mission, to cultivate relationships, and to translate the Bible follow a pattern based on lists of people in groups who lack self-sustaining and self-propagating Christian communities. Strategist Luis Bush coined the expression "10/40 window" to describe that portion of the world map

[3] Samuel Escobar, "Missions' New World Order," *Christianity Today* 38:13 (November 14, 1994): 48–52.

where most of the "least evangelized" people live today and where followers of this system are most likely to concentrate their efforts.[4]

The Family Model

What I will call the "family model" accepts, for the most part, the relationships that each denomination has inherited from its church's mission history and nurtures those relationships out of a sense of familylike relatedness and permanent commitment. New and additional relationships are forged, including for frontier mission work, usually in concert with members of the central family. The family model for transnational church relationships was embraced with special conviction by mainline Protestant denominations during the decolonization era after World War II. Earlier mission workers sent by these denominations had formed relationships and fostered the development of denominations, ecumenical ministries, and councils of churches.

It was believed that these relationships could be both the source and the venue for what God wanted to do with the parties involved for many years to come. It was believed—and this was influenced by the values of the cultures in which Western missionaries had worked—that our relational commitment was covenantal, including the traits of being open-ended and encompassing descendants. At its best this model holds what Christian ethicist Gilbert Meilaender calls the tension between *philia* and *agape*, that is, between preferential relationships and faithful permanent relationships.[5] This patient holding enlarges the "school for love," to borrow one of Calvin's memorable descriptions of the church, as Christ's disciples everywhere learn to be part of the ultimate community God is creating.

Describing the Family Model. I focus on the family model because it is the one I am most familiar with, and it is the ecosystem of transnational relations in which Princeton Seminary mainly lives. Another reason to fully describe it, tell some stories about it, and then make some remarks about its future is that this family model of transnational church relations concentrates enormous energy and resources on "giving friends." To understand the scope and impact of this model of relating is to assess one of the major responses given to Bishop Azariah by the descendents of the delegates present at the mission conference in Edinburgh in 1910.

[4] According to the AD 2000 and Beyond Movement's Web site, Luis Bush pinpointed the need for a major focus of evangelism in the "10/40 Window," a phrase he coined in his presentation at the Lausanne II Conference in Manila in July 1989 (http://www.ad2000.org/histover.htm; accessed July 1, 2008).

[5] Gilbert Meilaender, "Friendship and Fidelity," in *From Christ to the World: Introductory Readings in Christian Ethics*, ed. Wayne G. Boulton, Thomas D. Kennedy, and Allen Verhey (Grand Rapids: Eerdmans, 1994), 269.

The mainline churches' focus on long-term partnering relationships in mission has roots in the nineteenth century but experienced a milestone at the 1947 conference of the International Missionary Council. It was there that the expression "partnership in obedience" took hold and distinctions between older and younger churches were successfully challenged on theological grounds. During the ensuing geopolitical period of decolonization, the language and philosophy of "partnership" and "accompaniment" were elaborated in mission circles. For some, partnership is like a marriage. For some, accompaniment is more like an acceptance that in God's providence, we two are on the same road together as the disciples were on the road to Emmaus. Both philosophies are within the family model because of a de facto and long-term commitment to a known set of transnational relationships. New relationships are forged only at a pace befitting people who make a long-term commitment to one another.

In this context of choosing to be faithful in friendship with a given set of churches around the world, mainline denominations have developed systems and practices that do a great deal to "give friends." In addition to literally sending and receiving people, giving friends can also include mobilizing prayer, correspondence, advocacy, study, solidarity, and hospitality. To "give friends" to a church in another part of the world is to build an array of relationships that lead to many kinds of activities.[6] The theology and practice of right relationships in mission are subjected to trenchant review and improvement by scholars such as the PC (USA)'s Sherron K. George and Philip L. Wickeri, and are the subject of denominational policy statements such as *Presbyterians Do Mission in Partnership.*[7]

Area Specialists. A pivotal but almost wholly unstudied part of the system for giving friends grew mainly out of the need to change the way missionaries related to the churches that had become partner churches. Missions in various countries and regions had had their own leaders, usually chosen from among mission workers, and their own practices for relating to the "native workers," which is to say, the Christians in each place with whom the missionaries were working. To acknowledge the new status as a fellow denomination, it became important that leaders of the church in each place relate directly to the leaders of the sister churches and not just through their missionaries. This development

---

[6] Indeed, in the early 1970s, when it appeared to many in the U.S. churches that the day of sending missionaries might be coming to an end, there arose new forms of missionary life that focused precisely on transnational befriending, an excellent example of which is the association called "Bi-National Service."

[7] *Presbyterians Do Mission in Partnership* (Louisville: Ecumenical Partnership, Worldwide Ministries Division, 2001).

meant that denominational headquarters needed regional or area specialists for relating to this plethora of churches.

Variously termed "area directors," "regional leaders," "church relationship specialists," and so on, these multilingual and seasoned church statespersons have in common that they advise and shape most of the denominational processes that turn tens of millions of Americans toward specific Christian friends around the world for news, perspectives, and cooperation. The result has a significant impact on the voice for advocacy presented by U.S. denominations, the flow of people and resources, and at the level of members, the opportunities for spiritual transformation as part of the leavening action of God in the world.

In my own partial survey of Protestant denominations and conventions, I found five regional experts serving the combined offices of the Christian Church (Disciples of Christ) and the United Church of Christ, five with the Mennonite Mission Network, seven in the Evangelical Lutheran Church in America, four with the Reformed Church in America, and six with the PC (USA). There are eleven "regional leaders" serving the Southern Baptist Convention's International Mission Board today. Even in the denominations that function like global churches instead of national churches, one finds specialists in church relations who have regional assignments—seven of them, in the case of the United Methodist Church, for example.[8]

In all cases, the regional specialists are expected to help members of their denominations or constituencies relate to the Christian partners in each region. In addition, most of these church offices have at least one person who is a partnering consultant to help the grassroots of the church form good mission partnerships and promote formal programs designed to foster mission partnership relationships among the segments of each partnering denomination.

The most recent component developed to foster partnerships with old friends, at least in the PC (USA), is called "mission networks." These new networks provide individuals, congregations, and regional units a mechanism for coming together around the same partners, and they are therefore often focused on a particular country. Because of the repeated downsizings of central offices, the denominational staff members who helped form these networks attempted to ensure that long-standing partnership relations would continue to flourish even if the staff who nurtured them were no longer employed.

---

[8] The UMC's decision to be a global church rather than a national church affects its staffing for regions to some extent, and the UMC "Mission Contexts and Relationships" team includes more functions than providing area expertise for mission collaboration.

Indeed, the dedication of the partnership specialists comes in part from their being convinced that these relationships are crucial parts of what Princeton Seminary Dean Darrell Guder calls "the continuing conversion of the church." It is significant that Guder's book on that subject cites the impact of ecumenical work trips as one of his own early experiences of a congregation undergoing "conversion."[9]

To understand the scope and scale of the impact for friends around the world represented by denominations' retention of partnering specialists, it would be a mistake to look at the budgets of their offices. For the most part these people are brokers and persuaders, not grant makers or deciders.[10] A list of some of their principal functions in the family system of giving friends must at least include the following:

- Placing mission workers who are sent. Today, the majority of full-time and long-term mission workers sent by mainline churches are seconded at the request of long-standing mission partners or sent to places and ministries agreed upon by those partners, and area experts are active in these conversations. So in truth, mission workers are potential new friends sent by or because of old friends. They have a special role to play in incarnating the larger relationship, and that is why the best literature on friendship in mission emanates typically from them.[11] But at the system level, the family model's impact is that everyone who turns to mission workers for expertise, for prayer concerns, for devotional literature, and for mission interpretation work is hearing from someone whose life is profoundly shaped by a long-standing member of a particular transnational family of churches. Increasingly, mission workers from the United States are valued as much for being vectors (or "synapses") of relationships and partnerships as for being professionals in their own right, providing teaching, healing, and other services.[12]

---

[9] Darrell L. Guder, *The Continuing Conversion of the Church* (Grand Rapids: Eerdmans, 2000), 201.

[10] Many other staff supplement (and sometimes challenge) the expertise of the area specialists. In a 2006 survey to which fifty of eighty-three PC (USA) Worldwide Ministries Division staff responded, it was revealed that collectively these fifty worked in twenty-three languages, had lived 395 years in countries other than the U.S., had served 124.5 years under PC (USA) mission appointments, and had worked for the PC (USA) 704.5 years.

[11] Notably, see Philip L. Wickeri, "Friends along the Way: Spirituality, Human Relationships and Christian Mission," *Theology* XCIII:752 (March/April 1990): 101–8; and Philip L. Wickeri, "Friends along the Way: Attachment, Separation and the Way Forward," *Theology* XCIII:753 (March/April 1990): 179–90.

[12] Karla Koll uses the cognition-related term "synapse" in relation to mission workers, building on work by Sharon Erickson Nepstad, in Karla Ann Koll, "Struggling for Solidarity: Changing Mission Relationships between the Presbyterian Church (USA) and Christian Organizations in Central America during the 1980s," Ph.D. diss., Princeton Theological Seminary, 2003, 2.

- Requesting mission workers to be received. A small but growing function of partnerships is to recruit pastors and new church development specialists to come to the United States. Such requests often are conveyed by area specialists to a denominational partner in another country, who then may actually select, send, and even supervise these missionaries to the United States.

- Vetting grant proposals. Denominational programs and women's organizations in the church often use the tool of grants to support scholarships, fight hunger, collaborate in evangelism, and so on, and this kind of support adds up to scores of millions of dollars annually. Typically, regional experts are given an opportunity to comment on proposed uses of those dollars.

- Resourcing denominational advocacy. Whenever a denomination speaks out on an issue that affects members of its transnational family, often in response to a request originating with one partner church friend, an area expert's input is part of the process.

- Planning trips for leaders and press. When denominational executives, elected officials, and church-related journalists travel, their itinerary is developed by or in coordination with the area experts. Stories from these trips are therefore stories affected by long-standing friends.

- Shaping Web sites. Web sites have become a powerful tool for people seeking to connect in mission partnership. Denominations interested in giving friends in the family mode have responded by designing their sites so that people can easily find and support long-standing partners.

In summary, in the service of friendship and cooperation with brothers and sisters in Christ who have become family in a practical sense, an intentional ecosystem for "giving friends" has grown up in denominations, encompassing an impressive array of tools. These tools move attention, hearts, people, and funds toward specific relationships. They also give vitality to the large ecumenical family aggregations such as the World Alliance of Reformed Churches, the Lutheran World Federation, and others.

God's Leavening Work through Committed Friendships

With all of this investment in long-standing relationships, we must ask the "so what?" question. Where are the ethics of Christian friendship most embodied in transnational relationships and serving as yeast to transform the world in the powerful way of God in Christ?

Those of us who have a strong Calvinist streak in us know without being told that human depravity has pockmarked these friendships in a thousand ways. Mission partnership relationships have been the subject of many critiques. Often they are said to focus too much on the projects and needs of those with money and power and too little on mutual relationships and building up of those with less money and power.

But the persistence of the family system of committed friendships and mission partnering is about much more than needs and resources meeting each other in some sort of marketplace. Mutual transformation and world transformation are both to be found in the true Christian friendship and companionship fostered by this intentional ecosystem. I've chosen just a few illustrations from the large number at hand. A committed friendship is the key factor in each story.

The Starter Dough Returns

Let me start with an example that shows the long reach of the family model precisely because it shows a largely unintended effect of that model. Among the many yeasting influences of mission due to intentionally sustained mission friendships is the impact on how U.S. congregations deal with migration into their communities. Like the bread called friendship bread, for which starter dough is passed around, the yeast of historical mission relationships is circulated in the persons of migrants, and one finds congregations welcoming and sometimes even providing a "nest" for Christians with whom they have *learned* to feel connected.

A recent article in the Louisville *Courier-Journal* caught my eye. The article describes Crescent Hill Baptist Church, where the congregation is now joined every Sunday by about 100 refugees, Karen people from Myanmar who sought out fellow Baptists when they arrived. This congregation is probably only dimly aware that in distant offices generations of devoted church professionals very intentionally perpetuated the heritage of mission-related friendships that catalyzed this relationship by making the Crescent Hill Baptists and their new Burmese neighbors feel they belonged together. Baptist mission communications have kept alive the story of Ann and Adoniram Judson, early missionaries to Burma, evidence of which is the fact that the newspaper article cited the history of the Judsons.

To find out if this was an unusual story, I researched the resettlement of refugees in the United States. Since World War II, nearly 3.5 million refugees have been resettled in the United States with the help of Catholic and Protestant faith-based programs. In a typical year, there are about 56,000 resettlements of this kind. The executive of one of Kentucky Refugee Ministries estimates that congregations fully sponsor about 30 percent of these refugees. When the refugees are Christian, they often ask for a congregation that belongs to the refugee's definition of a transnational religious family. Many from Southern Sudan, for instance, want Episcopalian or Presbyterian help. If Kentucky's experience is typical, then as many as 15,000 U.S. congregations are sponsoring a refugee each year and finding the way eased by a previously developed sense of family.

At the close of the article about the Karen people at Crescent Hill Baptist, a church member is quoted as saying she is amazed to see the faith of the Karen despite the traumas they've endured. She recalls the time when these new arrivals led the singing of "What a Friend We Have in Jesus," and she comments, tellingly, "It just doesn't mean the same thing as when I sing it."[13] Is the world not being leavened when, thanks to a framework and tradition of friendships, one more person begins to see through new eyes her own friendship with Jesus Christ and friendship through Christ with people who lead very different lives? Multiply this experience by thousands, and we catch a glimpse of the reach of the Family Model's world-changing "leavening effects."

Ingredients Changing Each Other

One of the challenges of these transnational Christian friendships is finding the right mix of perspectives and priorities. Most of the time, it is best to give the greater weight to the friends in whose country the work will have the greater impact. They will live with the consequences of the mission cooperation. And they should be presumed in most cases to have the greater understanding; that presumption is part of what it means to live up to Bishop Azariah's criteria of coming alongside, building up, and being changed. For Americans in particular, given our culture that convinces us we are quick studies who are good at quick fixes, it is best to adopt the spiritual discipline of partnership and become transformed by learning to respect and trust people in other places regardless of how odd their timing and priorities may appear to be to us.

An example of this kind of circumstance can be found in the wake of the nationalization of the church-related schools in Pakistan in 1972. Many of these church-sponsored schools belonged, legally, to what we now refer to as the northern stream of American Presbyterians, great supporters of public edu-

[13] Peter Smith, "Church Opens Hearts to Karen Refugees," *Courier-Journal*, December 31, 2007.

cation and inclined to see nationalization of schools as a sort of progress for Pakistan. The public sphere appeared to be taking up its correct responsibility for education.

But from the perspective of our long-standing friends of the Presbyterian Church in Pakistan, the nationalization was a bad development that had to be reversed. For them, running the schools themselves provided a way to show the Muslim majority that Pakistani Christians are good citizens providing a service to the nation. For them, the schools were a place where Christians could safely say their own prayers instead of Muslim prayers. For them, the schools were a place where they were safe from discrimination in educational and employment opportunities.

They fought the first legal battles for denationalization on their own, but later, they needed their U.S. partner to insist on our rights to the school properties under a treaty protecting American properties from confiscation. This request would have felt large and uncomfortable to us even if we on the PC (USA) side had perceived our Pakistani partners as prepared to take over so many management and payroll functions at once and even if we hadn't seen denationalization as, possibly, a spark in the gas-filled chamber of rising Islamic extremism. Only the discipline of partnership could pull us beyond our concerns to use our power in the way that was being asked of us.

There were many factors in the success of this effort to denationalize. But the key impact of the bilateral church-to-church transnational friendship between the Presbyterian Church (USA) and the Presbyterian Church of Pakistan is undeniable. One should not idealize that relationship; it has been troubled. But school denationalization was a virtually unanimous desire among Pakistani Christians, and the PC (USA) cooperation with them bore the marks of accompanying, self-risking, and mutual transforming that Bishop Azariah articulated for true transnational Christian friendship under conditions of stark inequality.

Today, many Christian students in Pakistan are able to take a turn in leading classroom prayers. More faculty positions are held by Christians than before, perhaps slowing the emigration of the Christian presence. The schools and Forman Christian College are functioning well as a visible contribution of Pakistani Christians in partnership with supportive American Christians. The yeast of Christian presence and ministry remains and even grows in an unlikely place, thanks in large part to a well-developed system of "giving friends."

Keeping the Ingredients Together Long Enough

The kind of "cooperation between foreign and native workers" to which Bishop Azariah called us has been at its most difficult and perhaps most Christ-like when the circumstances have involved multiple old friends who are in conflict with one another. One of the more striking examples involves Taiwan and China. The PC (USA)'s relationships that led us into partnership with the China Christian Council, in the People's Republic of China (PRC), are very long-lived. Decades old as well, but not quite as long-lived, is our partnership with the Presbyterian Church of Taiwan (PCT). These two partners of the PC (USA) sharply disagree with each other on the question of the political status of Taiwan. An important element of that tension is the fact that Taiwanese Presbyterians are not marginal actors in the debates about Taiwanese political status. Officials of the PCT have been in the forefront of the human rights movement in Taiwan and in favor of formalizing statehood and United Nations membership for Taiwan.

The creative tension in partnership relations with both groups is especially acute among Christians in the United States, where the power of the United States in the UN and as a security guarantor for Taiwan gives the statements of U.S. Christian bodies extra geopolitical significance. The stakes, quite literally, include war involving the United States, and specialists on geopolitical hot spots see this one as an imminent threat to world security.[14]

There have been efforts to induce the PC (USA) to "take sides," but true friendship seems to demand something else in this circumstance; it calls for all parties to struggle to come and stay alongside one another and remain open. Of all the ways the PC (USA) has tried to be of service in this situation, it is likely that our best way of serving the cause of Christ has been our stand for family connectedness, for giving friends, in the body of Christ. Connectedness decreases the polarization and sense of different belongings that can lead to making human beings into objects and targets of violence. And so we work against the isolation of any group by working for the multiplication and strengthening of theirs and our transnational friendships, reinforcing a common belonging around the Eucharistic table.

Has transnational Christian friendship prevented war? That would be a grandiose claim, and one that could not be proved even if true. But these friendships are proving resilient and steadfast, and we pray they are serving the cause of justice and peace.

---

[14] See for example the Carnegie Endowment for International Peace's Michael Swaine in "Trouble in Taiwan," *Foreign Affairs* 83:2 (March/April 2004): 39–49.

Where Do We Go from Here Concerning Friendship?

Anecdotes are important but cannot convey the scale of the friendship phenomenon. A thorough study of the ecosystem of long-standing transnational mission friendships in the family model will reveal that this truly is a vast phenomenon touching virtually every country on the globe and every Christian tradition. It is not just about bilateral relationships between founders and the denominations they founded. Churches throughout the world are pursuing this means of relating to other churches, including in South–South relationships.

Next steps, however, need to do more than take the measurements. There are important issues to explore, many of which can be grouped into these three clusters: the church in new places, the church in places guarded by another religion, and the church in restricting places.

The Church In New Places

By the 1970s, the Family Model's focus on deepening the relationships with old friends was allowed to reinforce a mainline decline in ability and interest to develop new churches and engage in "frontier mission." In the past fifteen years, this imbalance has been significantly redressed in the PC (USA). There is much more PC (USA) mission and evangelism in new places and languages now, and we have managed in many cases to pioneer that work in partnership with old friends and with guidance from our area experts. But denominations such as the PC (USA) have not yet dealt head-on with some key matters related to this new wave of mission.

One of these matters is the perspective of our Orthodox brothers and sisters that brands many activities as "proselytism." We have been "living into" this situation, as they say, especially since the end of the cold war made large parts of the globe more accessible. Dialogues such as the Reformed–Orthodox one that Princeton Seminary's President Iain Torrance leads are building bridges. Principled stands will have to be made—collectively, one hopes—and those stands must be centered in missiology.

Another matter is to envision the day when the Holy Spirit breathes mightily on some of these frontier endeavors and suddenly large new Christian movements have enormous needs for Christian formation, leadership development, and perhaps solidarity in the face of threats. Will we repeat the history of founding denominations and related institutions? Also, if resources are scarce, will we have to ask old friends to excuse us while we turn to assist these new ones?

A third and final question related to frontier mission is whether mainline denominations today will move quickly and expertly enough to forge internal agreements on how to carry out frontier evangelism with integrity and with support from the pews. Strategizing for this work has, so far, been in the hands of a small number of busy persons operating without much oversight.

The Church in Places Guarded by Another Religion

Rabbi Jonathan Sacks, in his book *The Dignity of Difference: How to Avoid the Clash of Civilizations*, performed a service, first by holding out the possibility of avoiding that clash and second by calling on religions to present, as he does, a theological case for embracing variety instead of sameness and particularity instead of universality.[15] A related question must be posed about the Family Model. Even though it intentionally cuts across geopolitical boundaries, does it do so only to build up what Samuel P. Huntington called "civilizations" that are coming into greater tension with each other?[16]

I reviewed the list of 178 transnational partnerships the PC (USA)'s team of area experts created in 2003. More than 42 percent of these long-term friendships were with denominations in the Presbyterian and Reformed tradition. Close to 20 percent were with councils of churches and multidenominational seminaries that sometimes include Orthodox, Pentecostal, and Catholic Christians. Most of the remaining bilateral partnerships were with Protestants, Anglicans, and united churches, the latter usually having built upon previous Presbyterian mission endeavors. Only one partner listed had interfaith relations as its main reason for being. It is not unreasonable to suppose that the PC (USA) list is typical of mainline lists of partners. For all the striking variety of contexts and perspectives in the particularity represented by this family of partners, there is also a certain religious sameness, and we must ask how that relates to the thesis of clashing civilizations.

My experience mostly points to the Family Model being an important means by which wisdom about and progress within religious plurality is shared and used as leaven in the world church today. This can be true even when transnational church friendships are also helping beleaguered Christian minorities to be a bit

---

[15] Jonathan Sacks, *The Dignity of Difference: How to Avoid the Clash of Civilizations* (New York: Continuum, 2003).

[16] The title of the book by Rabbi Sacks is a reference to the title of the earlier book by Samuel P. Huntington, *The Clash of Civilizations and the Remaking of World Order* (New York: Simon & Schuster, 1996).

safer and less beleaguered. We could explore this topic in relation to any context where one religion dominates, but because I already talked about Pakistan, I will illustrate using majority-Islamic places.

The joint effort in Pakistan to denationalize church-related schools had a dimension to it that worried me. In the Pakistani context, where the Blasphemy Law, bombings, threats, employment discrimination, efforts to convert Christian children, and other aspects of the context add up to a hostile environment for Christians, many Christians see the transnational solidarity of Muslims as very prominent and powerful, and they sometimes feel tempted by the thought of having something similar for themselves, a world church that would respond in kind with strong support. In such a context, having a friend, and not just any friend but one with the letters "USA" in its name, claiming rights of school ownership, could, wearing one set of lenses, look like a step toward the clash of civilizations. Wearing other lenses—the ones that in the end I chose to wear—the same events created a bridge between Muslims and Christians that was an answer to audacious prayers, and perhaps not just Christian prayers, but also Muslim prayers. Instead of responding to each other as caricatures, people of both faiths met and worked out a particular way to cooperate for a common good.

In another Muslim-majority context, Egypt, our main mission partner, has, with our willing participation, used our PC (USA) visits as opportunities to approach Muslim religious and political leaders on a number of issues, such as church building permits and the increasing Islamic content of the education in Egyptian schools. At the same time, PC (USA) representatives have enjoyed and learned from the Muslim friends and colleagues of our Egyptian Christian friends, getting acquainted with the particularity of religious experience in Egypt. And in Indonesia, the PC (USA)'s Christian partner has placed one of our mission coworkers at a Muslim university to teach, an exploration of a way to build a bridge there.

In summary, it is fair to say that much of what U.S. denominational Christians learn about other faiths comes through the particularities of the lives of our long-standing Christian partners in many different contexts, as those lives are shared with us through the many ways that we give each other friends. Mission in partnership gives us ways to learn, to avoid oversimplification, and to experiment with bridge building. Increasingly, our challenge is to do more to extend the leavening effect of these friendships within the U.S. context, as the PC (USA) did for several years by itinerating mixed-religion pairs of speakers throughout the United States.

The Church in Restrictive Places

The third cluster of concerns arising from the heritage of giving friends in the Family Model, and the last one I will explore here, has to do with partnership in the context of political restrictions. For all the attention given today to restrictions on freedoms related to strong religious establishments, we must not forget those places where such restrictions come from secular governments.

The calling and craft of giving friends is greatly complicated by restricting contexts, and here one might think of the examples of Myanmar, Cuba, North Korea, China, and in earlier days, the Soviet Union. At the same time, governmental efforts to impose isolation on churches, restrict the dialogue among and outreach activities of churches, and use divide-and-rule tactics among Christian groups simply provide the world church with reasons to work extra hard at giving friends. Doing so brings considerable risk and pain, however, as efforts to partner are cast by some as approval of the regimes themselves, as leaders of churches become accused or suspected of being collaborators, and as those outside of a country are forced to choose from an artificially limited menu of options in our partnering. Christians living in these kinds of restricting political circumstances have expressed great gratitude for the costly efforts at friendship shown to them, and partnering has in many cases helped to open up the spaces available to the churches. One thinks, for instance, of the greatly increased spaces in Cuba and some very slightly increased spaces in North Korea for diaconal ministries of the church beyond the walls of worship facilities. That being said, this is another area where scholarship is badly needed. Political polemics have greatly hindered the world church's ability to assess the true history of our partnering under these kinds of circumstances, as difficult as that assessment would be even today in places such as Hungary, where many people still are reluctant to talk about this. Such an assessment would not provide us a clear guide to present-day or future circumstances, but it could help us to share some common understandings and vocabulary and reduce the level of acrimony as we discuss the relationships and dynamics that tend to develop because of religion-restricting regimes.

Conclusion

As we approach the centenary of Bishop Azariah's appeal, "Give us friends!" it continues to serve the cause of Christ for the churches to say "yes" to his appeal. A meaningful way to do that is to assess what we have done and learned in the past century and discern our focus for the future. To do so will require the efforts of students of mission who until now have inadequately studied the massive

Family Model means of relating, learning, acting cooperatively, and becoming a new thing through God's grace. To do so will require greater knowledge and involvement from members of denominations that provide the support for their national staff and programs and that tend to take too much for granted about the health and conduct of their transnational connections. To do so will require honest dialogue among representatives of denominations who participate in ecumenical processes such as the one leading up to Edinburgh 2010, avoiding facile criticisms of the transnational mission relationships of churches and pointing instead to viable ways to improve.

Few calls so powerfully characterize the commitments of the last century and the learning edge of the present one as the appeal of Bishop V. S. Azariah in 1910. It is fitting to close with it and let it move us to an ever better response, as yeast is moved in dough: "You have given your goods to feed the poor. You have given your bodies to be burned. We also ask for love. Give us friends!" ■

The Bible in China: Religion of God's Chinese Son

by Archie Chi Chung Lee

Archie C. C. Lee is a Professor of Biblical Studies and Asian Hermeneutics in the Department of Cultural and Religious Studies, and Dean of the Faculty of Arts at The Chinese University of Hong Kong. He is also associate editor of the Global Bible Commentary *(2004) and the* Cambridge Dictionary of Christianity *(forthcoming, 2009) and is the author of books and articles on biblical interpretation, cross-textual hermeneutics, and the Bible and Chinese classics. He delivered this Alexander Thompson Lecture on March 3, 2008, in Princeton Theological Seminary's Mackay Campus Center.*

I am honored to be invited to give the Alexander Thompson Lectureship, which was established to examine the Bible and issues relating to its interpretation. There are two aspects to the topic I have chosen. The first aspect concerns the introduction of the Bible to a nonbiblical land and its encounter with other religions, engaging in, or in most cases suppressing, other texts and scriptures. The second aspect, and the more specific focus, is the Taiping Bible, produced by the self-proclaimed "God's second son," Hong Xiuquan (1814–1864).

In 1847, Hong declared himself to be the younger brother of Jesus, and from 1853 to 1864 he established in China the so-called "Taiping Tianguo," the "Heavenly Kingdom of Great Peace." "God's Chinese Son" is a designation given by Yale historian Jonathan Spence in his history *God's Chinese Son: The Taiping Heavenly Kingdom of Hong Xiuquan.*[1] The Taiping Kingdom was condemned by the imperial power of the Manchurian Empire as a rebellion, uprising, and

[1] Jonathan Spence, *God's Chinese Son: The Taiping Heavenly Kingdom of Hong Xiuquan* (London: HarperCollins Publishers, 1996). Spence has presented two lectures at Baylor University on the Taipings and is the author of *The Taiping Vision of a Christian China, 1836–1864* (Waco: Markham Press Fund, Baylor University Press, 1998).

DOI: 10.3754/1937–8386.2008.29.1.4

insurrection and was disowned by the Christian world as a blasphemous and syncretistic religion.[2]

Because some fifty books and pamphlets were published by the Taiping government, including many proclamations, declarations, edicts, and poems with Christian themes and most significantly for biblical interpretation, a revised version of the Bible with eighty-two annotations written in the margins, I take it as one of the historical cases of the encounter of the Bible with a nonbiblical culture.[3] Most, if not all, of the scholars who studied the Taiping Heavenly Kingdom so far have neglected the Bible and undermined its legitimate place in biblical interpretation and the history of reception. I plan to expand on this theme and to explore several issues relating to the Bible in Asia.

Before addressing some of these questions, I will present a brief account of Hong Xiuquan and his Heavenly Kingdom of Great Peace. Then I will review how Hong dealt with the biblical canon in his context. Finally, I will closely examine the appropriation of some of the biblical themes and motifs in the Chinese religious world as Hong saw it. I will conclude with deliberations on some critical issues pertaining to biblical interpretation in the Chinese cultural context.

Hong Xiuquan and Taiping Tianguo

The Heavenly Kingdom of Great Peace (Taiping Tianguo), commonly referred to as the Taiping Rebellion, was basically a peasant revolt that developed in the 1850s in the southern provinces of China. The movement was aimed at the imperial government of the Manchus, who ruled all of China as the Qing Dynasty (1644–1911) from the capital in Beijing. The leaders of the revolt, Hong Xiuquan and his comrades, came from the Hakka villages of the economically deprived zones of southern China. They created a Chinese subculture by transforming the form and content of Christianity transplanted by missionaries and made efforts to adapt the Christian faith to traditional Chinese religious beliefs and to their political vision of building a heavenly kingdom on earth. They successfully conquered large regions of the southern parts of China, and the military conquest of the Taiping army extended as far as Nanjing. There,

[2] See the summary on the religion of the Taipings in Ssu-yu Teng, *New Light on the History of the Taiping Rebellion* (New York: Russell & Russell, 1966) 74–80.
[3] For an English translation of a selected list of these publications see Franz H. Michael and Chung-li Chang, *The Taiping Rebellion: History and Documents,* 3 vol., trans. Margery Anneberg et al. (Tokyo: University of Tokyo Press, 1966).

they took the city, renamed it *Tianjing* (the heavenly capital), and in 1853 established a new regime called the "Heavenly Dynasty."

Sociologically speaking, life in the poor Hakka community in Kwangxi had been harsh and people constantly struggled just to survive. The Hakkas were known as a rootless and powerless people who would agree to any religious views and political movements that promised a better life and a bright future. Like many rebellious movements in Chinese history, Taiping Heavenly Kingdom was religiously motivated and involved a pragmatic program aimed at improving the living conditions of the followers. Dreams and visions were taken seriously as media to decipher the divine will for the present. The Chinese government, like many of its counterparts in human history, was known for its intolerance toward heterogeneous religious factions beyond the officially recognized religious traditions and institutions. The government believed, therefore, that heterodoxical religious organizations and communities that threatened the existing order must be suppressed. Taiping Heavenly Kingdom had gone far beyond the set boundaries with its military campaigns and its political agenda, which was directed toward overthrowing the Manchurian regime of the Qing Dynasty. The establishment of the Taiping Heavenly Kingdom's capital in Nanjing had anticipated the violent military combat that eventually came in 1864 and that brought the kingdom to its tragic end, with the massacre of millions of people and the devastation of much land in China.

In Chinese, the religion of the Taiping Kingdom is called *Shangdijiao* (the religion of *Shangdi*). Although the term is not adopted by any of the present-day Christian communities, *Shangdi*, the Chinese name of God, is still widely used by most of the ecumenical churches. *Shangdijiao,* or *Bai Shangdihui* ("society of God worshippers"), was the religion instituted by Hong Xiuquan in 1843 as a result of his desperate disappointment after failing the civil examinations for public office several times. In 1836, Hong had some dramatic mystical religious experiences that took the form of a series of dreams and visions. In these visions, he was taken to heaven, where he was attacked by the devil and saved by God, who then commissioned him to return to the earth with the task of eliminating evil, protecting the righteous, and establishing the Heavenly Kingdom of Great Peace.

Although *Shangdi* is the name of the deity worshipped in ancient China, it did not present any problem to Hong Xiuquan.[4] The reason that Hong adopted the name *Shangdi* may go back to the first Chinese Christian convert and evangelist Liang Afa

[4] For a discussion on the nature of *Shangdi* in ancient China, see "Was There a High God Ti in Shang Religion," *Early China* 15 (1990): 1–26.

(1789–1855), whose book *Good Words for the Admonition of the World* exerted a tremendous impact on Hong's understanding of Christianity.[5] This *Shangdi* is both the Christian God of the Bible and the Chinese God of old. The name is found in numerous places in the Chinese classics, especially the *Shijing*, the Book of Poetry, and *Shujing*, the Book of Writings. *Shangdi* was formerly exclusively worshipped by the emperors and nobles. But in Daoism and various local Chinese religions, as a means, in some cases, of subverting political power, the name *Shangdi* was also commonly adopted in various forms to designate the divine beings of these religious traditions. In the past, there had been heated debates by the missionaries over the most appropriate term in Chinese for the Christian God.[6] The disagreement was between either adopting the ancient Chinese term *Shangdi*, or instead, using the generic term *Shen*. In the Protestant missionary movement in China in the nineteenth and twentieth centuries, the debate was known as "the term question," and it was also involved in the so-called "rite controversy" during the Jesuit Missions to China in the sixteenth and seventeenth centuries.[7] *Tianzujiao* (the religion of *Tianzu*) and *Jidujiao* (the religion of Christ) have become the conventional designations of the Catholic and Protestant churches, respectively. Hong adopted the name *Shangdi* for God, who is both the Christian God and the God worshipped by the Chinese ancestors in ancient times, the record of which can be found in the Chinese classics, especially *Shijing* and *Shujing*. Hong saw *Shangdi* as the Creator of heaven and earth and the universal Father of all human beings. Worshipping *Shangdi* and doing away with idols were taken as the only ways to salvation.

Contesting Canonicity and Hong's Appropriation of the Bible

In narrating the dramatic story of Hong, Jonathan Spence vividly describes Hong's assigned role as a scholar in his poor farming family, where he was expected to bring hope and to change fate. He dedicated himself to the intensive study of the

---

[5] George Hunter McNeur, *China's First Preacher Liang A-Fa: 1789–1855* (Shanghai: Kwang Hsueh Publishing House: Oxford University Press, 1934). In Liang's book there are a few names used for God. Some scholars therefore assume that Hong takes the name Shangdi from Karl Friederich August Gützlaff (1803–1851), whose translation of the Bible was the official text of the Taipings. On Gützlaff's Bible and the Taipings, see Thomas H. Reilly, *The Taiping Heavenly Kingdom: Rebellion and the Blasphemy of Empire* (Seattle: University of Washington Press, 2004), 67–73.

[6] On the debate of naming the Christian God in Chinese, see Archie C. C. Lee, "Naming God in Asia: Cross-Textual Reading in Multi-Cultural Context," *Quest: An Interdisciplinary Journal for Asian Christian Scholars* 3:1 (2004), 21–42.

[7] Sangkeoun Kim, *Strange Names of God: The Missionary Translation of the Divine Name and the Chinese Responses to Matteo Ricci's Shangti in Late Ming China, 1583–1644* (New York: Peter Lang, 2005); see also Linfu Dong, *The Search for God in Ancient China: James Mellon Menzies, China Missionary and Archaeologist* (Ph.D. thesis, York University [Canada], 2001. Dissertation Abstracts International, Volume 63–03).

Chinese Confucian classics in order to acquire a government office through public examinations. Although he was successful in the local examination, he failed the provincial ones. In China, the Confucian classics had come to be the driving force for the homogenization of the vast and diverse nation, and the government exercised its ideological control over any heterodoxy by using these texts. It is ironic that in 1836, outside the examination hall, Hong was handed another text with long sections of translation and commentary on Bible passages.[8] This book, as mentioned above, was *Good Words for the Admonition of the World,* which includes the nine Christian tracts written by Liang Afa, who abandoned Buddhism for Christianity. The book exerted a tremendous impact on Hong's understanding of Christianity and provided him with the key to interpreting his religious dreams.[9]

Through the Christian interpretations found in Liang Afa's book, Hong discovered his role and mission in life. The book consists of "fourteen occasions including fifty-three verses which are quoted from the Old Testament, whereas there are forty-eight occasions including twenty-one chapters and seventy-eight verses where the New Testament is quoted."[10] Hong found quite a few of the Christian doctrines from the quotations of the Bible in Liang's book; among them were the concept of God as the only God, the Supreme Creator, and a personal deity who can be approached for direct revelation. The book explained that human rebellion against God brought condemnation unless repentance was made through the abandonment of all idol worship. Only with the grace of Jesus the Savior, who had been sent down into the world to suffer for the sins of mankind and to give his life in redemption, could there be hope for salvation from the torture in hell. In Hong's visions, he had seen that Jesus was sent by God to the earth to eliminate Satan and all demons in order to save the righteous. This is very similar to the beliefs of most evangelical Christians.[11]

Liang Afa's book enabled Hong to interpret his dreams and not only gave meaning to his religious experiences but also confirmed the father–son relationship between Hong and God and prescribed a new mission for Hong's life on earth.

---

[8] The year Hong received the book has been debated by scholars, but 1833 seems to be the earliest acceptable date. See Luo Ergang, *History of the Taiping Kingdom,* vol. 2 (Beijing: Zhonghua Bookstore, 1991), 652, note 1.

[9] Spence, *The Taiping Vision*, 6–7.

[10] Teng, *New Light,* 76.

[11] Rudolf G. Wagner gave a good summary of the evangelical orientations and revival traditions of missionaries of the time in *Reenacting the Heavenly Vision: The Role of Religion in the Taiping Rebellion* (Berkeley: Institute of East Asian Studies, University of California, 1982), 6–16. See also Eugene P. Boardman, "Christian Influence upon the Ideology of Taiping Rebellion," *The Far Eastern Quarterly*, 10:2 (1951): 115–24; and Vincent Y. C. Shih, *The Taiping Ideology, Its Sources, Interpretations and Influences* (Seattle: University of Washington Press, 1967), 147–64.

Obviously, the Confucian text had to be reappropriated and reframed in order to make sense of his new religious existence. To complete his religious training, Hong went to the Baptist missionary Rev. I. J. Roberts in Guangzhou for three months to receive instructions in Christianity and the Bible. He then baptized himself in a river with his friends.[12]

Hong then declared that all ancient Confucian books were "demonic" and, based on this attitude, formed a policy of banning these books in the new heavenly dynasty.[13] He forbade his children and all the court women to possess the classics and requested that they read a chapter a day of the Old Testament and New Testament alternatively, in addition to reading his own poems. On the Sabbath, which the Taipings designated as the day for worship, he instructed that the Ten Commandments should be read as well and declared that punishment would result if anyone was reported to have failed in observing his rules. The order to read the Bible was also instituted in the Taiping army, which had to recite a chapter a day on rainy days. Biblical verses were even used as the password for army patrols.

These teachings had the effect of placing the Bible in a superior position and suppressing the Confucian texts. In addition, in one of Hong's visions, he saw Jesus descend to the earth and asked him about the situation of Confucius in heaven. Jesus told Hong that Confucius had been stripped and whipped by God for the errors in his writings, even though there was some truth in his sayings. Now, Jesus told Hong, Confucius was required to bow and be humble before God. In these visions, we can see the struggle between the two texts, the Bible and Confucian classics in the Chinese context. Even a Confucian scholar such as Hong had to deal with the two texts in confrontation and with their competition for loyalty from the people. During his descent, Hong said, Jesus instructed him to burn all Confucian books. He said he was told that because Confucius had been regarded as a good man, he was bestowed with blessings in heaven but would not be allowed to descend to the earth again.[14]

On the surface, the confirmation of Confucius being found in heaven does not seem to be significant, but put in the context of the missionary movement in China, it is extraordinary. Most, if not all, missionaries including the Jesuits who came to China in 1583, condemned the ancient Chinese sages and the great ancestors of China to suffer in hell because they did not believe in Jesus and accept the gospel.

---

[12] Ergang, *History of the Taiping Kingdom,* vol. 2, 678.
[13] "The Confession of the Young Monarch," quoted by Jonathan Spence in *God's Chinese Son,* 253, note 35. See Michael, *The Taiping Rebellion,* 1531.
[14] "Sacred Declaration of the Heavenly Brother," in Luo Ergang and Wang Qing, *Taiping Kingdom,* vol. 2 (Guilin: Guangxi Normal University Press, 2004), 248.

For the Chinese, who honor their ancestors and practice filial piety, the missionary condemnation of their sages and ancestors seemed horrendous, and some objected to accepting the gospel simply because of this. Hong's attitude on this matter was therefore regarded as rebellious. How could he state that the supreme and honorable Confucius could be under God's authority? Furthermore, how could he accuse Confucius of having committed errors and say that his books would have to be burned?

With respect to the attitude of the Taipings toward the Bible, the single most significant incident in their entire history is recorded in the *Sacred Declarations of the Heavenly Father*.[15] The book states that God appeared on July 7, 1854, in the person of Yang, the East King, to proclaim that the Bible is full of errors and should be revised before being printed for further circulation:

> The Heavenly Father sees that his children on earth are so stubborn and rigid about the Testaments to the extent that they undermine God's sacred declaration. Therefore God declares that there are errors in them that should be corrected. ... The Heavenly Father said: "Your God has come down to you today for one reason and one reason only: namely, to inform you that both the Old Testament and the New Testament, which have been preserved by the barbarian nations and currently circulated, contain numerous falsehoods. ... You are to inform the North King and the Wing King, who in turn will tell the East King, who can inform the Heavenly King, that it is no longer urgent to propagate these books."[16]

This incident clearly reveals the approach of the Taipings to the Bible, showing that direct revelation from God had more authority than the written text that had been passed on from the West. God seems to blame the missionaries from foreign lands for the transmission of the falsehoods. At the end of God's speech in this incident, God gives his final verdict on the biblical books:

> Those books are neither polished in the literary terms nor are they fully complete. You must all consult together, and correct them so that they become both polished and complete.[17]

---

[15] *Tianfu Shenzhi (Sacred Declarations of the Heavenly Father)*, bound together with *Tianxiong Shenzhi (Sacred Declaration of the Heavenly Brother)*, British Library 15293.e.29. It is published in *Taiping Tianguo*, vol. 2, 322–45.

[16] "The Divine Will of the Heavenly Father" (*Tianfu Shenzhi*), in Ergang and Qing, *Taiping Kingdom*, vol. 2, 329–30. The words of God in the quotation are a modified rendering of Spence, *God's Chinese Son*, 254.

[17] Ergang and Qing, *Taiping Kingdom*, vol. 2, 330. Spence, *God's Chinese Son*, 254.

This declaration confirmed that the Taipings had the right and responsibility to read the Bible closely and revise it. This declaration was delivered around the time when the British delegation, under Captain Mellersh of the ship *Rattler*, visited the East King and presented thirty questions about the different aspects of the life and beliefs of the Taipings. In essence, the questions expressed the foreign suspicion of the validity of the Taipings' doctrines and doubt about their biblical interpretation. These Westerners rejected Hong's claims of his being God's second son and pressed for biblical support of Hong's beliefs.[18] In response, Hong found it necessary to revise the Bible according to his new understandings. The result was the production of the imperial edition of the Old Testament, which includes the books of Genesis through Joshua and the entire New Testament.[19] The latter was renamed the Former Testament because the Taipings elevated some of their own writings and called them the "True Testament."[20] The True Testament presents the story of Hong's religious conversion and reveals the truth about his repeated ascents to heaven. The True Testament represents the divine act in the present time, whereas the "Old Testament" and the "Former Testament" contain the acts of God in the past. There are, according to Xia Chuntao, four books designated as the "True Testament" or the "Taiping Canon": *The Sacred Declaration of the Heavenly Father, The Sacred Declaration of the Heavenly Brother, The Gospel Jointly Witnessed and Heard by the Imperial Eldest and Second Brothers,* and *The Taiping Tianre (Heavenly Sun).*[21]

The first two books are records of direct divine revelation from God and Jesus, who descended to the earth thirty and 120 times, respectively. The latter two recount Hong's heavenly visions, his mandated mission to establish the Taiping Kingdom, and his status as the second son of *Shangdi*, whom he called Heavenly Father. In these books, Hong declares that Jesus is his elder brother, whom he calls Heavenly Elder Brother. The third book was written in 1860. The only surviving copy is located in the British Library and bears a written marginal note that says "Venerable Record of the Gospel."[22] These four books contain the revelation that "Father knows there are errors in the New Testament" and affirm and legitimatize the need for revising the Old and New Testaments. Hong added eighty-two anno-

---

[18] Spence, *God's Chinese Son*, 229–32.

[19] There is only one surviving copy each of the imperial edition of the Old Testament and the imperial edition of New Testament in the British Library: 15117.e.20 and 15117.e.19, respectively. The New Testament has the complete table of contents of its twenty-seven books except for the Gospel of John, which is missing.

[20] Xia Chuntao, *The Fall of the Heavenly Kingdom, The Religion of Taiping Tianguo Revisited* (Beijing: People's University Press, 2006), 157–59.

[21] Ibid., 159–66.

[22] The translation of this book can be found in Michael, *The Taiping Rebellion,* vol. 2, 7–18. Wang Qingzheng has a good summary of all surviving copies of the publication of the Taiping Kingdom in overseas libraries in his *Documents and History of Taiping Tianguo* (Beijing: Social Science Documents Publishing, 1993), 60–114.

tations to the imperial edition of the Bible, six of which are in the Old Testament.[23] Hong explained the function of the True Testament in terms of the symbolic "narrow gate" in Luke 13:24 and Matt 7:13–14, which leads to eternal blessing but grants access to very few. In using this symbol, he revealed his familiarity with the concept of "narrow gate" used in John Bunyan's book *The Pilgrim's Progress.*[24] The True Testament also provides the justification for Hong's revision of the Bible and claims a supreme position for the revision over every other publication of the Taipings. The establishment of the True Testament, and the revision of both the Old Testament and the renaming of the New Testament as the Former Testament, are significant steps that Hong took to affirm his religious and political authority independent of Western Christianity. The possession of a "Taiping Canon" empowered the Taiping regime and strengthened Hong's position in the community.

Hong made use of some of the ambiguous texts of the Bible to drive home his religious convictions and Christian beliefs. Mark 12:35–37 is one such case. Jesus, while debating with the scribes in the Jerusalem temple, quotes Psalm 110 to cast doubt on the idea that the Messiah is the descendent of David. Hong stressed that Jesus is the Son of God, but he is not one with God, neither in Heaven nor on earth. As Son he has his own separate existence vis-à-vis the Father. In Stephen's witness to the crowd before his martyrdom, as revealed in Acts 7:55–60, Hong found affirmation of the existence of God the Father and Jesus the Son. Stephen cried out: "Behold, I see the heavens opened, and the Son of Man standing at the right hand of God." Furthermore, in the Gospel of Luke, Hong was concerned with the theological understanding that the Holy Spirit is God, but Jesus, being God's son, has a separate existence distinct from God (Luke 1:35, 4:12, 7:16, 12:8–10; Acts 4:24; 7:55–60). When commenting on the healing stories, Hong repeatedly emphasized the presence and indwelling of God in Jesus or the divine action mediated through Jesus (Matt. 8:15, 9:29; Mark 2:3–5, 8:3).

Both in his first book of the Old Testament and in his New Testament, Hong identified himself as the light together with God and Jesus: "The Father is light. The Elder Brother is light. The Lord is light" (Gen. 1:1–5, p. 1a)[25] and "God is flame; therefore he is Holy Light. The Elder Brother is flame; therefore he is the Great Light. I am the sun; therefore I am also light" (Matt. 4:15–16, p. 5a). Hong claimed his position in the divine order as "God's Chinese Son." In his commentaries on the Bible,

---

[23] Michael, *The Taiping Rebellion,* vol. 2, 224–37.

[24] Hong's possession of the book has been testified to by Hong Renkan, "A Report by Joseph Edkins," *Western Reports on the Taiping: A Selection of Documents,* ed. Prescott Clarke and J. S. Gregory (Honolulu: University Press of Hawaii, 1982), 243.

[25] Translation is the author's modification based on the text taken from Michael, *The Taiping Rebellion,* vol. 2, 225.

Hong was clearly preoccupied with the dual issues of family relationships between Jesus, himself, and God the Father, as well as the uniqueness of God. It is repeatedly emphasized "that Jesus cannot be God, is not God, just as he Hong is not God, can never be, and will never claim to be."[26] The concept of Trinity applies to three children: Jesus, Hong, and Yang. The three are brothers born of the same Father.[27]

Purging of the Bible according to Chinese Ethical Values

After Nanjing was conquered and established as the capital, the religion of Shangdi continued to develop and Hong began to eliminate the presence of Confucianism. Some deep-rooted Confucian conceptions persisted, however, and influenced Hong's interpretation of the Bible. With the exception of a few minor editorial changes in terminology in accordance with the Taiping systems and the avoidance of certain words exclusively used for God, Jesus, and Hong as the Heavenly King, Hong's editorial changes to the Bible mainly emphasized ethical values and family ideals.

The inappropriate behavior of Noah in his drunkenness (Gen. 9:21) was edited to become "deep asleep," in accordance with Taiping's strict ban on alcohol. The story of Noah being naked in the tent (Gen. 9:21) after being drunk was edited to say only that he "fell from his bed." Verse 24, "Noah awoke from his wine," was then

---

[26] Spence, *God's Chinese Son*, 291.

[27] Spence, *God's Chinese Son*, 292; Michael, *The Taiping Rebellion,* vol. 2, 234; Jin Yufu, *Historical Sources of Taiping Heavenly Kingdom,* ed. Tian Yuqing (Beijing: Zhonghua Publishing Co., 1959), 85. On First John 5:7 it is said that "there are three that bear record in heaven, the Father, the Word, and the Holy Spirit: and these three are one." Hong labors on the verse to bring his reading of the different persons in the divine family. *Shangdi* is the only supreme God. Jesus is not to be confused with God; lest there are two Gods or there is no separate existence of Jesus as the Son of God. Jesus is God's first Son and Hong is the brother of Jesus, hence he is God's second Son. Only here it is said clearly that Yang, the Eastern King, is also God's son and that Jesus, Hong, and Yang are the Trinity from before heaven and earth existed. The Holy Spirit is God himself and God only issued an edict to appoint Yang as the comforter and the wind on earth in the same way that Jesus descends into the world in the West King. In this long annotation there are ambiguities on the identity of Yang as the Holy Spirit and as the wind. It is clear that Hong intends to challenge the validity of the New Testament on the Trinity, especially on the separate existence of the Holy Spirit and Jesus as God. "The Father knew that the New Testament contains erroneous records; therefore he sent down the Eastern King as a witness that the Holy Spirit is God, that the wind is the Eastern King. Further, knowing that people of the world mistakenly took Christ to be God, God sent down the Eastern King in order to make it clear that the Divine Father exists. Thus Christ descends on the Western King to prove the existence of the first son." There are misunderstandings and unclear renderings of the text in both of the two existing English translations of the text. Mote renders Jesus being the "first son" into "the heir," which though correct in the usual sense is very unclear in this context (Michael, *The Taiping Rebellion,* vol. 2, 234), and James Chester Cheng reads the word "wind" together with the previous sentence to arrive at "the Holy Ghost is the Wind of God" (James Chester Cheng, *Chinese Sources for the Taiping Rebellion, 1850–1864,* New York: Oxford University Press, 1963), 89.

slightly revised to read "Noah awoke from his sleep."[28] And because circumcision is contrary to filial piety according to the Confucian concept of taking good care of the body we receive from our parents, it was regarded as inappropriate behavior.[29]

All the indecent and obscene passages that are counter to traditional ethical standard and family ethics were also eliminated. The passage describing the forbidden incestuous relationship of Lot with his two daughters, in Genesis 19, was dropped altogether from the Bible. And the account of the sexual act between Judah and Tamar, in Genesis 38, was rewritten: Judah mistaking Tamar, his daughter-in-law, as a "harlot" became Judah mistaking Tamar to be a "woman"; the image of Tamar cheating Judah into having sex with her was reshaped into an obedient daughter-in-law pleading with Judah to get a wife for his son Shelah; and Judah getting Tamar pregnant was rewritten as Judah "got a wife for Shelah," his youngest son, and "the wife became pregnant after marriage with Shelah."

In Hong's interpretation, it was not the levirate marriage that necessitated the marriage of the second and third sons of Judah. Instead, Tamar urges Judah to marry off his second and third sons so that they could father a son who would be the stepson of the first brother. The Chinese custom of adoption is enforced to replace the Hebrew custom of levirate marriage: "And so Judah chose Perez to continue the elder brother's line, and Zerah to be the son of Shelah" (Gen. 38:30).[30] Hong himself had done the same to have his own son adopted as Jesus's son.[31] Genesis 38 is therefore used by Hong to support the Chinese concept of adoption of the first born of a younger brother by the elder brother.

Purging the Bible of the indecencies and immorality in the Old Testament was imperative in order to present the ancestors of Jesus in the genealogy of Jesus in Matthew 1 as moral exemplars. The lies told by Abraham and Isaac in denying their wives were recast so that the blame "falls on either their wives themselves or on other intermediaries."[32] Jacob's story is full of deceits and therefore too immoral to be redeemed by just making minor changes, so Hong rewrote it. In Genesis 25:31–34, Jacob is presented as one who lectures to Esau to respect his birthright and only agrees to "divide" it with him in exchange for the pottage that Esau deeply desires. Jacob's deceitful plan in Genesis 27 is said to be fully initiated by Rebekah, although Jacob had gently reproved her and only follows her

---

[28] Ergang and Qing, *Taiping Tianguo*, vol. 2, 9; Spence, *God's Chinese Son*, 256.
[29] See "Odes for Youth" in Michael, *The Taiping Rebellion,* vol. 2, 163 and *Publication of Taiping Heavenly Kingdom,* vol. 1 (Nanjing: Jiangsu People's Publishing Co., 1979), 59.
[30] Ergang and Qing, *Taiping Tianguo,* vol. 2, 42.
[31] Spence, *God's Chinese Son*, 258.
[32] Ibid., 256; Gen. 20:2–13; 26:7–9

plan out of filial piety. At the end, Jacob does not deceive Isaac at all. His father is moved to bless Jacob because of his filial piety in bringing him savory meat.

The laws in the Pentateuch also had to be altered to bring them in line with the Confucian traditions. Exodus 22:16–17 was rewritten to have Moses's laws fall in line with the Taiping rules against adultery, which was punishable by death. The seventh commandment was properly addressed and duly observed. In the following examples of the original biblical version, followed by Hong's version, it is obvious that the revised version has been changed to be readily acceptable in the Chinese context:

> And if a man entices a maid that is not betrothed, and lies with her, he surely endows her to be his wife. If her father utterly refuses to give her unto him, he shall pay money according to the dowry of virgin (Exod. 22:16–17).

> And if a man entices a maid that is not betrothed, and lies with her, *he is breaking the Seventh Commandment*. If her father knows of the matter, then *he must hand over both the woman and her seducer to the officials, to be executed*; *on no account may he, knowing what has happened, attempt to conceal it* (Exod. 22:16–17).

Hong's Annotations and the Impact of the Chinese Religious World

In the last section I show how cross-textual reading affects the selection and interpretation of themes and motifs of both the Chinese religious world and the Bible in the eighty-two annotations Hong made on the margins of the Bible. The longest annotations are on First Epistle of John 5 and Revelation 12, containing 419 and 321 characters, respectively. I highlight three areas: first, the portrayal of Satan and demons; second, the concept of God descending to the earth with a divine mission; and third, the pursuit of a utopian ideal of great peace and its fulfillment in the Taiping Kingdom of Great Peace.

According to Theodore Hamberg, the tracts of Liang Afa shed light on the foreign invasions, mass sufferings, and tragic deaths encountered by the people of the time.[33] The quotations from the prophet Isaiah in the tracts speak out loud

[33] Theodore Hamberg, "The Visions of Hung-siu-tshuen, and [the] Origin of the Kwang-si Insurrection," 1854. Reprint with Chinese translation by Jen yu-wen (Jian Youwen) (Beijing: Yanjing University Press, 1935). Hamberg assumes that Hong read Liang Afa's *Good Words for the Admonition of the World* in 1836. Jonathan Spence agrees to that date and gives a narration of the political and social catastrophes of Liang Afa's time in *God's Chinese Son*, 51–55.

and clear about the evils done to the land.[34] Now that evil, presumably the work of the devil, has infiltrated the human race, the slaying of demons remained the central task required to cleanse the earth. The annotations emphasize the divine mission and mandate from heaven given to Hong to "exterminate the demons and redeem the righteous" (Matt. 10:32–33). The parable of the tares (Matt. 13:24–43) and the parable of the net (Matt. 13:47–52) were interpreted along this line.

The search for the source of evil begins in the third chapter of Genesis in the Bible. It is from Liang Afa that Hong took the image of the serpent demon in the Garden of Eden, who embodies the devil and lures Eve into taking the forbidden fruit, which generates knowledge of devious ways.[35] Hong approved of this image and accepted the devil as having first appeared as the serpent in the Garden of Eden. Eve was tempted and believed the devil's words. In successive generations, the serpent deceived all women who deeply believed in the demon's word, bringing destruction to all human lives. The Father therefore decided to send down the flood.[36] God's plan to send his Son to earth was seen as necessary to save fallen humankind from evil. Liang explained that this messianic event is not recorded in the Chinese classics because the classics were completed before Jesus arrived.[37]

The command that Hong should kill the devil and all the demons provided the rationale for the kingdom's strategic military and violent punitive campaigns. The central message of the Taiping Kingdom was the fight against demonic power, which manifested itself in various forms in the religiocultural and sociopolitical context of China. Eliminating the "demon" is a radical call without any compromises.[38] The first task was to eliminate all idols and images of false gods. Confucianism, Daoism, and Buddhism were all condemned as false teachings and idolatrous. Confucian scholars worshipping the gods of literature were accused of imploring vanity. They "cling to their delusions" and are "obsessed by their ambitions."[39] "The Confucian examinations are worthless vanities, spreading false hopes, engendering false procedures."[40]

---

[34] Isaiah I:5–7; 28–31.
[35] Liang Afa, *Good Words for the Admonition of the World* (Taipei: Taiwan Student Bookstore, 1965), chap. 1:17.
[36] Hong's annotations on Gen. 3:1–2 and 6:5–13.
[37] Liang, *Good Words,* chap. 12:16.
[38] Spence, *God's Chinese Son*, 254.
[39] Ibid., 60. Taken from *Good Words,* 1:5–6.
[40] *Good Words*, 65.

In the long annotation on Revelation 12, the theme of the great red dragon as the serpent-devil named Demon *Yan-Luo*[41] is highlighted along with God's plan to save humankind by the descent of Jesus to earth and Hong's birth by a woman on the earth.[42] In this annotation, Hong also refers to two other annotations in the Old Testament. As part of God's plan of salvation, God sends Hong as Melchizedek to protect and bless Abraham, knowing that Jesus will be born from one of Abraham's descendants. In the Abraham and Melchizedek story, "King of Salem" becomes "King of Heavenly Dynasty" (Gen. 14:18) as Hong identifies himself with Melchizedek in the annotations. Hong's mission on earth was to fight against and eradicate the devil and bring peace on earth. This annotation stresses that Hong's mission was accomplished through the establishment of the Taiping Kingdom, the fulfillment of the scripture.[43]

The prediction of Hong's descent is explicitly stated in the annotation on God's covenant after the flood (Gen. 9:8–17), with the heavenly rainbow taken as the sign. It curves like a bow, symbolizing the sun in the Chinese character, with Hong himself as the shining sun. The rainbow that appears in heaven also "prophesies that God would send Hong the Sun to be the Lord."[44] The Chinese concept of *xiafan* (meaning "descending to the earth") and divine indwelling are central ideas used to understand the epiphany of God, Jesus's incarnation, and Hong's divine mission. The use of the term *xiafan* itself shows the impact of the traditional Chinese religious notion of "descending to the profane." In the annotation to Matthew 3:16 on the baptism of Jesus, it is written: "The Holy Spirit is God, and the Elder Brother is God's Eldest son. When the Elder Brother comes, God also comes. So it is that God and Christ have now descended into the world. Respect this."[45] In Jesus God has dwelt, and Jesus's word is therefore God's word, and Jesus's healing power is from God (Matt. 8:1–4; 14–15; 9:29–30).

The figure Melchizedek in Genesis 14:17–24 was interpreted by Hong as "none other than me." Hong made use of the Melchizedek passage to indicate that whatever God intends to do, God must give him a "premonition."[46] Melchizedek

---

[41] Hong uses the phrase "the Demon Devil Yan Luo and his minions" to refer to the power of evil and its company; see Spence, *God's Chinese Son*, 254. "Yan Luo" is the Chinese name for the master of hell, who controls the dead.
[42] Hong points out that a sign of the sun was made and he was clothed with the sun, a symbol of royalty and kingship in China.
[43] English translation in Michael, *The Taiping Rebellion,* vol. 2, 236–37. See also Cheng, *Chinese Sources,* 90–91, and the Chinese original in Yufu, *Historical Sources,* 86–87.
[44] My modification of Michael's rendering in *The Taiping Rebellion,* vol. 2, 225.
[45] "Respect this!" is a standard phrase used by the emperor to conclude the imperial edict that demands obedience from his subjects.
[46] The translation in Michael, *The Taiping Rebellion,* vol. 2, is "previous allusion," which is not appropriate in the context.

is historical proof of Hong's descent manifested in real events. The notion of premonition is further developed by the illustration of God descending in ancient times to deliver the Israelites from Egypt and the birth of the Elder Brother, Jesus in Judah, to save the world. Hong also refers to himself in these words: "In the past when I descended into the world to comfort and bless Abraham, it was a very good premonition."[47]

The theme of fulfillment seems to be purely Christian, but it is also combined with the Chinese shamanist concept of signs and portents to demonstrate the coming of a mandated ruler or savior. Hong claimed to be the one predicted by the Scriptures of both the Old and New Testaments to be sent by *Shangdi* and Jesus. Hong also believed that Jesus was referring to him in Matthew 27 when he talked about rebuilding the temple in three days. "Three" refers to the three dots of Hong's surname in Chinese characters and "days" indicates the "sun" ("re" in Chinese has both the meaning of "day" and the "sun"). Hong therefore interpreted "three days" as having the metaphorical meaning of "Hong the sun who will become the ruler and rebuild the destroyed temple."

The establishment of the Taiping Heavenly Kingdom secured its biblical foundation in Hong's interpretation of the Bible. The often-spoken phrase "Earthy Paradise," which refers to the "Heavenly Court" of Nanjing, the capital of the kingdom, is understood vis-à-vis the "Greater Heaven" awaiting the souls of God's followers. Being an earthly "Little Heaven," it represents man's temporal physical existence. Hong justified this belief through his interpretation of the texts of I Corinthian 15:49–53 and Acts 15:14–16. The divine revelatory status of Hong's "Heavenly Court" also was supported by the commentary about the new Jerusalem in the Book of Revelation 3:12. Hong's annotated note in the margin reads:

> Now the Elder Brother is come. In the Heavenly Court is the temple of the Heavenly Father, *Shangdi,* the True Deity; there also is the Elder Brother Christ's temple, wherein are already inscribed the names of God and Christ. The New Jerusalem sent down from Heaven by God the Heavenly Father is our present Heavenly Capital [Tianjing]. It is fulfilled. Respect these words.[48]

Building the heavenly kingdom on earth has been a tradition in certain Christian communities and theological circles. Hong regarded his heavenly

[47] Michael, *The Taiping Rebellion,* vol. 2, 225.
[48] Michael, *The Taiping Rebellion,* vol. 2, 235, quoted and modified by Spence, *God's Chinese Son,* 295. See also Yufu, *Historical Sources,* 86.

dynasty as the fulfillment of Jesus's word in the gospel. He says in the annotation on Matthew 5 that the "Kingdom is at hand" and the "Great Paradise" includes both the heavenly kingdom above and the one on earth. Hong saw his capital in Nanjing as the new Jerusalem coming down from heaven as it is revealed in Revelation 21. Furthermore, the songs of the angels, who appeared to the shepherds in the field during the birth of Jesus, are interpreted as being fulfilled in the present (Luke 2:13–14). "Glory to God in the highest and peace (*taiping*) upon humanity below" refers to "the establishment of the Kingdom of Great Peace." The new Jerusalem seen by John in Revelation 21 is therefore said to be both in heaven and on earth. According to the annotation, the heavenly capital of the heavenly dynasty is regarded as the new Jerusalem on earth.[49]

Whether Hong's motivation in setting off the revolution was genuinely based on his religious experience or he made use of Christianity only for his rebellious movement depends on how committed he was to these religious beliefs.[50] The eighty-two annotations and commentaries Hong wrote in the ample margins of the Bible may appear to some as "incoherent, meaningless, ramblings,"[51] but they are appropriations shaped by Hong's claim to be God's younger son and his convictions about the coming of great peace on earth. He believed that the Old Testament should be read, as in the Christian tradition of the missionary movement of the time, in the light of the New Testament. The former contains the prophecies of not only the prefiguration of the messianic mission of Jesus as the Christ but also the prediction of his own descent to earth to establish salvation through the Taiping Heavenly Kingdom.

Conclusion

The Bible is a powerful text that inspires readers to reach their own interpretations when they are free from the prescribed interpretation governed by traditional doctrines of the Christian community. Biblical themes, concepts, motifs, and literary structures provide the basic foundations for imagination and enable readers to engage with the text in their own differ that ways, which sometimes seem strange to the Christian communities that claim to

[49] Yufu, *Historical Sources*, 87; Michael, *The Taiping Rebellion,* vol. 2, 237; and Cheng, *Chinese Sources,* 91.
[50] Luo is of the position that Hong's political agenda came first and religion was only the outer garment; see his *History of the Taiping Kingdom,* vol. 2, 153.
[51] Michael, *The Taiping Rebellion,* vol. 2, 234.

own the text and assume an authoritative reading strategy. In this case, it is the utopian ideals that captured the minds and thoughts both of the poor peasants who had been oppressed by their corrupt government and of a disappointed scholar who failed the public examinations that could have guaranteed him a successful and respectable life. The Heavenly Kingdom of Great Peace that Hong described as a result of his imaginative reading of the Bible cannot be said to have been meaningless to the thousands of frustrated peasants in the southern part of China at the time. The new religion that Hong formulated was complex in its attempts to integrate Christianity, Confucian teachings, indigenous shamanistic beliefs, and the political agenda of the Taiping Heavenly Kingdom on earth. But as a result of its syncretistic approach and ideological concerns, Hong's religion was undermined by conventional Christianity and deemed heretical.

When I ponder the situation and experience of Jesus and his disciples in their quest for salvation in the midst of the Roman Empire, my mind is drawn to the challenging parallels between Jesus and Hong. Jesus read the Hebrew Bible and saw himself as the Son of God, fulfilling the text's promise of redemption of the people of Israel. Most contemporary Jewish communities find the ways the New Testament interprets the Old Testament to be offensive and blasphemous. The new religion and its text have survived to become the gospel. Perhaps it was its political agenda and massive military campaigns that eventually drove the Taiping Heavenly Kingdom to its destruction. The withdrawal of the colonial powers and the abandonment by the missionary boards facilitated the brutal suppression of the short-lived kingdom and the bloody massacre of not only the rebellious Taiping Army but also innocent citizens in all the cities that came under the rule of the Taiping regime. All things even remotely linked to the Taipings in China were utterly destroyed, and all publications were completely burned. No wonder the only copy of the imperial edition of the Taiping Bible that survives today is found in the British Library.

The Bible does speak through its readers, albeit sometimes to our surprise and in a strange voice not generally recognized by those who claim to be in possession of it, defending the authority of its interpretation and upholding the orthodoxy that presumably derives from it. The questions are: who has the power to set criteria for interpretation when the Bible leaves the familiar context of the conventional Christian community and encounters a foreign culture, with its plurality of texts and scriptures? How valid are the traditions of the "mother church" for the "younger churches" in the so-called mission field? Who should govern the process of reading the Bible in a new sociopolitical context? Perhaps for those who are interested in canonical criticsm, should the

Bible always be understood only as the canon in the traditions of the Christian community, as has been proposed by proponents of canonical criticism?[52]

The Bible is surely an open text that invites a variety of interpretations and inspires a plurality of readings in diverse contexts. Who should own the Bible and therefore possess the monopoly of the power to interpret? Many of us have, in one way or another, shown our appreciation of the creativity demonstrated by literature, visual arts, and music as they engage in and appropriate the Bible. The great challenge for us is: who can exercise the authority to keep the Bible within the Christian community and to not allow it to live out its life as a scripture of another religion or to liberate the human imagination for the "peoples of God" in a new context in Asia?

Hong's interpretation of the Bible is a typical example of the encounter between the biblical scriptures and the Asian texts in a non-Christian context in which readers possess numerous religious texts. Even if the local texts are being suppressed in principle, they still exercise some cultural influence on native readers. On the other hand, the power of the biblical text should not be undermined. The basic structure and motifs in the Bible do provide the imagination and inspiration for new readers in new contexts. ■

[52] See the representative works of Brevard S. Child, *Introduction to the Old Testament as Scripture* (London: SCM Press, 1979) and *Old Testament Theology in a Canonical Context* (London: SCM Press, 1985), as well as James A. Sanders, *Canon and Community: A Guide to Canonical Criticism* (Philadelphia: Fortress Press, 1984). James Barr, whom I regard as a great biblical scholar and for whom I had the honor of being invited to pay my respects in a memorial during the 2007 San Diego SBL session, engaged the canonical issues from a perspective different from the conventional canonical criticism in his books: *The Scope and Authority of the Bible* (Philadelphia: Westminster Press, 1980) and *Holy Scripture: Canon, Authority, Criticism* (Oxford: Clarendon Press, 1983).

Moral Theater in the Streets: The Role of Suffering in the Quest for Social Justice

by Peter J. Paris

Dr. Peter J. Paris, Elmer G. Homrighausen Professor of Christian Social Ethics Emeritus at Princeton Theological Seminary, gave this Dr. Martin Luther King Jr. Lecture on April 7, 2008, in Miller Chapel. Paris earned his M.A. and Ph.D. degrees at the University of Chicago, which honored him as alumnus of the year in 1995. Paris has served as president of the American Academy of Religion, the Society of Christian Ethics, and the Society for the Study of Black Religion. He is the author of Black Religious Leaders: Conflict in Unity *(1991) and* The Spirituality of African Peoples: The Search for a Common Moral Discourse *(1995).*

On this fortieth anniversary of the assassination of Martin Luther King Jr., it is altogether right and proper that Princeton Theological Seminary have a lecture in honor of the twentieth century's most respected civic leader. I have fond memories of Professor Mark Taylor devoting much energy to helping us develop the rationale for such a lectureship. Our aim was to have an annual lecture delivered in April by a scholar who would address King's legacy from an academic perspective. Your invitation to me to present this year's lecture is a great honor for which I am most grateful.

Since 1986 this nation has celebrated Dr. King's birthday as a national holiday, and it will forever be associated with the legacy of Congressman John Conyers from Michigan, Congresswoman Shirley Chisholm, and Dr. King's widow, Coretta Scott King. Conyers introduced the bill for a national holiday four days after King's assassination. He and Congresswoman Chisholm reintroduced it each year afterward. Mrs. King worked tirelessly for fifteen years to build public support for the bill and to raise monies to build the Martin Luther King Jr. Center for Nonviolent Social Change at the site of his family home and church in Atlanta.

DOI: 10.3754/1937–8386.2008.29.1.5

By celebrating King's birth, we recognize the promise of a great soul who would contribute much good to his nation and the world at large. By commemorating his assassination we recognize that the struggle for racial justice was a matter of life and death for all who had the courage to oppose the prevailing customs and mores of the day. Dr. King predicted that he would eventually be killed, and he lived every day anticipating it. In other words, he was haunted daily by the angst of constant terror. His home was bombed; he was beaten, stabbed, insulted, ridiculed, spied upon, abused, threatened, jailed twenty-nine times, and finally killed in broad daylight.

The so-called civil rights movement at mid-century was motivated by the Supreme Court decision of May 17, 1954, in *Brown v. the Board of Education*, which overturned the *Plessy v. Ferguson* decision of 1896 that had bestowed constitutional legitimacy on the racial doctrine of "separate but equal." Prompted by the gentle disobedience of Rosa Parks to give up her bus seat to a white man, King, a clergyman of twenty-six years of age, fresh from Ph.D. studies in theology, was called upon to lay the theological and moral foundation for a boycott of the buses in Montgomery, Alabama. No one could have predicted that that boycott would last for nearly thirteen months. And none could have imagined that its momentum would steadily increase and eventually culminate in the Civil Rights Act of 1964 and the Voting Rights Act of 1965, both of which restored first-class citizenship to blacks for the first time since the period of Reconstruction.

Along with others I view this notable struggle through the imagery of moral theater in the streets. With King as the major protagonist, the public drama took the form of nonviolent resistance comprising well-dressed students marching; singing the so-called spirituals of their ancestors while updating their lyrics; praying on the steps of the state capitols; shouting slogans; waving posters; gathering in churches for prayers, testimonies, and preaching; and, most of all, refusing to retaliate with violence. More often than not, these nonviolent demonstrators were confronted with the violence of the local and state police forces, hatemongers, and the nefarious activities of clandestine groups such as the Ku Klux Klan. Other collateral dramas inspired by the same ethos also gained visibility, such as the 1959 Albany campaign, the 1961 Freedom Riders campaign, the 1962 University of Mississippi desegregation crisis, the 1964 freedom summer campaign, and the 1964 appearance of the Mississippi Freedom Democratic Party at the Democratic Party's National Convention in Atlantic City, where Fannie Lou Hamer, the youngest of twenty-two children in a sharecropper's family who was badly beaten by her Mississippi jailers, gained national visibility by telling her story of suffering and ending with the song, "This Little Light of Mine."

Time does not permit a comprehensive analysis of the phenomenon of street theater in the civil rights movement. Rather, my aim is to discuss one dimension of that subject, which permeated every scene of those street dramas, namely, the role of suffering in the moral quest for racial justice. In fact, the experience of suffering has characterized the lives of African Americans ever since 1619, when our ancestors were sold into slavery for the first time in Jamestown, Virginia. They had come to this country not as hopeful immigrants but as human cargo, destined to remain in the cauldron of slavery for 244 years, followed by another century of racial segregation and discrimination. During every period of that brutal experience, the enslaved Africans displayed two major characteristics: one that aimed at survival, and the other that sought freedom and social transformation.

On the one hand, their drive for survival necessitated what appeared to be passive endurance of the incessant misery of forced labor: an experience that the poet James Weldon Johnson aptly described as a time "when hope unborn had died." On the other hand, their spirit of resistance involved a variety of actions that included clandestine meetings for spiritual nurture through music, dance, and song, and plotting either to escape or to rebel.

Subsequent to the abolition of slavery and the fall of Reconstruction, this nation descended into a moral quagmire, a condition that Rayford Logan called the nadir in American history. Throughout that time blacks adapted to their situation when they had no other choice, and they protested against it whenever they possibly could. Clearly, the civil rights movement led by Martin Luther King Jr., constituted a unique moment in the history of black resistance because the Montgomery bus boycott was the first sustained direct confrontation blacks had ever launched against the white power structure. The noted sociologist C. Eric Lincoln claimed that this significant action marked a radical change in the history of African American civil protest in the south. Henceforth, the Montgomery bus boycott would symbolize the death of the so-called Negro church as E. Franklin Frazier had understood it and the birth of the nascent black church.[1]

In the late 1960s, nascent black theologians sought to give theological meaning to the post–civil rights struggle for economic and political power. The provocative phrase "black power" emerged during that period. It was a term that originated from the radical rhetoric of King's rebellious follower, Stokely Carmichael. Along with his followers, Carmichael strongly believed that radical thinking and aggressive actions would persuade growing numbers of people

---

[1] See C. Eric Lincoln, *The Black Church Since Frazier* (bound with Edward Franklin Frazier's *The Negro Church in America*) (New York: Schocken Books, 1974).

that King's method of nonviolent resistance had become obsolete. Under the influence of both Marxist and black nationalist ideologies, they rejected King's ethics of love and reconciliation, which they mistakenly interpreted as passive acceptance of suffering coupled with an unnatural love for their oppressors. King tried in vain to remain in dialogue with these challengers, as seen in his last book, *Where Do We Go from Here: Chaos or Community,* in which he argued against the use of the words "black power" because of their inflammatory semantic effects.

Over the years and in varying ways, the problem of suffering has been a major theological concern in the religious thought of a wide range of theological thinkers, such as the black nationalist Malcolm X, long-time national spokesman for the Honorable Elijah Muhammad's Nation of Islam, commonly known as the Black Muslims; the black liberation theologians James Cone, Gayraud Wilmore, William R. Jones, and others; the womanist theologians Delores Williams, Jacqueline Grant, JoAnne Terrell, et al.; and white feminist theologians Judith Plaskow, Rita Nakashima Brock, and Susan Thistlethwaite, to mention only a few.

Rejection of Traditional Atonement Theories

Though very different from one another in many ways, black liberation, womanist, and feminist theologians all shared, both then and now, a profound dislike for the violence associated with those traditional theories of atonement that offered theological explanations for the meaning of Christ's crucifixion. The following are the most prominent of those theories:

- Origen's ransom theory in the third century, which was dominant in the church's teaching for the first millenium and was based on the necessity of God paying a ransom to Satan for the deliverance of humanity from the punishment for Adam and Eve's sin

- Anselm's satisfaction theory in the eleventh century, which modified the ransom theory by viewing the payment being made to God to satisfy God's law and justice rather than Satan

- the Reformation's penal-substitution theory in the sixteenth century, which emphasized God's mercy replacing God's wrath

- the liberationist/feminist/womanist theologies that totally reject all notions of violence as the means to salvation in favor of a moral emphasis on the life of Christ for that purpose.

In short, one or other of the traditional atonement theories have informed all the major Christian traditions. This is seen vividly in the annual liturgical remembrances of the passion of Christ leading up to Easter. Prior to the black theology movement, the black churches seemed to have uncritically embraced the atonement tradition. Yet it is important to note that although they always viewed the suffering of Christ as analogous to theirs, they were never comfortable with embracing those theories that claimed that God required the crucifixion as a necessary condition for human salvation.

Since blacks knew from their own experience that suffering was inevitable for all people who dared to oppose the reigning ethos of racial injustice, they tended to understand the suffering of Jesus similarly. Consequently, they always felt a close affinity with him for his prophetic criticisms of the religious and political systems of his day, and his opposition to injustice, which resulted in his crucifixion. Accordingly, the black church prophetic tradition has identified itself with the life and ministry of Jesus.

The nascent theologies that African Americans constructed in the late 1960s and beyond critically claimed that the traditional atonement theories were morally and psychologically crippling for all oppressed peoples and especially for African Americans and all women. Needless to say, perhaps, as those new theologies sought to ground their understandings of Christ's life and mission in the historical struggles of oppressed peoples for liberation, they collided headlong with the mainline theological traditions of the Christian churches: traditions that had been greatly influenced by the Hellenistic ethos of the so-called church fathers whose theologies virtually abstracted Christ from history altogether. Consequently, black theologians claimed that they had failed to demonstrate the meaning of the crucifixion for oppressed peoples.[2] By doing so they had created a vast divide between the cross of Christ and the Exodus event that Jesus referenced in his mission statement in the gospel of Luke, which black liberation theologians have always considered paradigmatic for their own constructive thought:

> The Spirit of the Lord is upon me,
> Because he has anointed me
> To bring good news to the poor.
> He has sent me to proclaim release to the captives
> And recovery of sight to the blind,

---

[2] The noted black theologian Howard Thurman's early book *Jesus and the Disinherited* (Nashville: Abingdon-Cokesbury Press, 1949) addressed that question by a careful rendering of Christian thought among enslaved Africans as seen in the so-called Negro spirituals.

To let the oppressed go free,
To proclaim the year of the Lord's favor. (Luke 4:18)

King's Understanding of Suffering

King frequently used the phrase "redemptive suffering," which he had inherited from the traditional substitution theory of the Cross. In my judgment, he used traditional atonement language in order to set forth an alternative view of suffering, which we will analyze carefully.

Condemnation of racial injustice and strong advocacy for racial justice was the substance of King's thought and action. Consequently, I contend that he was the forerunner of the black theology movement, which has never given him his due credit because of its blindness to his true understanding of suffering. Though most black liberation and some womanist theologians have made enduring contributions to our discourse about the relation of Christ's mission to the struggles of African Americans for racial justice, they have minimized the contribution of King's thought and action to theirs. In doing so they have misunderstood the prophetic tradition that Jesus explained in the Sermon on the Mount and that King embraced as the basis of his teaching and practice.

It is important to note that neither black liberation theology nor womanist theology was at the vanguard of the civil rights movement. Rather, they emerged after the movement had completed its work and achieved its primary legislative goal of first-class citizenship for African Americans. Henceforth, citizens of African descent would be protected by law and entitled to all the rights and privileges of full citizenship, including that of democratic dissent. Even the use of radical rhetoric by various black nationalists was protected by the accomplishments of the civil rights movement and the extraordinary leadership of Martin Luther King Jr.

For more than a decade King's leadership saturated the public arena with his prophetic diagnosis that racial injustice constituted a malignancy in the soul of America, a malignancy that he predicted would eventually destroy the nation if it were not eradicated. The image of a diseased nation implied only one possible cure, namely, the eradication of its cause. Thus, King viewed his mission as that of redeeming and saving America's soul. His prophetic witness courageously called upon the nation to live up to its ideals by expanding its democracy to include African Americans as equal citizens. His vision of a redeemed nation captured the imagination of a generation of people both in this country and around the world, where countless other oppressed peoples were inspired to challenge the prevailing systems of injustice that they experienced in their search for freedom and justice. King's persuasive rhetoric and courageous actions inspired men, women, and children of all races to participate in an unusual program of nonviolent resistance that he initiated, nurtured, and carried out faithfully through numerous church gatherings, mass rallies, and public demonstrations. Rarely had the nation ever seen such countless numbers of students, teachers, ministers, priests, rabbis, singers, musicians, comedians, movie stars, and little children gather in the churches and pour out into the streets of Albany, Georgia; Birmingham; Selma; and even Chicago as disciplined nonviolent resisters to the societal structures of racial injustice. In fact, many black doctors, lawyers, entrepreneurs, and others who did not march supported the demonstrators by paying bail money and providing pro bono defense services and medical attention when needed.

Furthermore, all those who participated in the many auxiliary activities of the movement—such as lunch counter sit-ins, freedom rides, voter registration campaigns, and the desegregation of the University of Mississippi—embraced and exemplified that same spirit of nonviolent resistance. Though King was widely criticized by both whites and blacks for his method of nonviolence, it nonetheless characterized all aspects of the civil rights movement throughout the entire decade of its existence (1955–1965).

In every campaign much blood was shed by the participants. Most important, however, each participant was a willing active agent in the resistance movement and not a passive recipient of suffering as most black nationalists, including black theologians, mistakenly thought. Because of the novelty of the event, most whites and blacks failed to comprehend its power and significance. For the first time in the nation's history, blacks and whites deliberately chose to work together nonviolently in their resistance to the evil practices of racial segregation.

Both observers and participants alike easily discerned that the purpose of the movement was to provoke the mean-spirited forces of racism to reveal their true nature in confronting the protestors who, in turn, would take upon themselves the resulting pain and suffering inflicted upon them. Though none believed that God required such suffering, each knew that their goal was fully in accord with God's will. The suffering inflicted on them represented the resistance of evil forces whenever they are threatened by the possibility of change. The willingness of the resisters to endure the suffering represented the divine character of love, which always implies forgiveness and reconciliation as the foundational principles of racial justice.

Thus, the protestors willingly offered their bodies to absorb the brunt of the physical force that was leveled against them. As anticipated, their resistance provoked the municipal and state authorities to attack them with brutal force. Like prisoners, blacks had always been expected either to stay in their place or risk the violence of the state police, which was reinforced by terroristic white citizen groups, such as the Ku Klux Klan. Unwittingly, various southern sheriffs, such as Bull O'Connor and Jim Clark, supported by state governors and congressional senators like George Wallace, Senator James Eastland, and many others, cooperated beautifully in the unfolding drama. Television cameras carried the images of their cruelty into American living rooms nationwide and to the world at large.

The nonviolent resisters had assumed that the nation's conscience would respond appropriately to the images of innocent people being severely beaten and abused as they asserted their right to protest racial injustice. The redemption of a nation that was proud of its democratic tradition necessitated the expansion of that tradition to include blacks as full citizens. Alas, that goal would not be realized aside from the pain and suffering inflicted on the protestors by the ruling authorities.

Certainly, not all blacks were willing to affirm King's method of nonviolent resistance. As students became exposed to and influenced by the notions of cultural pride that were implicit in the black nationalist ideologies they were discovering, and as they began viewing violence as justifiable in self-defense according to the teachings of Malcolm X, they gradually began turning away from King's unusual method of nonviolent resistance. Their rejection of that method was intensified each time they heard King's oft-repeated teaching that "unmerited suffering is redemptive." Under the influence of black nationalism, black theologians persisted in viewing King's philosophy of nonviolent resistance as a legacy of white slave-holding Christianity and, correspondingly, the habits of accommodating themselves to racial insult, abuse, and exploitation.

In my judgment, if he had lived to experience it, King would have objected strongly to James Cone's teaching that blacks are justified in fighting for their liberation "by any means possible." In fact, Cone argued that King's method of nonviolent resistance and his concern for the reconciliation of the races constituted an accommodation to a white value system that denies ontological status to the liberation of black people prior to any move toward reconciliation. By contrast, King would have argued as he often did that his commitment to nonviolent resistance was motivated by the spirit of the Sermon on the Mount, which proclaimed an alternative approach to violence as the only way to break its circular effect. Thus, he said:

> To meet hate with retaliatory hate would do nothing but intensify the existence of evil in the universe. Hate begets hate; violence begets violence; toughness begets a greater toughness. We must meet the forces of hate with the power of love; we must meet physical force with soul force. ... The end is redemption and reconciliation. The aftermath of nonviolence is the creation of the beloved community, while the aftermath of violence is tragic bitterness.[3]

No one ever doubted King's uncompromising commitment to the method of nonviolent resistance that he claimed was regulated by the biblical principle of love as *agape*. Furthermore, he believed that those who practiced nonviolence habitually would become nonviolent people, and even those who merely observed its practice would be transformed similarly by its power. He also taught that the final goal of his method was reconciliation and redemption, because the struggle they were waging was not against people but against the forces of evil that victimized all concerned, including the oppressors themselves.

Thus, King's theology resonated well with the black liberation theology of J. Deotis Roberts as well as that of various womanist theologies. Though Cone has striven valiantly to sustain a positive assessment of King's integrative theology, he has only been able to do so by holding him in dialectical tension with the thought and practice of Malcolm X. In my judgment, the dialectical relationship he sees between the two is not a resolution but a juxtaposition of two contraries. Because most blacks appreciate many of the teachings of both King and Malcolm, and though they may have been influenced in different ways by each of them, the attempt to hold them together in a dialectical manner is neither a theological nor a moral solution. King's uncompromising commitment to nonviolence constituted an irreparable divide between him and Malcolm and between him and Cone.

King's Diagnosis of Racism

Let no one suppose, as some have implied, that King provided a weak diagnosis of the problem of either racism or the suffering it entailed for blacks. Fully acknowledging the painful and tragic history that African Americans endured for several centuries, he called upon the nation to eradicate all forms of racism from its midst. In his Palm Sunday sermon in Washington, D.C., a few days before his assassination, he said the following in the language of the day:

---

[3] James M. Washington, *A Testament of Hope: The Essential Writings of Martin Luther King, Jr.* (San Francisco, Harper and Row, 1986), 17–18.

> I must say this morning that racial injustice is still the black man's burden and the white man's shame. ...
>
> It is an unhappy truth that racism is a way of life for the vast majority of white Americans, spoken and unspoken, acknowledged and denied, subtle and sometimes not so subtle—the disease of racism permeates and poisons the body politic. And I can see nothing more urgent than for America to work passionately and unrelentingly to get rid of the disease of racism.
>
> Something must be done. Everyone must share in the guilt as individuals and as institutions. The government must certainly share the guilt, individuals must share the guilt, even the church must share this guilt.[4]

Furthermore, King provided a vivid picture of why blacks should not be expected to pull themselves up by their own bootstraps, as European immigrants once did. He drew a sharp difference between the experience of African Americans and that of white European immigrants. The former had the unique distinction of being enslaved for two and a half centuries, followed by the unwillingness of the government to render them any kind of material assistance whatsoever. King described the situation thusly, which I quote extensively:

> No other group has been a slave on American soil. ... the nation made the black man's color a stigma; but beyond this they never stop to realize the debt that they owe a people who were kept in slavery for 244 years.
>
> In 1863 the Negro was told that he was free as a result of the Emancipation Proclamation being signed by Abraham Lincoln. But he was not given any land to make that freedom meaningful. It was something like keeping a person in prison for a number of years and suddenly discovering that that person is not guilty of the crime for which he was convicted. And you just go up to him and say, "Now you are free," but you don't give him any bus fare to get to town. You don't give him any money to get some clothes to put on his back or to get on his feet again in life.
>
> Every court of jurisprudence would rise up against this, and yet this is the very thing that our nation did to the black man. It simply said, "you're free," and it left him there penniless, illiterate, not knowing what to do. And the irony of it all is that at the same time the nation failed to do anything for the black man—through an act of Congress

---

[4] Ibid., 270.

> it was giving away millions of acres of land in the West and the Mid-West—which meant that it was willing to undergird its white peasants from Europe with an economic floor.
>
> But not only did it give the land, it built land-grant colleges to teach them how to farm. Not only that, it provided county agents to further their expertise in farming: Not only that, as the years unfolded it provided low interest rates so that they could mechanize their farms. And to this day thousands of these very persons are receiving millions of dollars in federal subsidies every year not to farm. And these are so often the very people who tell Negroes that they must lift themselves by their own bootstraps. It's all right to tell a man to lift himself by his own bootstraps, but it is a cruel jest to say to a bootless man that he ought to lift himself by his own bootstraps.[5]

Like all struggles for social justice, the struggle for civil rights in this country was no cakewalk. During the decade, approximately forty people died as martyrs in the cause of racial freedom and justice.[6] Thousands carry the marks of physical wounds on their bodies today. As a matter of fact, my good friend and colleague, Professor William B. McClain, who teaches homiletics and worship at Wesley Theological Seminary in Washington, D.C., walks with a slight limp because of a gunshot wound in his hip that he received while kneeling in prayer with King at the statehouse in his native Birmingham, Alabama. In the year 1963 alone, children from six years old upwards, and their mothers, were attacked with fire hoses and snarling dogs. Two months before the historic march on Washington, D.C., Medgar Evers was assassinated on the steps of his home by a sniper. Eighteen days following that march, four little girls were killed at Sunday school in the Sixteenth Street Baptist Church, Birmingham. On November twenty-second of that year, President John F. Kennedy was assassinated after pledging his support for a civil rights bill.

Clearly, King had good reason for constantly reminding his wife, family, and followers that he did not expect to live through the civil rights movement. When President Kennedy was assassinated, King once again reminded those around him that he expected a similar death. Not invited to the funeral, he traveled alone to Washington and stood on a side street weeping as the cortege moved along its way to the Arlington National Cemetery.

---

[5] Ibid., 271.
[6] The names of those martyrs are inscribed on Maya Linn's Civil Rights Memorial at the Southern Poverty Law Center in Montgomery, Alabama.

King believed that much of the suffering blacks have endured was inflicted on them by the nation. Few African Americans have doubted the accuracy of that diagnosis. Most important, he knew as we all do that suffering deliberately caused by an external agent is not only ignoble but totally void of any positive value. It is analogous only to torture. No one can rightly call such suffering redemptive even though some African Americans like Phyllis Wheatley, the most prominent of such proponents, once interpreted slavery as intended by God so that Africans could be converted to Christianity and return to Africa to evangelize the continent. Fortunately, such a divine pragmatic scheme was never widely adopted by African Americans.

Nonetheless, their suffering has been ubiquitous, and virtually none has escaped its pain. As a life-threatening phenomenon, white racism unfailingly considers every person of African descent genetically stained as an inferior destined for unequal treatment. Those who have spoken against it in public have always run the risk of retaliation by the stakeholders of the status quo. Those who try to transcend it by focusing on their own personal achievements never succeed because both whites and blacks place them under the lenses of perpetual scrutiny and disdain. Those who blame their own people for their suffering serve the spirit of racism best of all because they justify those who create and sustain the problem. These also repudiate all who advocate reparations or affirmative action programs.

Let us hasten to say, however, that African Americans have also striven to overcome their suffering through countless artistic expressions, such as the blues, spirituals, jazz, and hip-hop. In his book *Race Matters*, philosopher of religion Cornel West speaks of the blues as tragicomic hope, an essential ingredient in sustaining one's humanity:

> The tragicomic is the ability to laugh and retain a sense of life's joy—to preserve hope even while staring in the face of hate and hypocrisy—as against falling into the nihilism of paralyzing despair. This tragicomic hope is expressed in America most profoundly in the wrenchingly honest yet compassionate voices of the black freedom struggle; most poignantly in the painful eloquence of the blues; and most exuberantly in the improvisational virtuosity of jazz.[7]

King was nurtured all of his life in the black church's gospel music. He loved to hear Mahalia Jackson and similar artists sing those old familiar songs. In

---

[7] Cornel West, *Democracy Matters* (New York, Penguin Press, 2004), 16.

fact, while standing on the balcony of the Lorraine Hotel just minutes before he was killed, he asked Ben Branch, director of Operation Breadbasket's orchestra, to sing at the service that night Thomas Dorsey's hymn, "Precious Lord, Take My Hand."

King never ceased believing that even the worst racist person had the capacity to change and hence should be loved because everyone is a child of God. Thus, Marshall Frady quotes King speaking in 1964 to a group of people in Greenville, Mississippi, whom he discerned had lived their lives in fear of white racists:

> Mississippi has treated the Negro as if he is a thing instead of a person. But you must not allow anybody to make you feel you are not significant and you do not count. Every Negro here in Greenwood, Mississippi, has worth and dignity—because white, Negro, Chinese, Indian, man or woman or child, we are all the children of God. You are somebody. I want every one of you to say that out loud now to yourself—I am somebody.[8]

King frequently said that one of the best accomplishments of the movement was the evidence that blacks who had been afraid of whites at one time now had courage and those who had viewed themselves as having no dignity now had a renewed sense of pride. He believed beyond a doubt that all the accomplishments of the movement were due to the method of nonviolent resistance regulated by *agape* as taught and lived by Jesus. That love ethic loves without counting the cost. Thus, King was able to say during times of great crisis and mourning, like the funeral of the four little girls in Birmingham, "We must not lose faith in our white brothers. Somehow we must believe that the most misguided among them can learn to respect the dignity and worth of all human personality."[9]

I am convinced that it was pleasing to God that King and his followers should resist racial injustice nonviolently. Most important, they expected and prepared themselves for the suffering that they would encounter because it is the method that oppressors use to retaliate against those who threaten the benefits and privileges they derive from maintaining the status quo. Such suffering is evidence of the evil. To retaliate in like fashion merely perpetuates the brokenness of human relations. The resistance of the police and other state officials demonstrated the unjust violence of the system toward the healing goodness of the protestors. The function of the protestors was to provoke the custodians of the status quo to reveal the concealed violence that controlled the social system of racism with

---

[8] Marshall Frady, *Martin Luther King, Jr.* (New York: Penguin, 2002), 146.
[9] Martin Luther King, Jr., "Nonviolence and Racial Justice," in Washington, *A Testament of Hope*, 9.

the expectation that its appearance in public view would prompt the nation to make the necessary correctives.

Analogously, this is quite similar to the history of Jesus's prophetic encounter with the religious and political authorities of his day. His teachings and practices of mercy, love, and justice challenged the social system to reveal its violent methods in confronting all such endeavors. The suffering that ensued in the forms of an unjust trial, physical abuse, public disdain, and the horrors of crucifixion were predictable and not determined by God to appease God's anger as a necessary condition for divine forgiveness.

All those who characterize the nonviolent resistance of either Jesus or King as cowardice, passivity, or masochistic love for one's tormentors fail to understand the essential nature of the Christian prophetic tradition as exemplified by those who are moral exemplars of authentic Christian ministry. The moral theater in which each was a primary actor revealed the tragic dimension of human existence because their respective confrontations with oppressive evil forces resulted in predictable and inevitable suffering: suffering not required by God but the predictable outcome of righteous spirits struggling against evil forces. Jesus expressed that argument well in the beatitudes by stating that all advocates of justice, mercy, and peace would be persecuted:

> Blessed are those who hunger and thirst for righteousness for they will be filled.
> Blessed are the merciful for they will receive mercy. …
> Blessed are the peacemakers, for they will be called children of God.
> Blessed are those who are persecuted for righteousness' sake, for theirs is the kingdom of heaven. (Matt. 5: 6, 7, 9, 10)

Martin Luther King Jr. expressed similar viewpoints equally well:

> This, in brief, is the method of nonviolent resistance. It is a method that challenges all people struggling for justice and freedom. God grant that we wage the struggle with dignity and discipline. May all who suffer oppression in this world reject the self-defeating method of retaliatory violence and choose the method that seeks to redeem. By using this method wisely and courageously we will emerge from the bleak and desolate midnight of man's inhumanity to man into the bright daybreak of freedom and justice.[10]

---

[10] King, "Nonviolence, " in Washington, *A Testament of Hope*, 9.

What We Have Learned from Martin Luther King Jr.

We have learned that the use of nonviolent resistance in protest activity is not only morally sound but also effective because it can aid greatly in mobilizing widespread public support, especially when suffering is inflicted on the protestors by the law-enforcing authorities. Nonviolent resistance serves both a moral and political purpose: morally it causes those who use the method to become nonviolent people and politically it respects the humanity of those against whom it acts. Thus, the spirit of forgiveness and reconciliation is implied by the method.

We have also learned from King that history is sometimes made by those at the bottom of the social-economic pyramid, though not without struggle and the suffering that attends the process. Invariably such struggle is in pursuit of justice, which, in turn, invariably provokes anger and violence from those whose material benefits and social privileges are threatened. Such violence causes much suffering, pain, and death. Thus the process of social change is cyclical: the initiative of nonviolent resistance; violent response from defenders of power and privilege; resultant pain, suffering, and death by the resisters; public visibility of a formerly concealed problem; moral outrage by citizens and people of good will everywhere; a corrective by the public authorities motivated by sentiments of citizens and people of goodwill demanding change.

Clearly, the prophetic witness cannot by itself win the battle for social justice. It must join in coalitions with others, and Martin Luther King Jr. was a master at motivating others. The prophetic role is to articulate the vision of the good, give public visibility to social injustice, persuasively proclaim the call for change, join in solidarity with the victims of injustice, encourage them in their nonviolent resistance, and persuade all people of goodwill to join in the struggle for social justice. Such coalitional work may be supported by people of diverse theologies and religions, and even those who make no such profession of faith. It is sufficient that they be people of moral virtue who are able to discern the nature of justice and be committed to its realization. These are the things we have learned from Martin Luther King Jr. They should be taught to every generation, and the teaching should begin in our seminaries. ■

Reflections on Pluralism

by Oliver O'Donovan

Oliver O'Donovan is Professor of Christian Ethics and Practical Theology at the University of Edinburgh, Scotland. He delivered this lecture on April 17, 2008, in Princeton Theological Seminary's Miller Chapel as the 2008 recipient of the Abraham Kuyper Prize for Excellence in Reformed Theology and Public Life. His most recent book is Church in Crisis: The Gay Controversy and the Anglican Communion *(2008), and he is the author of* The Ways of Judgment *(2005) and* The Just War Revisited *(2003). He is also past president of the Society for the Study of Christian Ethics.*

In order to think about pluralism, let us begin with the tail of the horse: the suffix, *ism*. One should not be tediously verbal in discussing big ideas, for language is too spontaneous and circumambulatory to be a very detailed guide to what we think. But it is interesting all the same that we have formed this epithet with a suffix that almost always denotes a *philosophical* idiosyncrasy, as in "skepticism" or "deconstructivism." As students forty years ago, we would be pulled up sharply by our elders if we referred to a "pluralist" society: it was a vulgar mistake; the proper term was "plural." But intuitively we thought of pluralism as *a way of seeing* social relations, a perspective on them. It is not a fact that Britain is a plural/pluralist society. There are many facts underlying that assertion, some of them startling, but the proposition *interprets* fact, it does not itself *assert* it. How does it interpret it? In the first place, obviously enough, by letting the spotlight fall on social difference rather than on conformity. But the interesting thing is how it conceives this difference, which is as *plurality*. What is implied in understanding social difference as plurality?

Pluralism conceives of difference as a *danger*. To raise the question of pluralism at all is to frame social reflection with anxiety. Not every difference would, or could, make us anxious. *Linguistic* difference is not alarming in itself (witness the Swiss example), neither is *class* difference (witness eighteenth-century England), nor even *racial* difference, as contemporary North America makes plain.

DOI: 10.3754/1937–8386.2008.29.1.6

Not every difference, then, and not even an assemblage of differences invites the construction of "pluralism." Pluralism singles out for attention something inherently worrying, which is *a difference of practical principle.* When sectional cultures in society act on contrary assumptions and pursue divergent courses in their relations with each other, when there are incompatible modes and expectations of public conduct, then we are anxious. But this still fails to get to the bottom of the anxiety.

The nineteenth century knew of highly differentiated societies and the dangers associated with them. Even today there is nowhere in the Western world where we begin to approach the diversity of cultural and religious plurality, with the accompanying social fragility, that prevailed in nineteenth-century India. But if you asked our colonial ancestors what the danger was, they might talk of Muslim fanaticism, Hindu superstition, Sikh persecution complex, or even Christian arrogance and incomprehension, for one may fear all these threats to a given society, and a thousand like them, without fearing what we fear in pluralism, which is a danger posed by the very constitution of society. In raising "pluralism" to a topic of discussion, we present practical difference as a *foundational* problem, given in the very nature of social interaction.

But then pluralism anticipates a proposal, or a family of proposals, for coping with the danger. The family likeness in these proposals is the positing of *different orders* of practical principles to govern conduct. If each one of us, or each community, thinks about our activity in such idiosyncratic ways that our neighbors lack all practical understanding of us, it is necessary, so it is alleged, to deploy a different kind of thinking to govern our interactions. And so there is proposed a distinction between *first-order* and *second-order principles,* the latter a regime of practical thinking detached from all fundamental principles of action—to use a term that has now become widespread, a "public reason."

But there is an odd feature about this picture: the *object* of anxiety and the *proposal for coping* with the anxiety are, in fact, one and the same: an "ideal type" of society, which is fissile, segmented, held together by principles belonging to none of its component parts. The meaning of this, I take it, is that pluralism is something rather more than a practical anxiety that anticipates a practical proposal. It is a metaphysic of society, at once a way of reading the world and a way of reacting to it. It is as though the coming of new cultural demographics were a moment of metaphysical disclosure, an underlying reality we had overlooked became suddenly clear, and we are disillusioned by our simple idea that society is based on things held in common. It has in view something more than a modification of practice in response to determinate risks, possibilities, hopes, and fears. It has in view a conversion of disposition, enabling us to accept our ontological situation gracefully.

The proposal for a regime of "public reason" has been intensively discussed over the past quarter of a century, yielding a formidable philosophical literature of considerable complexity, and any observation I make about it will inevitably be overgeneral and probably overfamiliar. But it is necessary to review in general terms the problems inherent in the proposal if we are to throw light on the problems of the original anxiety that prompted it, what I have called "difference as plurality." The questions commonly put to public reason can be summed up as: *In what sense is it public?* and *In what sense is it reason?*

In What Sense Is It Public?

The concept of the *public* is formed as a polar opposite to the concept of the private. You cannot have public without private or private without public. But the private is defined negatively, by privation, as the very form of the word betrays; that is to say, by walling off, excluding, refusing entry. Private thought, domestic privacy, property, private associations, and so on are those withheld from universal access. By contrast, the public is the negation of the negation, defined by the absence of barriers, by opening up, by extending communication. The public is where we venture out from our different privacies and discover what we have universally in common. Of course, public and private are not absolute opposites; they are the poles of a relative scale. A school may admit all children residing in the neighborhood as pupils and so be a "public school" while at the same time it excludes from its premises all members of the public who are not either pupils or staff. This phasing off between the more private and the more public makes social life possible. It enables society to be organic rather than mechanical, a living interaction of living social identities. Without the more secluded private we could have no moral identity to bring to the public realm; without the more open public we could have no use for our moral identities, no wider commonality in which they might emerge in action and reaction. But when we look at the philosophers' "public reason" in the light of this thumbnail sketch, we find an oddity about it. This "public" seems to be constructed by privation, like another kind of private sphere. It refuses to admit moral identities formed behind its back, in private. The publicity of public reason, it appears, is less like the town square we imagine lying before our front door, more like a walled and barbed-wired garrison, bristling with warnings against entry by unauthorized personnel. It is a public conceived of as another kind of privacy. But whereas the whole point of real privacy is to establish and protect identities, there is, or so it is claimed, no *further* identity that these inhibiting public restrictions are meant to protect.

It is, of course, essential to the general interplay of private and public that there be *disciplines* for making the transition from one to the other. We do not walk into the public square in bedroom slippers nor wear an overcoat in the bedroom. Disciplines of public behavior secure possibilities for moral identities to meet. If we are to pay attention to one another, listen to one another, discuss with one another, we cannot treat one another in public with the *immediacy* that we use in private. Our practical principles are refracted through our various roles. A journalist conducting an interview asks questions a neighbor would never ask. A police officer enquiring about a young offender's conduct betrays no emotion at what he learns, while a parent may be expected to betray emotion, and so on. Most adults occupy many roles, public and private, and the style of behavior they adopt at any moment varies with the role. But the variations will be morally explicable, to themselves and to others, within a second-order account of how different roles require different interpretations of the same practical principles.

When public and familial responsibilities and duties of conscience converge on concrete situations, a resolution must be found that saves the essential demands of each. That means that the rules governing *public* conduct must be coherent with the rules governing *private* conduct, allowing our moral identities to encompass the stretch so that we move between the different spheres of action without annihilating ourselves in the process. We may put the point at issue this way: human society requires its members to sustain what Bernd Wannenwetsch has happily termed a "homologous identity," linking the performance of any individual in public and the same individual's performance in private. And that means that public disciplines, too, must arise from within the same moral traditions that shape the identities that move among the practical spheres. Where they become separated from those traditions and absolultized, they assume the character not of disciplines (that is, aspects of an acquired wisdom) but of arbitrary prohibitions, what Foucault calls *prélèvements*. In France today, a *prélèvement* is what in Britain we call a "direct debit": the money leaves the account before we have time to decide whether or not to pay it. In the same way, the impositions of an absolute public reason must bypass the moral reasoning of those who participate in it. This is defended in the name of ideological neutrality, escaping the influence of any "hegemonic" tradition that might interpret the relations of human beings in ways that might be more native to some than to others. But this means it is devoid of reasons that could lead us to act. So what it presents as "second-order" reasons are, in fact, not reasons at all, because they do not derive from, or connect with, first-order reasons. They are simply *prélèvements.*

Christian reason will complain that this bare, stripped-down conception of public reason is devoid, above all, of charity. Charity is a hegemonic principle; that is to say, it generates not only private but public forms of conduct, shaping a homologous identity that can move between the private and the public. If hegemonic traditions are to be expelled from society, charity, a tradition born of the Christian gospel, must be expelled. And if all hegemonic traditions are to be expelled, why, in the last resort, should an exception be made for a humanist tradition of Aristotelian provenance based on distributive proportion? Unless we declare an outright prejudice for nonhegemonic principles, even that one must quit the public square, leaving the war of all-against-all as the only truly pared-down, pure, and presuppositionless public order!

In What Sense Is it Reason?

That brings us to the second question: to what extent is public reason reasonable? We speak of "practical principles" only in relation to trains of reason. Practical principles are rational dispositions, and like all rational dispositions, they are culturally rooted, which is to say that they are attributes not of individuals in isolation but of whole communities and their traditions. They are not merely separate strands of reasoning but community beliefs that generate a universe of reasons. What prompts our pluralist anxiety is the prospect of conflict among such community traditions of reasoning. September 11, 2001, would not have been half as threatening an event to the Western world if those who destroyed the World Trade Center had not been acting out of beliefs they had been taught. Our alarm was focused not on the bare fact that the perpetrators believed in what they were doing but that they might have had reasons for believing in it, reasons deeply woven into traditions of thinking and acting in which they had been nurtured. Pluralism pits the reasons of "society" (*Gesellschaft*) in sharp opposition to the reasons of "community" (*Gemeinschaft*). It is "foundationalist" in its account of reason, conceiving of belief systems as grounded upon posited axioms and proceeding to conclusions by deductive inference from them. Against communal reason, thus alarmingly conceived, it posits a social reason, also conceived in this positivist fashion, independent of community axiom.

Our experience as religious believers ought to tell us how wrong an account of reasoned belief this is. Religious belief does not produce moral practices deductively, like premises that produce a conclusion in a syllogism. Neither does it simply turn around in its own space, refusing questions posed to it from the world in which it lives. And what we can say about religious belief can also be said about wider, unreligious moral enquiries and convictions. Here, too, moral thought aspires to internal coherence and universality. Moral disagreement does not arise simply because individuals and communities belong to different cultures. The difference between morality and custom is precisely that morality does have universal aspirations; it refers to the place of human beings in the world, responsive to the nature of things and the will of the Creator. Thoughtless people, it is true, fail to distinguish their customs (such as eating bacon at breakfast) from their moral obligations, (such as protecting their children from danger). But it is the first requirement of moral consciousness, a requirement as old as civilization itself, to warn us against such thoughtlessness. A reflective culture finds its final justification of human acts outside local tradition or custom, however sacred. Moral thought conceives of action as *representative.* When we act conscientiously, we act *as humanity,* like Adam deciding for the human race as such. We recognize ourselves in others' acts and learn about ourselves from others' acts. The good in any action I perform is never mine in a private sense; it is an aspect of the good that belongs to everybody, *the human* good, as it is traditionally called, because it is the goal of human action. We could perfectly well broaden that term and call it "the *world's* good."

Rational communication is directed to "persuasion" broadly understood, that is to say, it is concerned with communicating *reasons* for acting, *reasons* for believing, and so on. It is the means by which each of us is drawn into the perspective of other human beings and enabled to see the world through their eyes. It is as a result of being morally capable that we have come to be persuaded of certain things through this traditioning process. But our persuasions, though nurtured within a tradition, are not confined within its community walls. Without coercive restrictions on the movement of argument, juxtaposed communities of tradition learn from one another. There are cross-fertilizations, conversions, etc. Alasdair MacIntyre understood that fact better than most of those who have lightly taken up his talk about plural traditions.

What makes the contemporary account of reasoning unreasonable is the failure to understand or allow space for learning. Wisdom is always the object of search. And because beliefs *must* engage in a search to perfect themselves, because they *must* engage with the challenges thrown up by alternatives, disagreements may disappear as well as appear. The unstable and eclectic character of our society does not make moral agreement *less* likely. Because agreement in the truth is what human beings are made for, they will search for it wherever the possibility arises and we will encounter new and intriguing coalitions of thought. To free ourselves for the search, we need only liberate ourselves from determinist theories of society that think they can tell us in advance just which agreements are and which are not possible.

The concept of an absolute public reason is therefore incompatible with the terms of any open practical enquiry and especially with a Christian one. Christians may sometimes be tempted to suppose that this approach may be serviceable to the *confessional* and *doctrinal* character of their faith. But it cannot be so, for Christian confession and Christian doctrine understand themselves correctly only when they understand themselves as "faith seeking understanding." Anselm's famous phrase perfectly captures the true posture of reason. Belief is itself the root and fruit of a search for God's will, and it is held only in the context of such a search. It may lightly be assumed that to be open to exploration is to be hesitant about one's convictions and vice versa, but that is actually skepticism. The one who said, "He who seeks finds" also said, "To him who has, shall be given."

All this is by way of an overgeneral and perhaps overfamiliar reflection on the *proposal for coping* with danger, "public reason." Now we return to that diagnosis of the danger that we named "difference as plurality."

Society is founded on plurality. Only a plurality can understand and connect themselves as *socii,* "associates." Adam in the Garden of Eden was not, and could not be, a society, because there was no associate found for him. But what kind of entity can be plural and therefore in a position to enter into society? Entities can be *plural* if they can be *numbered alongside* one another. And entities can be numbered alongside one another if their mode of being is as individual members of a kind. We can, if we wish, count the rocks by the seashore, but our counting will be arbitrary. The pounding of the waves that broke the cliff into so many chunks, particles, and granules could quite as easily have broken it into one or a trillion chunks, particles, or granules, more or less. It is not *rock* we are counting when we teach our child numbers by picking up one, two, or three of the more conveniently sized of these pieces. Rock is not constituted in individual units. But human persons, like other animals, are constituted in units; they are essentially particular, members of their kind, and therefore in a position to enter society. The first association, we read in Holy Scripture, was that of Adam and his wife, who was "bone of my bone, flesh of my flesh." But it is not only individual persons who can be plural—human communities also may be. An older theory of political constitution, prior to the emergence of the individualist contract theory of Hobbes and Locke, held that political society was formed as an association of families and tribes. These units of human cohabitation could share in a society, and when they did, that society belonged to no one of them more than to any other. It was indifferently common among them.

Now, the theory we have been discussing has claimed to identify a new kind of entity among those things that can be plural, can be numbered alongside one another, and can therefore enter into association. In the phrase made famous by John Rawls, this is a "comprehensive doctrine." Although Rawls may have invented the phrase, he did not invent the idea. In 1938, Heidegger was already arguing that human knowing was constituted in modernity by the *Weltbild,* "world picture," and that this mode of knowing must become a *confrontation* or *struggle* of world pictures. Heidegger did not conceive this plurality as a plurality of equals. He thought that the world picture was *essentially* one, constituted by the model of scientific knowledge as "representation." But he also thought that this one world picture—this representational world picture—could only establish itself eristically and so had to generate others—the medieval Christian world picture and the classical world picture—even though such world pictures had never existed in their own times. A plurality of world pictures was necessary in order to have one dominant world picture. Now confrontation and struggle are, of course, also modes of association. No two things can compete unless there is some common thing for which they compete. They must share, at any rate, a common view of winning or losing. Even if they strive to destroy each other, they must share a common expectation of how this destruction may be effected. A competition of worldviews, then, supposes terms indifferently common to them, terms that do not belong to one of them more than to another. This association is unequal and unstable, but it is an association. And that is the logic, it seems to me, of the progression from Heidegger to Rawls. The instability of the competitive world picture demands a stable association of *plural comprehensive doctrines,* just as the belligerent national-socialist society that formed Heidegger's environment demanded the bureaucratic-juridical rights society that formed Rawls's.

I refer to these hypothetical intellectual entities irreverently as "isms," a reminder of the point from which we began, that "pluralism," in addition to being a doctrine about isms, is also one of the kind itself. It is a reflexive doctrine of doctrines that insinuates a view of itself and its own status into its account of the status of other doctrines. But do such entities as isms, possessing the ontological structure implied in treating them as members of a kind and in association with one another, actually exist? Do we confront here, as with a plurality of animal kinds, a basic datum of the created universe, or, as with plural languages, do we confront a fruit of providence in response to Babel? Or do we confront only an imagination? Are we dealing only with an intellectual fallacy, a version of the pathetic fallacy, that has treated human doctrines and beliefs as though they were concrete things instead of abstract?

Heidegger was right, at least about the *modernity* of pluralism. Offered as a universal description of all societies, pluralism is easily rebutted. There are, or have been, doctrinally homogeneous societies. And indeed pluralism in this form would be self-rebutting, for the only demonstration it can have for its claim about the competing plurality of isms is to contrast modern society with older homogeneous ones. Pluralism, then, can and does answer only for a limited segment of the total social experience of mankind. It is part of that wider philosophical enterprise that attempts to account for how human existence as we know it today differs from human existence in the past. But granted this point, we see that pluralism cannot merely *posit* the plurality of isms. It is obliged to account for how plurality has emerged from homogeneity. How can the many isms that enter into a competitive association with one another have arisen from the "pre-ism," the homogeneous unifying doctrine that once constituted society in an age loosely described as premodern?

More clearly, perhaps, than most of those who have propounded a plurality of isms, Heidegger recognized that this question had to be answered, that pluralism could not be asserted as though it were a fact observed by journalists or statisticians. But his answer to it is a shockingly brutal one—a mere assertion of historical *fiat,* a philosophical strong-arm tactic. It is our fate as moderns to will our knowing as science, by representation. This form of knowing is given to us, and the reason we cannot resist it is that our will demands that we be the subjects of our knowing. We cannot, he sternly observes, "dawdle about in the mere negating of the age. The flight into tradition … can bring about nothing in itself other than self-deception and blindness in relation to the historical moment." I think that there are reasons why serious democrats must resist that answer, and I also think there are reasons why serious Christians also must do so. Let me, in conclusion, suggest what these reasons might be in both cases.

It is clear that many defenders of pluralism think of themselves as defending democratic polity in so doing. Democratic polity depends on a strong notion of social equality, a notion extending much further than the mere admission of adult citizens to the polling booth. But equality cannot be applied independently of ontology. The question underlying every concrete decision about equality is *what* entities make a recognizable demand for equal treatment in this situation. (This is why a democracy that thinks of itself as independent of ontology is doomed to be the most *confused* age there has ever been, for it begs all its own questions, seeking to establish equality without ever having to determine what is equal to what. Let us talk, however, of what "democrats" think, without committing them to this wild flight from ontology.) Equality is upheld within society by organs of government, and the fundamental organ of government is the court. Democracy must be, before being anything else, a doctrine about the equality to be observed in courts of law. Courts have their own ontology. To be a subject of equal treatment in a court you must be a "legal person," which is to say, capable of being party to a case, distinct from another legal person. Courts are impartial among legal persons.

But courts are by no means impartial among legal reasons. A court must reach a resolution of every dispute while also treating all legal persons equally. It does so precisely by treating the arguments unequally, by deciding that one set of arguments is inherently superior and must therefore prevail. Reasons enter court in competition, that is, in an unstable association, which it is the court's business to terminate by giving effect to their inequality. Reasons enter court in order to eliminate one another. The very practice of adjudication, then, assumes that the equal respect required by legal persons cannot also be extended to legal reasons.

How, then, do isms stand before the equalizing regime of democracy? When isms confront one another in common life, they do not have to eliminate one another, and indeed usually cannot do so. If they enter court, they may do so in one of two different ways. Either they appear as legal reasons, in which case they are in no different situation from other legal reasons, or they appear *as practical traditions* of some community that is a party in court. When the courts are presented with isms as reasons, they are bound, as in any other case, to resolve whether they are, in terms of legal coherence, superior reasons, and so allowed to stand. But when a community defined by its doctrine and practices appears before the courts, that community will have equal standing with any other legal person. The argument made recently by the Archbishop of Canterbury to introduce an element of Sharia law into British law, which met with much controversy, is not an argument for *doctrinal* equality. It is an argument for the legal standing of communities that do, in practice, resolve some of their problems in the light of their doctrines. Neither in this case nor in any other can doctrines be accorded the status of legal persons, so the apparatus of government adopts a position of indifference in respect to them. And the fact that the courts cannot give them this status explains why it is in the courts that the unfulfillable promises of pluralism to provide for the equal treatment of all beliefs have been most spectacularly disappointing.

In asking why Christians will have difficulty accepting pluralism, we must pay our respects to that great tradition of Christian pluralism derived from Abraham Kuyper, after whom this prize and this lecture are named, even while parting company from it at this point. By taking the epistemic dimension of original sin seriously, the Kuyperian theory invites us to expect deep social division at the level of "worldview," which may have to be coped with politically. And we should not, of course, ignore that advice. But there are two important questions to be asked. If it is accepted that ruptures of original sin are a given in any Christian account of the moral situation of the world, and not in the moral situation of the individual alone, how are we to justify the assumption that this rupture will normatively take an *ideological form* within society? A Christian cannot answer the question with the philosophical brutality with which Heidegger answered it: we are moderns, and therefore we cannot but will that it should be so! That strife and bitterness, the bile produced by Adam's apple, have assumed ideological forms in modern society is undeniable. But why should this fact be more than an accident? "Sin," as Aristotle said, "is manifold." And to identify one pattern of human sin as somehow normative is paradoxical, open at least to the temptation of willing it be so. Must the Christian pluralist play the part of the serpent in Eden, proffering the apple of ideological discord in order to bring sin, too, up to modern standards?

The second question brings me to back to the point I have been circling around. Why is *difference* of doctrine to be construed in terms of *plurality?* More theologically, we might ask this: how is the reconciling Word of God thought of as working within the ideological sphere? The Word of God, we are told, runs swiftly. The Spirit-sent message, the promise of deliverance, the suggestion of hope, all encounter us predoctrinally before they take form within a Christian worldview. Must this not have the effect of reconciling ideological differences and eroding the boundaries that mark the separation of plural worldviews? There is no need to think of this in terms of some big picture of the "global ecumenism" kind. The point is more modest: in a world where the Holy Spirit is alive, we may expect to see his workings in moments of reconciliation and agreement. And whereas two people whose differences are reconciled remain two people, two communities whose differences are reconciled remain two communities, it is not the case that two doctrines whose differences are reconciled remain two doctrines. That is because doctrines were never plural in the sense that people or communities are plural.

The complex intermingling of different beliefs and practices so typical of our culture cannot satisfactorily be thought of as a plurality of competitive isms. How, then, are we to conceive it?

Let us take the case that forms a horizon, acknowledged or unacknowledged, to a great deal of our discussion—ideological terrorism. It dramatically illustrates the thread of anxiety running through the pluralist theory, reminding us that disagreement in practical principles is never safe but always perilous. But it also illustrates a feature of all practical principles, which is that they connect our beliefs into a chain of practical reasoning. The Islamist terrorist holds together a belief that Allah is great and a belief that innocent lives may be intentionally destroyed in pursuit of justified religious ends. For myself, I cannot help being more sympathetic to the one belief than to the other. But for him, they are mutually implicated. That means that his practical principles are *discursive*: they take the form of a connected chain of reasoning from one point to the other. For the purposes of analysis, we may itemize his separate beliefs, but in its lived texture his thought moves from one to the other to establish a connection. There is a logic to be preserved in this movement between beliefs. Both beliefs are action-guiding, and the conduct of his life seeks a practical equilibrium that expresses both equally. There is also an order to be preserved between them. A religious belief commands a moral belief; the latter is answerable to the former, held up to question before it. And there is a universal claim implicit in his moral belief. In asserting the right and duty to conduct terrorist operations, he will maintain something as true for and on behalf of the whole world, so the validation of his beliefs is an intellectual task that constantly engages him.

Once we appreciate the discursive character of moral thought, the concept of disagreement itself becomes all the more complex. Presented with an isolated proposition, I can accept it or reject it outright. Presented with a series of propositions woven into a train of thought, I may find points of approximation and points of divergence. I may explore the logic of the way beliefs are held together, the implication by which they are derived. But in disagreeing I have something more to offer than a bare counterproposition. As I enter into a kind of counterpoint to the train of reasoning that the other is engaged in, I begin to accompany him as I challenge him and question him. I enter the sequence of his reasoned propositions, governed by a logic of moral thought from which neither he nor I can be exempt. Two people may have different viewpoints, but their different viewpoints are not two as the people who hold them are two. They are in a complex differentiation, with moments of greater distance and moments of greater proximity.

Just as public reason cannot accommodate Christian charity or Christian faith, so difference-as-plurality cannot accommodate Christian hope. Christian social theory will be known by the place it accords to mission. Mission is the work of public advocacy of the gospel in whatever form, looking for the coming of the kingdom of God, for the dawning of that universal consent to God's will in which "God shall be all in all." And that is why we may look for persuasion, conciliation, and agreement in the interim, too; but because the kingdom of God is the work of the spirit of God, not our own work, we cannot prescribe its specific dimensions or content before the event. It is therefore an object of hope, not prediction. Christian mission in the patristic period evoked unexpected civilizational agreements, which still provide important points of reference for our own very different civilization. Responses to the gospel in our own time, too, may afford new points of social cohesion, though we do not seek them for that end alone but as a sign of the greater unity still to come. ■

Whose Text Is It?

by Katharine Doob Sakenfeld

Katherine Doob Sakenfeld, William Albright Eisenberger Professor of Old Testament and Director of PhD Studies at Princeton Theological Seminary, served as the 2007 President of the Society of Biblical Literature (SBL) and is the General Editor of the New Interpreter's Dictionary of the Bible *(Abingdon Press, 5 vols., 2007–2009). She delivered this presidential address at the SBL annual meeting on November 17, 2007, and it appeared as "Whose Text Is it?" in the* Journal of Biblical Literature *127:1 (Spring 2008): 5–18.*

It was exactly twenty years ago that Professor Elisabeth Schüssler Fiorenza gave her landmark presidential address [to the Society of Biblical Literature] titled "The Ethics of Biblical Interpretation: Decentering Biblical Scholarship."[1] In her speech, she argued for the need for biblical scholarship to "continue its descriptive-analytic work … for understanding of ancient texts and their historical location" while also "exploring the power/knowledge relations inscribed in contemporary biblical discourse and in the biblical texts themselves." In such an approach, the work of those "traditionally absent from the exegetical enterprise would not remain peripheral or non-existent for biblical scholarship," but "could become central to the scholarly discourse of the discipline."[2] My address to you this evening is intended to further this call for a shift in our self-understanding of our scholarly work. We have made progress in the past twenty years, but work remains to be done.

---

[1] Elisabeth Schüssler Fiorenza, "The Ethics of Biblical Interpretation: Decentering Biblical Scholarship," *Journal of Biblical Literature* 107 (1988): 3–17; reprinted in Harold W. Attridge and James C. VanderKam, ed., *Presidential Voices: The Society of Biblical Literature in the Twentieth Century* (Atlanta: Society of Biblical Literature, 2006), 217–31; subsequent references are to the reprint edition. For a more extensive and updated treatment of her perspective, see her volume *The Power of the Word: Scripture and the Rhetoric of Empire* (Minneapolis: Fortress, 2007).
[2] Schüssler Fiorenza; "Ethics of Biblical Interpretation," 230–31.

DOI: 10.3754/1937–8386.2008.29.1.7

My particular focus was provoked in a session I attended at the SBL annual meeting two years ago. In introducing a session on feminism and postcolonialism, a moderator reported that she had been asked why the session had been organized around a book on African women's voices published a few years earlier (i.e., not hot off the press), to which her response had been "because nobody seems to be listening." The authors experienced their claim to ownership of the text, at least within the guild, as being discounted or overridden. Attempting to listen to global feminist voices within biblical studies has been a key theme of my own work, but developing viable modes of engagement between white Euro-Atlantic feminists and global feminism remains a challenge. That challenge, however, is but one component of the much larger question of how we all as scholars engage one another over a wide range of dividing lines, since we all claim texts as our own through our acts of interpretation.

I will first approach the question of "Whose text?" and competing claims to ownership in a wide-sweeping overview and then turn more specifically to feminist postcolonial interpretation as a particular example. Before launching into the overview, let me note that I will use more "I" language and anecdotal material than is usual for the presidential address. I want the style of my speaking to reflect my perspective that being more self-consciously contextual, more public rather than less so about the personal in our work, is critically important to a way forward in any mutual engagement across dividing lines.

"Whose Text?" in Our Descriptive Analytical Work

The question "Whose text?" as I am posing it has two principal dimensions: first, who claims a particular text as important; and, second, how are competing interpretive claims to be negotiated when more than one group has a stake in the same text. I find it helpful to remember that the question, thus conceived, has actually been with us for a long time in our traditional descriptive and analytical research. In the field of text criticism, for example, the degree of differences among manuscript families, as well as evidence of intentional scribal emendations, has led to theories of different schools or centers with different manuscript choices. Here interpretive claims are expressed through variations in the text itself, and scholars ask what kind of contextual hermeneutical and identity claims may lie behind the different manuscript traditions.

Studies of canon formation, whether of the TNK [Tanakh, the Old Testament] or the NT [New Testament], are a second, well-established locus of exploration of

"Whose text?" The emphasis on Judaisms (plural) of the Second Temple period and beyond, and our knowledge of the many extant Christian writings as well as those that were lost to us and not canonized, provide rich fodder for exploring ancient ownership claims to different texts and competing interpretive claims for texts held in common.

A third example of our scholarly historical inquiry into "Whose text?" is found in the recent heightened interest in the history of interpretation. Biblical scholars are increasingly collaborating across disciplines of history, music, and art to discover more about the religious-social-political-cultural contexts that have affected interpreters' selection of and perspective on texts over the centuries. The good questions that we have tried to ask and answer over many decades about the ancient biblical texts in their own compositional contexts are now being asked about subsequent readers and readings.

In short, the question "Whose text is it?" with its attendant issues of contested identities and hermeneutics is scarcely new to our discipline. But the question has seemed safe so long as it applied to the past and so long as the questions of why we ourselves as scholars choose to study particular texts or ask certain questions or reach certain conclusions were not part of the discussion. However heated the debates about the ancient world of the texts and their meanings within that world of the past have been (and we know those debates can be fiery), the conversations about our own places in relation to our work turn out to be more difficult.

"Whose Text?" The Current Landscape

Recent discussion of our own places in relation to our work is multidimensional; I have organized it under five headings, each of which represents a major fault line across which issues of ownership ("Whose text?") are in tension. These five are: academic methods; religious/secular interpretation; Jewish and Christian/other readers; sociocultural traditions, including cultural, ethnic, gender, economic, and political dimensions; and "ordinary"/"expert" readers. This schema is obviously porous, and after commenting on each of the five I will hasten to reiterate the inevitability of their interaction.

The first set of divisions concerns academic methods. None of us would even pretend to be able to control all of the subspecialties of method in biblical scholarship, even if we restricted ourselves to a particular smaller corpus of the material such as pentateuchal narrative or Johannine literature. I include this category not because we are unwilling to recognize the expertise of others but to raise the question of how we value that expertise. To the extent that hermeneutics says to textual criticism, "I have no need of you," or vice versa, a fault line is made visible. To the extent that those engaged in comparative study of ancient texts speak of literary critics as too lazy to learn cognate languages, or literary critics disparage or ignore possible illumination from extrabiblical sources, a fault line is present. Perhaps the widest fissure in method lies between those who are committed to focusing on identity hermeneutics and those who are disinterested in this broad approach or continue to question its academic value.

My second category, the division between religious and secular interpretation, is sometimes also described as between confessional and nonconfessional or between devotional and academic interpretation.[3] Whatever the nomenclature, the central issue is how (and, for many people, whether) the text can be introduced, discussed, and interpreted in a manner that does not privilege the perspective of a particular religious or faith tradition. Our Society [the SBL] for many decades has sought to provide a forum for such a nonconfessional approach, and much of our work as a Society has been predicated upon the assumption that we can engage in such work. Here in the United States, we associate this fault line also with the controversies around teaching the Bible in our public (government-owned and funded) schools. The SBL is currently cooperating in efforts to help local communities discern what the academic study of the Bible apart from contemporary religious claims might look like in local high school classrooms. Yet we are aware that many of us are adherents of Judaism or Christianity and that a great many of the college undergraduate teaching posts in our field in the United States exist because students (mostly Christian in this case) want or are required by their church-related institutions to learn something "academic" about the basic document of the Judeo-Christian tradition.[4] How this divide between religious and secular interpretation should be maintained and whether that is even possible are matters of continuing and sometimes heated debate.

---

[3] For confessional/nonconfessional language, see, e.g., Philip Davies, *Whose Bible Is It Anyway?* 2nd ed. (London: T&T Clark, 2004), esp. 13–15, 33–35. For devotional/academic language, see, e.g., "The Bible and Public Schools," in *Finding Common Ground: A First Amendment Guide to Religion and Public Schools,* rev. ed., ed. C. C. Haynes and O. Thomas (Nashville: First Amendment Center, 2007), 121–33. Online: http://www.firstamendmentcenter.org/PDF/FCGchapter11.pdf (accessed November 11, 2007). The SBL is one of many signatories to the position statement on this topic printed in this chapter.

[4] See American Academy of Religion, "AAR Survey of Undergraduate Religion and Theology Programs in the U.S. and Canada: Further Data Analysis: Summary of Results" (paper presented at the annual meeting of the AAR, Atlanta, Nov. 24, 2003). Online: http://aarweb.org/Programs/Department_Services/Survey_Data/Undergraduate/dataanalysis-20040309.pdf (accessed October 25, 2007).

My third broad category takes note of the fault line between those who acknowledge biblical texts as a part of their own faith heritage and those who study biblical texts out of curiosity about a religious tradition other than their own and often from a culture other than their own. Here I have in mind particularly the divide between Jewish and Christian (but predominantly Christian in terms both of numbers and of cultural influence) interpreters on the one hand and readers from other cultural and religious traditions on the other; I include the question of how biblical interpretation may be informed by comparative work growing out of other living religious traditions and their texts. What place do readers from other cultural and religious traditions have at the table of biblical interpretation? And what responsibility do Christian and Jewish biblical scholars have to become more engaged with other religious texts and traditions? The matter is of theoretical scholarly significance and also of practical import here in North America and especially in a global perspective. Scholars as diverse as Wayne Meeks and R. S. Sugirtharajah have identified this as a key frontier, urging its importance upon Western biblical scholars.[5] Those of us who teach in North America and Europe are challenged to prepare our students to engage rather than to ignore this divide. This fault line points us in two directions: it points back to my previous consideration of the debate about a secular or nonconfessional academic discourse; it also points ahead to my fourth category of sociocultural divides. Religious differences could be theoretically erased under the former category or incorporated into the latter; I have lifted out religious pluralism for separate notice to underscore the need for more sustained attention to other sacred texts and to perspectives from other religious traditions.

My fourth fault line, then, is sociocultural, which may include diverse religious traditions but in which I am focusing, as I indicated earlier, on the broad range of racial-ethnic, political, economic, gender, and cultural differences among interpreters and the resulting multifaceted tensions in claims to "ownership" of texts. If the dividing lines internal to my first four broad categories were complex, here they become even more so, since each interpreter, whether using one academic method or another, whether working in a religious or a secular context, whether working with his or her own faith documents or other texts, participates in this whole range of dimensions of sociocultural experience. The issue is not whether any one of us participates but how that reality impacts our work. Among those who speak and write from a perspective of identity hermeneutics,

[5] See Wayne A. Meeks, "Why Study the New Testament?" *New Testament Studies* 51 (2005): 168–69. In numerous publications, R. S. Sugirtharajah has urged the importance of comparing selected biblical themes and motifs to materials from Asian religious texts (see, e.g., *Postcolonial Reconfigurations: An Alternative Way of Reading the Bible and Doing Theology* [St. Louis: Chalice, 2003], 107–8).

fragmentation of perspectives is on the increase. No longer, for example, are categories such as Asian voices or even Southeast Asian voices adequate, but groups and individuals from different subcultures of many regions are distinguishing themselves. It is my own judgment that such fragmentation is a positive sign, even as it was a positive first step when black or liberation or white feminist interpretations (categories that we now recognize as quite broad) initially arose some decades ago. Ever smaller and more focused groups are considering their identity in relation to and/or in resistance to the text, seeking to make their own meaning and challenging what could become hegemonic interpretations even by their nearer neighbors. In the face of such fragmentation, however, constructive mutual engagement becomes even more difficult to achieve.

The fifth and last fault line that I would identify is that between so-called ordinary and so-called expert readers. The more usual discussion of this fault line has identified "expert" readers as those such as ourselves (members of the SBL) who have special academic training in the guild's methods of approaching biblical texts. Depending on our particular training we may rightly be viewed as more expert than ordinary interpreters in our various technical specializations. Gerald West, Musimbi Kanyoro, Hans de Wit, and others remind us, however, that all readers bring some sort of expertise to the text.[6] Thus, this divide may be better identified as between academic and nonacademic readers, recognizing that even with such a label there will be a continuum. Nonacademic or ordinary readers bring their own life experiences to the text, offering expertise often very different from ours, and the experiences of these nonacademic, sometimes nonliterate, readers may open up remarkably fresh avenues of analysis. Vincent Wimbush's important Institute for Signifying Scriptures project is drawing our attention to the significance of this approach to expertise in all cultural settings, including North America.[7]

As I indicated at the outset, these five categories of fault lines are heuristic and reflective of major threads of discussion in recent literature about the character of biblical scholarship for the twenty-first century. I expect that most of you have found your own resonance with the question of "Whose

[6] See, most recently, Gerald West, ed., *Reading Other-Wise: Socially Engaged Biblical Scholars Reading with Their Local Communities* Semeia Studies 62 (Atlanta: Society of Biblical Literature, 2007), esp. 1–3; Musimbi R. Kanyoro, *Introducing Feminist Cultural Hermeneutics: An African Perspective* (London: Sheffield Academic Press, 2002); Hans de Wit et al., eds., *Through the Eyes of Another: Intercultural Reading of the Bible* (Elkhart: Institute of Mennonite Studies, 2004). West emphasizes that among "ordinary readers" his particular interest is in "the poor, the working class, and the marginalized" (p. 2), and de Wit offers an extended discussion of the category of "ordinary reader" (pp. 5–19).

[7] See the Institute's Web site at http://iss.cgu.edu/about/index.htm (accessed November 12, 2007).

text?" primarily in one or two of the categories, although the interpenetration of the categories should be apparent.

In the face of this complexity it is a natural temptation for each of us to proceed with doing whatever interests us without worrying much about these fault lines. I say "for each of us," but I think that temptation, such as it is, is mostly for those of us who find ourselves by reason of birth and circumstance in relatively more privileged positions as part of the white Eurocentric academy. For many others in our midst, however, the struggle to find a venue for their work, and the struggle to have it taken seriously, is part and parcel of their academic life. It is their experience that, again in the words of the moderator of that panel two years ago, "Nobody seems to be listening." The effort to gain recognition for their claim to ownership of the text remains an uphill battle.

A Possible Way Ahead

In acknowledgment of that uphill battle, I want to focus now on possibilities for recognizing the claim to ownership of those who are not part of the privileged majority, for having their interpretive voices taken seriously, with special attention to the global context of our work.

Our society has taken structural steps in the right direction. Subsidies for bringing international scholars and specifically international women scholars to the North American annual meeting are to be applauded, although six to eight guests among several thousand attendees hardly form a critical mass. Our international meetings are potentially another step, insofar as they do not simply export Eurocentric presentations to holiday locations but rather enable scholars from outside the West to participate in more significant numbers. We have begun a project of making scholarly papers in native languages from across the world available electronically on our Web site, with the selection process conducted by local or regional associations of biblical scholars in Asia, Africa, and Latin America. Beyond such structural steps, what strategies may be helpful?

In approaching this question I recall one of my most difficult evenings in Asia. The women who joined me for conversation had agreed to be present as a courtesy to my host, but they were nonetheless quite frank. "We are tired of Westerners coming to tell us what to think," they said, and then added, "we are equally tired of being asked what we think. We need dialogue, a two-way conversation." On that we were agreed, but how to proceed eluded us. What might enable us to meet, as Kwok Pui-lan eloquently puts it, as equal subjects for sharing of our treasures?[8] In my subsequent experience, focusing conversation around a particular text has proved to be one helpful way of addressing such an impasse. With that in mind, let me sharpen my question of "Whose text?" Thus far in asking "Whose text is it?" I have spoken about "text/texts" rather generically. It is my conviction, however, that we can often proceed further toward mutual engagement if we focus the question of "Whose text?" not on the Bible as a whole (whatever its boundaries in various religious traditions) but rather on individual texts or on much smaller bodies of texts that introduce particular characters or political or sociocultural topics.

A Test Probe

Given this perspective on the value of a focal text, I turn now to offering a brief postcolonial reflection on a particular biblical story and character. As postcolonial feminists from among the colonized are calling for women like me (and men as well) to engage their work and their approach, I as a first-world, white feminist can perhaps best make clear my sense of my place by describing myself as a "pro-postcolonial feminist" (on the analogy of a "pro-woman man" entering into white feminist biblical interpretation).[9] I emphasize that I am making no claim to "having it right" in what follows. My goal is to model publicly the risk that I invite other first-world interpreters to take: recognizing global ownership of biblical texts by attempting to engage biblical interpretation across difficult dividing lines.

I have chosen for my test probe Judges 4–5, the story of Deborah and Barak, Sisera and Jael, chapters that have received extensive treatment by numerous white first-world feminists. Although postcolonial feminist writers have already produced an impressive body of work on selected biblical texts, most notably within the OT [Old Testament] on the story of Rahab and on the story of Ruth, Naomi, and Orpah, I have not yet uncovered publications from a specifically postcolonial perspective on Judges 4–5.[10] It is possible that this apparent lacuna

[8] For the image of shared treasures, see Kwok Pui-lan, "Discovering the Bible in the Non-Biblical World," in *Voices from the Margin: Interpreting the Bible in the Third World*, new ed., ed. R. S. Sugirtharajah (Maryknoll: Orbis Books, 1995), 303; reprinted from Semeia 47 (1989).

[9] See, e.g., Kwok Pui-lan, *Postcolonial Imagination and Feminist Theology* (Louisville: Westminster John Knox, 2005), 127, 167; Musa W. Dube, "Toward a Post-Colonial Feminist Interpretation," in *Reading the Bible as Women: Perspectives from Asia, Africa, and Latin America*, ed. P. A. Bird et al., Semeia 78 (Atlanta: Scholars Press, 1997), 20, 22.

[10] On Ruth, see, e.g., Musa W. Dube, "The Unpublished Letters of Orpah to Ruth," in *The Feminist Companion to the Bible*, vol. 3, *A Feminist Companion to Ruth*, ed. Athalya Brenner (Sheffield: Sheffield Academic Press, 1999), 145–50; Dube, "Divining Ruth for International

is not a reality, since the sources included in database searches are still limited largely to North Atlantic languages and publications (yet another sign, of course, of the hegemonic interpretive context I am highlighting here).[11] There may well be publications in Asia, Africa, or Latin America that do deal with Judges 4–5 from a postcolonial perspective, and there may be various forms of oral communication to which access is even more difficult.

My choice of this text and of the figure of Jael in particular may be an awkward selection. For me as a white first-world feminist to offer any postcolonial reflection before others have spoken may seem out of place. Yet I choose this text because of a prior experience that does place it for me squarely in this domain, with the hope that postcolonial feminist writers will choose to explore it further in response and correction. That experience, as I have recounted elsewhere, took place some years ago in discussing this story with Korean women church leaders.[12] I expressed the discomfort that I and many women peers in North America experience with Jael's murder of Sisera, to which the response came swiftly: "your place as a U.S. woman is with Sisera's mother, waiting to count the spoils." In retrospect this was surely a postcolonial (or neocolonial economic) reading and challenge, although none of us marked it as such at the time. I note also, and not insignificantly, that this observation was offered by a so-called ordinary (i.e., nonacademic) reader. She was not a biblical scholar; she had never, to my knowledge, studied Hebrew. But she was certainly an expert in relating the text to her life and the political context of our two nations.

With her response in mind, let me explore further how I imagine the story might be viewed through a postcolonial lens. My hermeneutical strategy, following a range of postcolonial writers, will be to explore possible points of contact between

---

Relations," in *Other Ways of Reading: African Women and the Bible*, ed. Musa W. Dube, *Global Perspectives on Biblical Scholarship 2* (Atlanta: Society of Biblical Literature, 2001), 179–95; Laura E. Donaldson, "The Sign of Orpah: Reading Ruth through Native Eyes," in *A Feminist Companion to Ruth*, 130–44; on Rahab, see Musa W. Dube, *Postcolonial Feminist Interpretation of the Bible* (St. Louis: Chalice, 2000), esp. 76–80, 121–24. Uriah Y. Kim considers the significance of postcolonial interpretation for Judges generally but without focused attention on chs. 4–5 ("Who Is the Other in the Book of Judges," in *Judges and Method: New Approaches in Biblical Studies*, 2nd ed., ed. Gale A. Yee [Minneapolis: Fortress, 2007], 161–82)

[11] Hans de Wit observes the tendency to overlook Spanish-language scholarship in his comparison of Latin American and non-Latin American treatments of Judges 4 ("Leyendo con Yael," in *Los caminos inexhauribles de la Palabra: Las relecturas creativas en la Biblia y de la Biblia: Homenaje de colegas y discipulos a J. Severino Croatto*, ed. Guillermo Hansen [Buenos Aires: Lumen-ISEDET, 2000], 11–66).

[12] See my "Deborah, Jael, and Sisera's Mother: Reading the Scriptures in Cross-Cultural Context," in *Women, Gender, and Christian Community*, ed. Jane Dempsey Douglass and James F. Kay (Louisville: Westminster John Knox, 1997), 13–22.

biblical actors and contemporary readers, even as did my Korean conversation partner in pointing me to Sisera's mother. This approach resonates, for instance, with the concept of "story field" as a locus for negotiating readings as proposed by postcolonial interpreter Laura Donaldson.[13] I choose it also because it fits closely with the way in which many "ordinary" (i.e., nonacademic) readers typically engage the Bible, thus providing an important bridge of contact across that divide.

I begin by stepping back from the character of Jael in order to problematize the place of Israel relative to the Canaanites. To be sure, these chapters, like the OT generally, view the situation through Israelite eyes. But the situation in Judges is not exactly the same as the picture in the book of Joshua, where the invading Israelites are taking control of Canaanite land. In Joshua, the experience of the Canaanites provides a connecting point of identity for contemporary peoples whose land has been or is being taken over by outside forces. As Robert Alan Warrior, among others, has emphasized, this is the Joshua narrative's portrayal of Israel and Canaan, regardless of what happened historically, and this has been the portrayal used as warrant by land-grabbing colonizing powers.[14] The scenario in Judges, however, is potentially more complicated. From the narrowest viewpoint on our narrative, it is now the Israelites who are under the oppressive hand of the Canaanites, without regard for how the Israelites came to be present. At this narrative level, a contemporary subject people might read this story in a liberationist mode alongside the exodus story and identify with the Israelites in their effort to throw off an oppressive yoke, even if those same readers have identified themselves with the Canaanites in the context of Joshua.[15]

Such an initial view of Judges 4–5 is immediately complicated, however, by the theological framing of the text, since it is Israel's deity who has allowed Israel's oppression, and it is Israel's deity who will accomplish Israel's deliverance. Does this theological stance inevitably make Israel actually the dominant cultural and political power in the story? I would propose that this is not necessarily the case; the story can still be read as a story of a weak Israel rejecting the temptation to participate in the Canaanites' religious-cultural hegemony, to which they have thus far succumbed, and trying to stake out their own sociocultural as well as physical space. On the other hand, we know enough of modern colonial history to see how readily

---

[13] Laura E. Donaldson, *Decolonizing Feminisms: Race, Gender, and Empire-Building* (Chapel Hill: University of North Carolina Press, 1992), 139.

[14] Robert Alan Warrior, "A Native American Perspective: Canaanites, Cowboys, and Indians," in *Voices from the Margin: Interpreting the Bible in the Third World*, 3rd ed., ed. R: S. Sugirtharajah (Maryknoll: Orbis Books, 2006), 235–41; reprinted from *Christianity and Crisis* 49 (1989).

[15] De Wit finds examples of such liberationist readings of Judges in Latin American sources (in ("Leyendo con Yael").

the story of Judges 4–5 can be read from the perspective of Israel's dominance, all the more so as the theological framing ties the themes of Judges back to Joshua. The image in Judges is still one of recent arrivals, now pictured as a weaker/small group, trying to establish themselves in the midst of powerful but despised native inhabitants, inhabitants who have temporarily, but only temporarily, overrun the intruding outsiders. In such a reading, the colonized are again the Canaanites. Parallels are legion to modern stories of "setders" who described themselves as "beleaguered," and to original inhabitants who have resented and resisted their presence.

Thus far I have suggested that it might be possible for contemporary postcolonial subjects to identify with either of the two sides in the conflict, depending on what level of the narrative and what points of contact are selected. The corollary is that those like myself who live on the side of Empire, of the colonizers, historically and/or at the present moment, must consider our own place.[16] On my first, narrower level of reading, we may find ourselves as Canaanites, as my Korean respondent had powerfully pointed out. At the second level, however, we will find ourselves instead as Israelites, participating in a sociopolitical and even religious community that imagines itself as rightly called to the role of colonizer even while experiencing a temporary setback. I suspect that for those of us who are a part of Empire yet seek to resist its impulse, this latter identification with Israel is more difficult. To be a Canaanite in this story, for me to be Sisera's mother, means to be in the wrong: reading with the grain of the text, the Canaanites are in the wrong, and the connection is straightforward. However, to identify myself as an Israelite in this story while maintaining a postcolonial lens requires first that as a colonizer I view Israel's weak and overrun position nonetheless as one of Empire, already a difficult mental step for a relatively privileged first-world reader to hold on to, and second that I must choose whether and how to resist that identity for the sake of the Canaanites. As one who is immersed in the Western Judeo-Christian faith tradition, the mental gymnastics of standing within yet against ancient Israel as it seeks to defeat Jabin and Sisera are complex, to say the least.

These potential connecting points are subject to even further complication if we ask after ancient Israel's own possible perspectives on the story and how Canaan may have been a cipher for imperial powers for some ancient hearers. If we

[16] Postcolonial scholars have varying ways of distinguishing between imperialism and colonialism, as well as neocolonialism; see, e.g., Dube, "Toward a Post-Colonial Feminist Interpretation," 15; JR. S. Sugirtharajah, *The Postcolonial Biblical Reader* (Oxford: Blackwell, 2006), 16–17. None of these concepts, of course, is precisely parallel either culturally or geopolitically to the situation of the Israelites and Canaanites as portrayed in Joshua-Judges. The issues of control of land and resources, emphasis on cultural distinctiveness, and regarding the other as inferior are features shared by the biblical narrative and imperial/colonial impulses.

undertake an experiment in historical imagination, overhearing the story late in the monarchy in the era of Judah's King Josiah, we find Judah as a small blip on the world scene dominated first by the Assyrian Empire but soon by the rising Babylonians.[17] Perhaps, as Judah dreams of some degree of independence from Mesopotamian might and Egyptian pressure, we can imagine the story of Deborah and Barak as a warrant for Josiah's mysterious decision to go to battle against Pharaoh Neco at Megiddo. A people and leader who have recently turned afresh toward devotion to YHWH, at least as the narrator of 2 Kings portrays them, seek to throw off a foreign yoke. This time, however, the battle ends in quite the opposite way with the death of Judah's leader rather than defeat of the enemy, and Judah's status as puppet or pawn of imperial powers remains unchanged.

If we move ahead in our imagination into the Persian era, when Judah is officially part of another empire, a standing army is no more, and prophecy has taken a quite different shape, perhaps the story becomes colonized Judah's nostalgia for bygone days, or perhaps a call to repentance in hopes of restoring former glory, or perhaps even part of the Persian colonizer's strategy for maintaining order—if Judah's deity has not sent another Deborah in these latter days, then submission to Persia/Canaan must be the intent of Judah's god.[18] Each of these readings equates ancient empires with Canaan, but now there is no deliverance for the subjugated. Even if the story wants to portray Israel as the powerful center, even if it is resistance literature rather than a tool of Empire, it is preserved in a community that experiences its life as colonized and without serious prospect of change. Attention to historical context seems to make a pipe dream of the hope implicit in an anticolonial reading. In the absence of prospects for change, Empire becomes more secure, and the effort to resist complicity with Empire, whether from within or from without, becomes correspondingly more difficult.

Thus far my proposed patterns of reading have bypassed Jael and the Kenites; I turn now to the question of Jael's social location. Jael is presented to us in the usual rendering as the wife of Heber the Kenite, who is not Israelite yet by

---

[17] For an important treatment of Josiah and 2 Kings from a postcolonial perspective, see Uriah Y. Kim, *Decolonizing Josiah: Toward a Postcolonial Reading of the Deuteronomistic History*, Bible in the Modern World 5 (Sheffield: Sheffield Phoenix, 2005). For a more abbreviated interpretation of Jael, along with Rahab and Ruth, from the perspective of colonized Judah, see my "Postcolonial Perspectives on Premonarchic Women," in *To Break Every Yoke: Essays in Honor of Marvin L. Chaney*, ed. Robert B. Coote and Norman K. Gottwald (Sheffield: Sheffield Phoenix, 2007), 192–203.

[18] For an approach suggesting that some biblical texts functioned to support the interest of the Persians, see Jon Berquist, "Postcolonialism and Imperial Motives for Canonization" Semeia 75 (1996): 15–36; Berquist, *Judaism in Persia's Shadow: A Social and Historical Approach* (Minneapolis: Fortress, 1995), esp. 131–36.

tradition would be affiliated with Israel as a descendant of Moses' father-in-law. Yet Heber had separated himself from his kinfolk, moved his tent into Canaanite territory, and "made peace" with the king of the Canaanite forces (4:17). Heber (who never personally appears in the story) is thus a borderland figure, both geographically and ethnically, one who cannot belong fully to either side, who has eschewed his ties even to his own liminal Kenite group, and who apparently has chosen to align himself with the seemingly dominant side (Canaan) rather than with the kinship side (Israel).[19] On this reading of the text, we are told nothing explicitly about the ethnicity of Jael or of her personal loyalties, despite the assumption of many commentators that she is a loyal Kenite. It is conceivable that Heber had married outside his clan, either an Israelite woman or a Canaanite woman.[20]

Some scholars have argued that the word "Heber" is not a proper name but a common noun.[21] In this case Jael would be presented to us clearly as a Kenite, but with no reference to her marital status. For my purpose here, however, the central point is that none of these readings suggests that Jael as a woman had any part in the decision to encamp away from other Kenites or from Israel or to join in alliance with Canaan. The text does not tell us anything about her loyalties. No matter which ethnicity we presume for Jael, Israel's victory in battle and Sisera's appearance at her tent force her to make a choice.

Although white feminist interpretations of Jael are enormously diverse, a number tend to interpret her killing of Sisera as an act of self-defense. Themes include Jael's defense of herself against a male intruder into women's private space (especially in the poem) and thus against a threat of rape, and Jael's defense of herself against being discovered harboring the enemy (especially in the prose account), and thus against a threat of death.[22] This "defense" or implicit justification of Jael's

---

[19] Baruch Halpern has suggested that the Kenites may have been working for Israel, despite appearances ("Sisera and Old Lace: The Case of Deborah and Yael," in *The First Historians: The Hebrew Bible and History* [San Francisco: Harper & Row, 1988], 85–87).

[20] If we imagine Jael as a Canaanite, we might align her intertextually with Rahab; if we imagine her as Israelite, connections with Judith of much later tradition might be more apt. For comparison of these other characters, see Musa W. Dube, "Rahab Says Hello to Judith: A Decolonizing Feminist Reading," in *Toward a New Heaven and a New Earth: Essays in Honor of Elisabeth Schüssler Fiorenza*, ed. Fernando Segovia (Maryknoll: Orbis Books, 2003), 54–72.

[21] See Susan Ackerman, "What If Judges Had Been Written by a Philistine?" *Biblical Interpretation* 8 (2000): 37–38, and bibliography there.

[22] For the former, see Ann Wansbrough, "Blessed Be Jael among Women: For She Challenged Rape," in *Women of Courage: Asian Women Reading the Bible*, ed. Lee Oo Chung et al. (Seoul: Asian Women's Resource Centre for Culture and Theology, 1992), 101–22; for the latter, see Danna Nolan Fewell and David M. Gunn, "Controlling Perspectives: Women, Men, and the Authority of Violence in Judges 4 & 5," *Journal of the American Academy of Religion* 58 (1990): 396.

need to kill Sisera for her own survival serves to defuse some readers' discomfort (even revulsion) with the tent-peg scene, but it also can lead to downplaying the poem's explicit celebration of Jael's action—"most blessed of women be Jael" (5:24). The "defense" theme also stands in contrast to oral reports of women from other cultures who compare Jael to women in their own traditions who are celebrated for assassination of enemy leaders in times of military crisis.[23]

As my Korean conversation partner suggested, women who champion the overthrow of oppressors can identify with Jael. Given Jael's complex liminal status and its possible permutations, however, I would covet more conversation about Jael with women reflecting on their varied positions as postcolonial subjects. Imagining us gathered around a table, I hope we could consider questions such as these: Stepping back from the specific circumstance of war and murder/assassination, how might Jael's liminality illuminate ways in which you find yourself caught between colonizer and colonized because of gender structures in either or both cultures? Where does Jael's lack of agency in finding herself placed between Israel and Canaan resonate with you as an individual or with the circumstances of your community as colonized? When may your circumstances have meant that you have found no home on either side? In the moment of crisis, does Jael's action represent genuine agency or only forced choice? Does Jael's predicament mirror choices you have been forced to make, and what have been the possibilities and costs of refusing to choose? Is there reason to resist identifying with Jael simply because she takes sides so quickly? Does her action simply reinforce and reinscribe the construction of "absolute, incompatible contrasts" that postcolonial analysis seeks to dismantle?[24]

And what of myself, or of other first-world white feminists? Is our only place with Sisera's mother? I hesitate to consider any additional option without postcolonial conversation partners at the ready to correct my blind spots. I have asked myself whether I dare to claim any place with Jael as a woman whose tent inevitably lies between the camps. I can interpret my catalogue of questions about Jael in a way that allows me to speak of my own liminal place in a kyriarchal world.[25] But the risk of taking over (colonizing) yet again a space that may better belong rightly to my colonized sisters seems great. So for now I ask instead whether there is another

[23] I heard such comparisons from several groups of Asian women; Gale A. Yee also reports such a comparison ("By the Hand of a Woman: The Metaphor of the Woman Warrior in Judges 4," Semeia Studies 61 [1993]: 106).
[24] See John J. Collins, "The Zeal of Phinehas: The Bible and the Legitimation of Violence," *JBL* 122 (2003): 18.
[25] The term "kyriarchy," coined by Elisabeth Schüssler Fiorenza, gathers up the multiple and intertwined hierarchies of a world of Empire.

place of liminality that could arise from committing oneself to hearing and advocating for the Jaels of the postcolonial world. Might there be an unnamed woman of Israel, or of Canaan, depending on where a first-world white woman places herself in the story, an unnamed woman who supports Jael in some small way by resisting the power and the strategies of her own people? Such a midrash I would like to explore with the guidance of my postcolonial sisters.

Whose story is it? Whose text is it? I have claimed this particular text for myself in the hope of giving it away and in the hope of receiving eventually a gift from other interpreters in a mutual sharing of treasures.

Conclusion

In conclusion, let me quickly pull the zoom lens back from postcolonial feminism and this one text to the wide angle on the question of "Whose text?" with which I began. Each year, as I greet new students entering my institution's Ph.D. program, I begin with that phrase more traditionally used only at the conferral of the doctoral degree, "Welcome to the company of scholars." In those remarks, my primary emphasis is on the word "company." The challenge I put to them, and now to you, is this: Acknowledging our need for the gifts and contributions of sister and brother scholars, let us not decide so easily that the contribution of the "other" does not count as worthy scholarship, whether because we perceive its method and data as too politically motivated (read "postcolonial") or alternatively too old-fashioned and even hegemonic (read "Eurocentric" or "patriarchal") or whether because we perceive the work as nonacademic (read "too much reporting on 'ordinary' readers"), or whether because we reject the method as too vague or too psychological or too whatever else causes any of us to "other" that approach and its practitioners.

Each text really does belong at least potentially to all of us and to people across the world who may never know anything of the work we do in these halls. But text by text, each text will belong to different ones of us in vastly different and sometimes painfully different ways. Given this reality, let us not be content with a state of static tolerance in which we simply ignore one another. Rather, let us be on the move toward that ethical calling to become a company of scholars who rejoice in working with and learning from those least like ourselves and who show special generosity of spirit to those whose struggle to be heard is more difficult than our own. ■

The Folly of Secularism

by Jeffrey L. Stout

Dr. Jeffrey L. Stout, Professor of Religion at Princeton University, delivered this lecture as the 2007 President of the American Academy of Religion. Dr. Stout earned his PhD in religion from Princeton University and has taught there since 1975. He is the author of Democracy and Tradition *(2004) and* Ethics After Babel *(1989), both of which won the Award for Excellence from The American Academy of Religion. This address was first published in the* Journal of the American Academy of Religion *(*2008 76(3):533-544; *doi:10.1093/jaarel/lfn042) and is reprinted here with permission.*

Many people who care about democratic practices and institutions are worried by the power of the religious right in the United States and the rise of militant Islam elsewhere. They fear that democracy will give way to theocracy if these forces triumph, and they want to know how to prevent this from happening. One increasingly popular answer to this question is secularist. It says that striving to minimize the influence of religion on politics is essential to the defense of democracy. My purpose in this essay is to raise doubts about the wisdom of this answer.

The ideal of a democratic republic holds that political power is to be shared by the entire citizenry and that no one is to be denied citizenship simply because of his or her religious beliefs or lack thereof. Theocracy holds that God's representatives on earth should rule everyone else. Democracy and theocracy are therefore at odds. Wherever theocracy catches on, even among a sizable minority, democracy is in trouble. Sooner or later, theocracy disintegrates into conflict over who God's earthly representatives really are. Each band of

---

NOTE: I dedicate these remarks to Richard Rorty and Mary Douglas—two dear friends who died within a few weeks of each other when I was writing this address, friends from whom I have learned much and with whom I continue to argue. I had hoped to bring Mary Douglas to San Diego for a plenary address, but it was not to be. My remarks aim to combine Rorty's love of democracy with Douglas's suspicion of secularism.

DOI: 10.3754/1937–8386.2008.29.1.8

theocrats takes itself to be God's elect, claims for itself the right to hold earthly power over others, and declares its opponents deluded by sin.

American theocrats appear to have grown in numbers since the 1970s, and they probably played a significant role in the election of George W. Bush. The long-term objective most American theocrats harbor is a Christian America. They seek to use democratic means to achieve an antidemocratic end. What they ultimately seek is the dominance of non-Christians by Christians. Everyone who is committed to democracy has a stake in opposing the new theocrats, however many or few of them there might be.

But not all religious people are theocrats. Why, then, should we take religion *as such* to pose a threat to democracy?

Secularism comes in many forms, but what they all have in common is the aim of minimizing the influence of religion *as such*. Secularism comes into focus only when we notice that it takes *religion*, rather than some particular religion or type of religion, to be the problem. If, however, some forms of religion are in fact committed to democracy and have evidently promoted democracy in the past, why oppose *them*? Why substitute whole for part and then oppose the whole?

Lenin and Mao were unrestricted secularists; they sought to minimize the influence of religion on all aspects of human life. They considered religion essentially irrational and politically regressive, so they sought to eradicate it. Their antipathy for religion went hand in hand with their reluctance to trust the masses with political power. Democracy will become justifiable, according to Lenin and Mao, only when religious false consciousness and similarly retrograde tendencies have been overcome. Until then, the revolutionary avant-garde must exercise political authority on the people's behalf.

Richard Rorty, in contrast, was a *democratic* secularist. He saw democracy not as a distant possibility to be achieved in a future classless society but rather as an existing heritage of reform and social criticism in danger of being lost. This heritage rests, he thought, on "the Jeffersonian compromise that the Enlightenment reached with the religious."[1] Religion will be tolerated, according to this compromise, only insofar as it steers clear of politics. Mark Lilla refers to the outcome of this compromise as the Enlightenment's "Great Separation" of

[1] "Religion as Conversation-stopper," in Richard Rorty, *Philosophy and Social Hope* (London: Penguin Books, 1999), 169.

religion from politics.[2] The trouble, as Rorty and Lilla see it, is that the Great Separation is fragile and under assault. Its emergence was contingent, not inevitable, and it will pass away if citizens stop honoring the compromise on which it is based. Without it, however, there can be no democracy.

When Rorty spoke of the need to "enforce" the Jeffersonian compromise by keeping religion "private," he was not simply referring to legal enforcement of the First Amendment's establishment clause. Rorty was right to think that the government has no business giving tax dollars to religious groups, let alone adopting a religion on behalf of the people. I agree with him, moreover, that any religious organization should lose its tax-exempt status if it explicitly endorses a political candidate or party. But the U.S. Constitution does not say that religion must be a wholly private matter, and I see no evidence that most religious citizens ever agreed, even tacitly, to treat religion as if it were.

Rorty's secularism is a practical proposal, a claim about how democracy can best be safeguarded, a claim that goes well beyond taking a stand on the jurisprudence of the First Amendment. Many other intellectuals are nowadays endorsing roughly what Rorty proposed. Like other practical proposals, this one needs to be evaluated pragmatically, in terms of the acceptability of its ends, means, and likely consequences. If the end is to safeguard democracy, we had better determine what means are being recommended in pursuit of that end and what the likely consequences of adopting those means will be.

In Rorty's address at the 2003 Annual Meeting of the American Academy of Religion in Atlanta, he said that atheists make better citizens than do theists. This explains why many of his writings project a utopia in which theists not only keep their religious convictions private but eventually pass from the scene altogether. The Jeffersonian compromise turns out to be a stop-gap measure. Democracy will not be truly safe until theism gives up the ghost. It should be noted that this position almost perfectly mirrors that of the new theocrats. Neither the secularist nor the theocrat will be content until everyone agrees with their basic convictions.

Arguments against belief in God have been in circulation for a long time. Many people are unmoved by those arguments and are unlikely to be moved by them in the future. If the eventual eradication of theism is part of the secularist program for saving democracy, it would seem that something more than rational persuasion will be required. But what might that be? Although Rorty was fond of quoting

---

[2] Mark Lilla, *The Stillborn God: Religion, Politics, and the Modern West* (New York: Alfred A. Knopf, 2007), 55–103.

Voltaire's dream of the day when the last king would be strangled with the entrails of the last priest, I doubt that he was actually recommending strangling George Bush with the entrails of Pat Robertson.

If privatizing religion is essential to safeguarding democracy now, and eradicating belief in God is essential to achieving the utopian democracy of the future, then these goals will have to be accomplished somehow: if not by rational persuasion alone, then by some other means. If secularism confines itself to rational persuasion while granting that this means it is unlikely to succeed, the strategy boils down to a mere *ought* expressing the secular intellectual's alienation from a disturbingly religious present. It thus implicitly concedes its futility as a politics, as a strategy for achieving some desirable public end.

Rorty's argument up to this point raises three questions: (1) If part of the long-term objective is the *eradication* of theism, how is this to be accomplished, assuming that most theists are not about to change their minds? (2) If the stop-gap measure is to keep theists from *acting on* the apparent political implications of their religious beliefs, how is *that* to be accomplished? (3) If the Jeffersonian compromise is to be *enforced*, what are the means of enforcement going to be and how are they supposed to be squared with such democratic ideals as freedom of religion and freedom of conscience?

Rorty offered no answers to these questions and seems to have been reluctant to advance his cause by using force. Democratic secularists need to do their best, he thought, to narrate the history of the Great Separation in a way that makes the benefits of privatizing religion both salient and attractive. They should project a secularist utopia in which all good citizens have overcome the desire for the consolations that theism provides. They should strengthen their hold on the institutions of higher learning and convert as many young people to democratic secularism as possible. But in the end they will have to admit that these discursive means of advancing the secularist cause are likely to fail.

Democracy appears, from Rorty's point of view, to be slipping through our fingers. Theocrats and plutocrats are jointly bringing about democracy's demise. Rorty's realization that there may not be much that democratic secularists can do to prevent this unfortunate outcome accounts for the wistful tone of his later writings on religion and politics.

Sam Harris is a secularist who seems less inclined to confine himself to mere suasion as a means to his ends. He shares Rorty's hope that theism will someday wither away but doubts that it can in the meantime be privatized. In a book called

The End of Faith, Harris claims that religious faith is inherently intolerant.[3] He is aware that religious faith comes in "moderate" forms, as well as in the "extreme" forms that are overtly intolerant of everyone who differs from them religiously. But a central thesis of his book is that moderates are actually undermining democratic society by protecting extremists from the criticism they deserve.

"While all faiths have been touched, here and there, by the spirit of ecumenicalism," Harris writes, "the central tenet of every religious tradition is that all others are mere repositories of error or, at best, dangerously incomplete. Intolerance is thus intrinsic to every creed."[4] Religious moderates disguise this fact, often from themselves as well as from others. They fail to realize that their own moderation is actually derived from sources alien to their faith. They pretend that their scriptures do not contain and sanction horrors. Their calls for toleration of religious faith actually provide cover for their extremist brethren. In a world where religious extremists already exercise considerable political influence and move closer every day to acquiring nuclear weapons, such toleration becomes an unaffordable luxury.

Belief, Harris says, is never a merely private affair. Generally speaking, to believe a proposition is to be disposed to *act* on the supposition that the proposition is true. Theistic belief, being inherently intolerant, tends by nature to express itself in overtly intolerant behavior unless commitments arrived at independently of theistic premises complicate the process of reasoning. For extremists, there are no such complications. For moderates, the complications lead not to a benign form of tolerance but a misplaced tolerance of extremists. It is only to be expected that much of the resulting behavior on the part of both extremists and moderates has implications for public life. Therefore, privatizing faith is not the answer, even as a stop-gap measure.

The nuclear age, in other words, has rendered the Jeffersonian compromise unworkable. The problem we face, Harris says, "is not merely religious extremism: rather it is the larger set of cultural and intellectual accommodations we have made to faith itself. Religious moderates are, in large part, responsible for the religious conflict in our world, because their beliefs provide the context in which scriptural literalism and religious violence can never be adequately opposed."[5] Harris provides no evidence for his claims about how religious moderates behave and what effects their actions have. One wonders what his grounds for believing these claims might be.

---

[3] Sam Harris, *The End of Faith: Religion, Terror, and the Future of Reason* (New York: W. W. Norton & Company, 2005).
[4] Ibid., 13.
[5] Ibid., 45.

On the next page Harris asks, "Should Muslims really be *free* to believe that the Creator of the universe is concerned about hemlines?"[6] Two pages later he affirms a more general conclusion: "We have simply lost the *right* to our myths, and to our mythic identities."[7] What is Harris hinting at here? If theists, be they extremists or not, have no *right* to their convictions, it seems that people who know better, people like Harris, will be within *their* rights if they use the coercive power of the state to suppress theism.

What, then, should secularists *do* to acquire the power they need to save civilization? And once they have that power, what exactly does Harris want *done* to theists? He does not answer these questions. As in Rorty's case, at the crucial point in the argument everything becomes vague. There is no strategy being articulated here at all.

Harris is aware that most of his fellow American citizens are theists. The very thought of them brings him to the brink of despair. If they are as irrational as he claims them to be, they are not going to be persuaded by his appeals to reason. Rational persuasion, for all the value he places on it, must therefore not be the only thing his strategy involves. Secularists are rational but vastly outnumbered. They constitute a small island of sanity in a vast sea of unreason. What are they to do?

Harris's proposal to his fellow nonbelievers is to stop tolerating the faithful. The pragmatic effect of this proposal in the contemporary American context is clear: there will be no political alliance between nonbelievers and moderate theists. By undermining such an alliance, however, secularism deprives itself of the only available *democratic* means for delaying or preventing the triumph of theocracy in the United States. It also deprives itself of democratic means for achieving other important democratic objectives, such as preventing the triumph of plutocracy.

Harris makes clear that he wants to prevent the triumph of theocracy. As we have seen, one of the things he dislikes about even the nontheocratic forms of theistic faith is their alleged proclivity to tolerate the intolerant. But the upshot of his argument is that secularists should be less tolerant. It is not clear in the end that democracy is Harris's preferred alternative to theocracy under present circumstances. His hints about the need to stop granting rights to theists brings him at least into the vicinity of Lenin's view that until the day when faith gives way to reason, an enlightened avant–garde must rule on the people's behalf.

---

[6] Ibid., 46 (italics added).
[7] Ibid., 48 (italics added).

Harris might protest that I am reading too much into his vague hints. It is not my purpose, however, to prove that he actually has antidemocratic ends and means in mind. I am trying to show that sincerely *democratic* secularists face a dilemma. Either (a) they are merely *warning* us about the dangers of allowing religion into politics, in which case, by their own account, their arguments are likely to fall on deaf ears and therefore fail to achieve the desired objective; or (b) they are proposing some more *aggressive* strategy for curtailing the influence of religion on politics, in which case they owe us a concrete explanation of what that might be and how it is to be made consistent with democracy.

Option (a) is obviously futile. The people being warned are highly unlikely to heed the warning. But what about option (b)? If we're supposed to get tough on the believers and this involves something more than distancing ourselves from them symbolically, shaming them with words, and refusing to enter into coalitions with them, what restrictions are being proposed, and how are those restrictions going to be adopted and enforced? Again, an American secularist must face the fact that most U.S. citizens believe in God. A largely theistic majority is hardly about to elect representatives who openly promise to rescind the constitutional rights of believers to believe and to act on their beliefs as they see fit.

When Rorty said that atheists are better citizens than theists, he must have had particular people in mind, but what he uttered was a generalization. When challenged for evidence, he said that for every Martin Luther King Jr., there are a thousand Jerry Falwells. It is true, of course, that no other Christian leader's speeches and deeds have caught the nation's imagination and instructed the nation's conscience to the extent that King's did. In that sense, there was only one King, whereas there probably are a thousand somewhat influential preachers who will use their pulpits and television studios tomorrow morning to dismantle some portion of King's democratic legacy.

But what does democratic secularism do to thwart the influence of the most hateful among those preachers? As far as I can tell, they are among the last people on earth who are going to privatize their religious commitments, let alone drop those commitments altogether, as a result of the arguments put forward by secularist intellectuals. They will continue believing what they believe and acting on the apparent political implications of their beliefs, regardless of whatever liberal advice they hear to change their ways. If, by some miracle, laws were passed to constrain the hateful preachers whom secularists love to hate, and judges were installed to uphold those laws, what would become of those preachers? The most courageous of them would go proudly to jail as martyr-patriots, clutching a Bible in one hand and a copy of the Bill of Rights in the other. A day later, their churches would contain multitudes.

So far I have been arguing that democratic secularists are unlikely to achieve their objectives by democratic means. Now I want to ask what *unintended* consequences are likely to flow from pursuing secularist objectives. The first of these unintended consequences is to strengthen the hand of the preachers who hope to undo King's legacy. The social context of their conservatism is anxiety over immigration, rapidly changing relationships among the races and the sexes, poor economic prospects for the middle class, the demise of the union neighborhood and the family farm, the dislocations caused when people move away from home to get work or a university education, uneasiness about the content of popular entertainment, and the realization that isolated individuals have little chance of influencing or contesting the decisions of bureaucratic elites. Secularist resentment fuels that anxiety rather than raising it to self-consciousness. It presents the hateful preacher with a fattened scapegoat, primed for rhetorical sacrifice.

As Mary Douglas would hasten to point out, secularists too have a social location. They are employed mainly in segments of the economy devoted to information, education, entertainment, and government. They live mainly in places where organizations devoted to these functions are concentrated, which is to say, in the counties colored blue on the electoral maps of 2000 and 2004—the same places where one finds most of the people who describe themselves to pollsters as "spiritual but not religious."

Now imagine yourself as a relatively *moderate* red-county preacher considering what sort of sermon to preach on Sunday morning. You were raised to love your neighbor but not to tolerate attacks on faith and virtue. What are you going to make of the claim that atheists make better citizens than do theists, or the fantasy of strangling the last king with the entrails of the last priest, or the notion that believers are *essentially* irrational and intolerant, or the idea that the purpose of a liberal education is to produce as many democratic secularists as possible, or the dream of a day when faith has passed from the face of the earth, or the advice that you should, in all fairness, keep *your* religious convictions behind the church door while secularists pursue *their* long-term objectives?

It seems to me that you will treat such dicta as evidence that secularists are your avowed enemies, that they are plotting the eradication of your way of life, that they are less than wholeheartedly committed to democratic practices and the Bill of Rights. You will quote the textual evidence to your congregation and draw the conclusions that follow from it: that secularists cannot be trusted to hold political office, to educate the children of believers, or to give citizens the news. You will wonder out loud whether it makes sense anymore to be a moderate.

Secularist resentment is grist for the hateful preacher's mill, and it pushes religious moderates into the arms of their extremist brethren. It further polarizes a political community in which polarization is a primary impediment to democratic action on behalf of the poor and the oppressed. If the most important threat to democracy in our time is not theocracy but plutocracy—not rule by God's self-anointed representatives on earth but rule by the economically lucky—then nonbelievers won't be able to combat that threat without help from religious moderates.

Theocracy will triumph in places like the United States, where the population is both religiously diverse and for the most part committed to theism, only if the religious moderates are forced to move rightward to find allies. Theocracy will triumph in the Islamic world only if democracy continues to be indistinguishable there from imperial domination, unconstrained capitalism, and secularism. A potential Muslim theocrat can be defined as someone who opposes those forces and is looking for a movement to join.

At this point, the religious right in the United States is not predominantly theocratic. Its theocratic strand is miniscule but vocal. The new theocrats have clout only because of the arithmetic of swing votes in close elections. Their numbers are unlikely to grow unless believers who remain committed to democracy decide that they have to choose between theocracy and secularism. Secularist rhetoric gives them reason to think that they face that choice. It has the ironic effect of making theocracy more attractive to religious moderates.

If I am right in holding plutocracy to be the most significant contemporary threat to democracy, then the pressing question is how to build a coalition to combat that threat. The answer, I submit, is *not* to exclude religious moderates from the antiplutocratic coalition by telling them that they are essentially incapable of excellent citizenship and declaring them inherently intolerant. If a new coalition is going to succeed in breaking the hold of billionaires and bosses on our political institutions, it will have to include millions of theistic moderates as well as a lot of people more like me, who consider themselves atheists, agnostics, or "spiritual but not religious."

The failure to build such a coalition in the years since 1970 has tilted our society dangerously toward plutocracy and militarism. Many children of the religious right sense this. They suspect that their parents were duped by the neoliberals and neocons who lured them into the conservative alliance. People who sincerely wanted conservatism to be compassionate and American foreign policy to be just and humble are wondering who their true friends might be in the age of Katrina and Guantánamo Bay. They were shocked by the realization that their leaders were dividers, that the prosperity that was supposed to be trickling down to the poor was actually getting sucked upward by the richest of the rich, and that the official reasons given for invading Iraq were neither wholly true nor motivated by a desire to track the truth.

As a result of these disappointments, some sort of realignment is under way. It is too early to know what it will look like. But it is *not* too early to ask what it *should* look like. Nor is it too late to influence its formation.

The only form of democracy worthy of our allegiance consists of a tradition of reform in which the responsibilities and rights of political and civil society were expanded to include people who used to count for little or nothing—such people as slaves, women, factory laborers, new immigrants, migrant farm hands, the unemployed, the working poor, blacks, Catholics, and Jews. The aspirations and ideals articulated in the great democratic reform movements of the past add up to something that can be distinguished from the characteristic ills of the modern era. Those movements accomplished something. One shudders to think what our society would be like if they had failed. How, then, were they set in motion, and how did they attain their central aims?

Abolitionism was born in the revival tents of the Second Great Awakening. There was formed a coalition that included secular intellectuals such as Ralph Waldo Emerson, religious moderates such as Theodore Parker, and people labeled religious extremists such as David Walker and William Lloyd Garrison. Lincoln admitted that he belonged to no church, but the evangelicals of his day made him their candidate anyway. Why? Because they considered slavery a horrendous evil, a violation of sacred value, and they understood that Lincoln did too. There were millions of religious people on both sides of the slavery question. Many of them considered their religious convictions relevant to their political conclusions and behaved accordingly. This should surprise no one.

The struggle for women's suffrage was another product of the Second Great Awakening. The labor movement was rooted in the Social Gospel. During the civil rights movement, there was only one Martin Luther King Jr., but there were thousands of ministers mobilizing their churches in support of civil rights. Black Muslims played a role, and so did liberal Jews. Countless churches ran citizenship classes. Secular organizers such as Ella Baker went door to door—without holding their noses in the presence of believers. James Baldwin was our Emerson. Baker and Baldwin were secular, not secularist.

One wonders what the Great Separation comes to in light of this history. There is not a word about such movements in Lilla's *The Stillborn God*, which focuses only on the likes of Hobbes, Hume, Kant, Hegel, Rosenzweig, and Barth. Lilla eloquently describes the emergence of "a new approach to politics focused exclusively on human nature and human needs." This approach, he says, "remains the most distinctive feature of the modern West today."[8] But the story he tells turns out to be all about intellectuals, not about the societies on which those intellectuals were reflecting.

Perhaps a Great Separation of religion and politics did occur in the minds of the northern European intelligensia. No doubt secularist political theory has had an influence on the political life of some societies, including our own. Yet I see little evidence of its influence in the history of democratic reform in the United States since the middle-third of the nineteenth century. As for Harris's claims about the reluctance of religious moderates and their secular allies to criticize religious extremists, I wonder what he might make of Emerson's "Self-Reliance," Stanton's *The Woman's Bible*, Rauschenbusch's *Christianity and the Social Crisis*, Baldwin's *The Fire Next Time*, or hundreds of lesser-known works expressing similar sentiments.

It is daunting but inspiring to contemplate the degree of cooperation among religious and secular individuals and groups that made possible each of the great American reform movements. I do not mean to suggest, however, that American democratic striving is unique. The South African triumph over apartheid had much the same structure. Would Nelson Mandela have been well advised to adopt a secularist stance? Doing so would have cost him the support of the South African Council of Churches and the World Alliance of Reformed Churches, whose spokespersons were Desmond Tutu and Allan Boesak, respectively.

The Polish triumph over Soviet oppression was founded on a similarly inclusive coalition. One of its principal architects was a secular intellectual named Adam Michnik, who read King as a young man, was a key figure in the Worker's Defense Committee, and in 1979 published *The Church and the Left*, which criticized secularism as a dead end for Poland.[9]

What these examples suggest, it seems to me, is that democratic reform may indeed be achievable by democratic means in places where the majority of the citizens

---

[8] Lilla, *The Stillborn God*, 58.
[9] Adam Michnik, *The Church and the Left*, ed. David Ost (Chicago: University of Chicago Press, 1993).

are religiously active *if* citizens are prepared to build coalitions of the right sort. If major reform is going to happen again in the United States, it will probably happen in roughly the same way that it has happened before. It will not happen *because* of secularism but *in spite* of it. And it had better happen, because if it does not, our political life will cease to be democratic in anything but name.

Does democratic reform remain possible in our day? In a plenary address delivered at the 2007 annual meeting of our academy in San Diego, Nicholas Wolterstorff reflected on how justice came to be a central theme of his academic work. (This piece is included in the *Journal of the American Academy of Religion* [2008 76:3]). Wolterstorff is a theologically conservative philosopher of religion; he practices our trade. He was also one of Boesak's American allies in the struggle against apartheid and thus part of a vast international network of activists who jointly increased the cost of maintaining the institutions of white supremacy in South Africa in the 1980s. It was not long ago that South Africa seemed headed toward a bloody revolution, but in fact apartheid was overcome there largely by nonviolent means. Today, of course, South Africa faces the woes of a new era, including the ravages of AIDS and the devastation caused by the economic policies of the World Bank and the International Monetary Fund. Those woes are depressing not only because of the number of people and degree of suffering the woes involve but also because of the patterns of complicity that come into view when we reflect on the uses of American power abroad. But this only shows that there are new forms of injustice to oppose. It does not show that new democratic coalitions, if we manage to build them, will fail to make a difference.

Two other plenary sessions at the 2007 annual meeting are equally relevant to the question of whether democratic reform remains possible. In one of them, the journalist Tavis Smiley reflected on the Covenant with Black America. Cornel West, Eddie Glaude, and Emilie Townes responded. In the other session, Ernesto Cortés, the most successful broad-based organizer in the United States, described his work with churches, synagogues, labor unions, and schools throughout the southwestern United States. Smiley and Cortés are both engaged in constructing nonpartisan democratic coalitions and in reviving practices of accountability. They have had much success in encouraging religious citizens to take responsibility for the condition of the poor in their midst. In the work of such figures, it seems to me, one can discern some grounds for hope that democratic reform remains possible *here*. Cortés, in particular, can point to many concrete victories, many examples of ordinary people achieving democratic ends by democratic means against great odds.

Only time will tell whether these efforts will eventually produce changes as fundamental as the abolition of slavery or the enfranchisement of women. No such change seems likely in advance. That is why hope is a central political virtue.

It should be clear by now that I do not share the theological convictions of a Wolterstorff, a Smiley, or a Cortés. But who among us surpasses *them* in the excellences of citizenship? Not I. Far be it from me to advise them to keep their religious convictions to themselves. Far be it from me to dream of a future in which they and others like them have passed from the scene. ■

Dedication of the Marion and Wilhelm Pauck Manuscript Collection

Historical Theology Done in the Radical Liberal Mode: The Story of Wilhelm Pauck

by Hans J. Hillerbrand

Dr. Hans J. Hillerbrand, Professor of Religion and History at Duke University, spoke at Princeton Theological Seminary on May 23, 2008, to mark the opening of the Marion and Wilhelm Pauck Manuscript Collection to the public. Dr. Hillerbrand has written numerous books and articles on the Reformation and the history of modern Christianity and served as editor-in-chief of the Oxford Encyclopedia of the Reformation. *His most recent book is* The Division of Christendom: Christianity in the 16th Century *(2007). Wilhelm Pauck was a German-American historian and theologian. He taught at Chicago Theological Seminary, the University of Chicago, Union Theological Seminary, and Vanderbilt University, and was professor emeritus at Stanford University. He died on September 3, 1981.*

I first encountered Wilhelm Pauck light-years ago, in 1953, when I was a German undergraduate exchange student at Goshen College—the sole Lutheran at the Mennonite College—and had great aspirations not in church history but in the diplomatic service. It was the heyday of the new way of looking at the long-despised Anabaptists of the sixteenth century. Harold S. Bender of Goshen College, then dean of Anabaptist historians, had convened a conference with Wilhelm Pauck as the main speaker. I do not recall his topic, but I do remember vividly that when the conference was to begin, with

DOI: 10.3754/1937–8386.2008.29.1.9

Wilhelm Pauck, University of Chicago, 1937

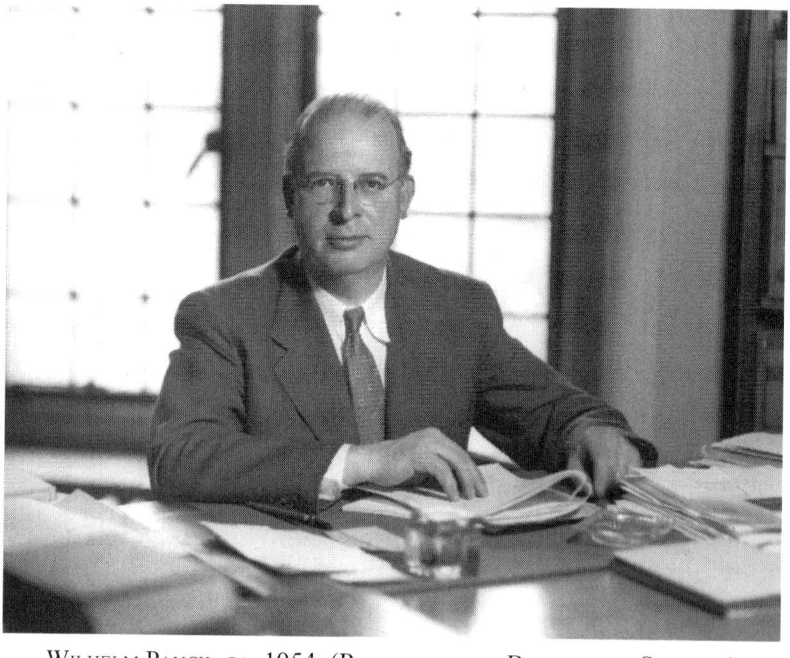

Wilhelm Pauck, ca. 1954. (Photograph by Blackstone Studios.)

his lecture first on the agenda, Pauck was nowhere in sight. After an interval of embarrassed waiting, Harold Bender took the lectern and began to read his paper. Some thirty minutes later, the door to the assembly hall in the main building on the Goshen College campus opened, and Wilhelm Pauck stormed in. Harold Bender dutifully finished the sentence or paragraph he was reading and, after a brief introduction, turned the microphone over to Pauck, whose opening words were: "I am sorry I'm late. I won't tell you how it happened." Needless to say, I was baffled, but I suspect that Pauck had forgotten the time difference between Chicago and Goshen.

In the three decades that followed, Wilhelm Pauck and I stayed in touch, both indirectly and directly. Most encounters were indirect, facilitated by his students and colleagues. They claimed a rich reservoir of Pauck stories, all terribly funny and all irreverent, if nothing else proof positive of the impact Pauck made as teacher. Thus I learned that one should never sit in the front row in his courses because Pauck would animatedly position himself in front of you and lecture only to you, periodically stabbing his index finger and showering you with saliva. And that Pauck urged a female graduate student to attend a meeting of the American Society of Church History at Union, warning her "when you walk into the room you will only see old men. Don't let that discourage you, but I fear that is not going to change." Glen Stassen, now a distinguished ethicist at Fuller Theological Seminary, told me that when he was a Duke doctoral student in the 1960s, Pauck's introductory church history lecture at Union Seminary was the most brilliant way to learn the relevance of the Christian past. Because I myself have always had students in my church history course who showed no interest in the Christian past, not to mention its contemporary relevance, I felt challenged. Not familiar with Pauck's lecture, however, I was handicapped, but I did some reflecting and for the past forty years my introductory lecture in church history has featured chopsticks, a spoon, and an excursion into the British habit of driving on the left side of the road. I am not sure Pauck would have entirely approved, but nonetheless, his spirit has hovered over my pontifications.

Later I realized that the fountain of this rich lore was frequently none other than Pauck himself, such as when he demonstrated how he dealt with a terribly shy first-year Chicago Divinity School student who appeared in his office and requested permission to write the term paper for the introductory church history course in Latin. Imitating both the student and his own response, Pauck eventually revealed that the student was none other than George H. Williams, later the prolific church historian at Harvard.

My direct relationship with Wilhelm Pauck paralleled these indirect encounters, with me taking the role of a junior scholar while he served as a revered mentor. I increasingly appreciated Pauck's erudition—his rich knowledge of all periods of church history and its primary and secondary literature, and, indeed, his vast background in art, literature, and culture. After I had given a paper on Menno Simons at a Washington meeting of the American Society of Church History, he informed me that my interpretation of Menno was correct and my style of presentation was "mature." I must have been thirty-one at the time. He also warned me, during a long walk at the Luther Congress in Jarvenpoo, Finland, in 1960, not to write a history of the Reformation as a junior scholar—a warning I promptly ignored, though I hoped to assuage him by dedicating the book I eventually wrote to him. All the same, on that Finnish summer day I probably was more baffled by the sight of the crème de la crème of Luther scholars nude in a Finnish sauna than by his advice. Later, he scolded me for writing in an essay that Dietrich Bonhoeffer was "confused" during his 1939 stay in this country. In all of these encounters, it was clear who was the student and who the mentor. At the same time, he was unfailingly poignant in his criticism and uncommonly generous in his praise.

I offer these recollections—including the cryptic reference to chopsticks as a tool to introduce church history—in the interest of full disclosure. I do not speak as an outsider, in other words, but as someone who knew and admired the church historian Wilhelm Pauck. My admiration, and the dedication of one of my books, derived from my own growing sense that my trajectory as teacher and scholar was not unlike his, not the least because of our shared German heritage, our ambivalence about it, and our mutual interest in focusing on the big picture in the story of the church.

When Wilhelm Pauck arrived at the Chicago Theological Seminary in 1925 as a twenty-four-year-old visiting postdoc from Germany, the theological revolution triggered by the second edition of Karl Barth's Romans commentary was just getting under way in Europe. Few in this country had then heard of Barth, who had received his first academic appointment in 1921 in Göttingen, where Pauck encountered him. This was Pauck's fleeting exposure to nascent dialectic theology, and the record shows that he was not impressed, which—given the fact that he had already been exposed to the thought of Adolf von Harnack and Ernst Troeltsch—should not come as a startling surprise. A comparison with Dietrich Bonhoeffer, Pauck's junior by five years is instructive, for when Bonhoeffer came to study in Berlin in the mid-1920s (Pauck was already in the United States), neoorthodoxy had become a successful insurgency and had taken the younger generation of students and theologians by storm. Tellingly, a Berlin observer noted that the lectures of that liberal idol Adolf von Harnack were hardly attended by students but mainly by elderly matrons of Berlin society.

Nonetheless, it speaks for Pauck's keen awareness of the emerging theological turn that his second book was his 1931 *Karl Barth: Prophet of a New Christianity?* Pauck's book, more than anything else, introduced Barth (and what came to be called neoorthodox theology) to North American Protestantism. H. Richard Niebuhr's review aptly noted Pauck's "admirable exposition" and called attention to the question mark at the end of the title. Comments such as "intolerable skeleton-dace" tellingly conveyed Pauck's view of the Swiss theologian. Pauck collegially sent Barth a copy of the book, itself an act of considerable self-assurance. This triggered an exchange of letters between the two, marked by Barth's equally self-assured, not to say aggressive, rebuttal of Pauck's book, including Pauck's supposedly blasphemous use of the biblical term "prophet" in the title. Pauck thereupon apprised Barth of the several uses of the word in the English language, which prompted Barth to acknowledge his cursory competence in the English language.

Pauck's book thus intimated that, to use a well-worn phrase of dialectic theology, *zwischen den Zeiten* (Between the Times), his was a theological understanding that sided neither with the Lutheran confessionalists, such as Werner Elert or Paul Althaus, nor with the new neoorthodoxy of Thurneysen, Gogarthen, or Brunner. Pauck's theological understanding remained grounded in the Historicist school, even though, at least in Germany, it was falling more and more into disrepute. The fact that he turned so late in his active scholarly life to two "historical theologians"—Troeltsch and Harnack, who had so profoundly influenced him—and that, together with the indispensable support of Marion Pauck, he undertook to focus on Paul Tillich reveals the line of continuity so important to understanding his approach to the past. It was never nontheological or antitheological.

Pauck's move to the United States meant that he was not swept up in the Barthian neoorthodox revolution that was initially confined to academic circles—leaving the people in the pews and even pastors altogether unaware—but eventually had an important impact on Protestant theologizing in Germany. Pauck found a more hospitable climate in this country than he would have experienced in Germany. His move to the United States also spared him from involvement in the German church struggle after the Nazis took power in 1933.

Pauck was a historical theologian, which was how he described Harnack and Troeltsch. On occasion he dabbled, so to speak, in narrowly historical topics, but he was not as comfortable with institutional history as he was with ideas, theological issues, and topics. Moreover, he always saw ideas and developments on a grand scale and with refreshing self-confidence. After all, who would have the nerve (or courage) to offer an assessment of Karl Barth's *Church Dogmatics* in eight pages, devoting a portion of those pages to an anecdote about the young Barth spending one day in a barn to write his "collected works."

The "big" topics engaged Pauck's attention—Luther and Melanchthon, Luther and the Reformation, the nature of Protestantism, Protestantism and democracy, the outlook for religion. There are no narrow monographs here, on such topics as "Luther's understanding of the doctrine of the church in his first Psalms lectures." Instead, Pauck's discussions had broad contours, and he used broad brushstrokes. And no matter what the topic, he made a vigorous plea for commitment to the historical-critical method of understanding the Christian past and presented a vigorous partisanship for what he called radical liberal theology.

It is now over a quarter of a century since we lost Wilhelm Pauck, since we last heard his wise comments, were last exposed to his erudition, or indeed, last heard the stories that he punctuated with his infectious laughter—stories that he seemed to enjoy even more than his listeners did. Wilhelm Pauck exuded the conviction that what he was teaching was of fundamental importance to understanding the history of Christian self-consciousness and thus the Christian faith. In his 1936 presidential address for the American Society of Church History, when he was thirty-five, he tackled the topic "The Nature of Protestantism," and his essay is clearly a theological confession rather than a historical analysis. After acknowledging the threat of the totalitarian state to Protestantism, he pointedly challenged Protestants to "avoid a resuscitation of antiquated theological and ecclesiastical heteronomies as well as reliance upon secular autonomies."

His distinguished contemporaries—John T. McNeill, Ray Petry, Shirley Jackson Case, Harold Bender, Matthew Spinka, Harold Grimm, and Roland Bainton—are also long gone, and the ranks of the next generation of church and Reformation scholars—Jaroslav Pelikan, Robert Handy, Cyril Richardson, Heiko Oberman, Lewis Spitz, Robert Kingdon, Brian Gerrish, Jane Dempsey Douglass, and Hans Hillerbrand—are thinning.

It thus should not be at all surprising that Reformation scholarship is not what it used to be: a new cohort of scholars has come to occupy center stage. Changes in methodology and perspective, already in the making in the 1970s, have become commonplace. The dominance of the theological perspective of the Reformation, prevalent in the heyday of neoorthodoxy, has been challenged, and most work on the Reformation, certainly in this country, has recently come from scholars employing the categories of social history in order to understand the religious phenomena of the sixteenth century. We now have new names and new head turners.

Wilhelm Pauck did not witness this development, but if he had, I am sure he would have made some trenchant observations. He would have pointed to his essay on the ministry in the time of the Reformation to convey that the kinds of questions recently raised by social historians were not at all new to him. He would have pointed to his editorship of the Library of Christian Classics volume on Luther's Romans commentary and Martin Bucer's *De Regno Christi* as proof positive of his expertise in Reformation thought. With that twinkle in his eyes—and his inimitable German accent—he would have informed us of the difference between a historical theologian and a confessionally bound historical theologian. In fact, he would have reminded us of Harnack's famous dictum—which was at once his own motto as a scholar—that "we must overcome history with history." In other words, the past must be creatively appropriated—neither rejected nor embraced wholesale. And the ambition and exuberance of the young have continued to challenge the maturity and wisdom of the old, as each older generation is challenged by the younger, with the younger inescapably winning out. Martin Luther put it quite simply: "the young must come and take over for us."

Of course, once you think about it, there always is a pivotal connection between one generation and the next. The point of departure for the new is the consensus of the old. The older and the younger generations of scholars, the young and the old, are intimately conjoined. The windows in the north transept of the cathedral of Chartres depict the New Testament apostles standing on the shoulders of the Old Testament prophets, visually revealing the complex and inextricable connection of generations. Physiologically, this posture cannot last long, but still, what a splendid way to depict the relationship of one generation of scholars to the next! Thus, a whole generation of Reformation and church historians has stood on the shoulders of Wilhelm Pauck—Jaroslav Pelikan, George Williams, Klaus Penzel, Bill Clebsch, David Lotz, Lewis Spitz. Some of these scholars gave us new scholarly insights, while others labored in the vineyard of "teaching." But none of them, none of us, would be what and who we are were it not for our dependence on the generation that has gone before.

There is yet another point, which tells us something about the transition of generations. Given Wilhelm Pauck's eminence in his time, the dearth of monographs during his active career must come as a surprise. By the time of his retirement, he had published his study of Bucer's *De Regno Christi* and his assessment of Karl Barth, plus a number of articles. Yet he exerted enormous influence and was universally respected; he was a former president of the ASCH, and a member of the American Academy of Arts and Sciences.

How different from today, when we tend to measure scholarship quantitatively, like a grade school counting exercise, making two books being better than one, three books better than two. The days when tenure decisions were made by deans only in brief conversation with the deity are long passed. There are, of course, colleagues who do not have an unpublished thought (I resist the temptation to name my favorite example). The German Reformation scholar Rudolf Stupperich was explicit about his determination to publish 1,000 journal articles in his lifetime. Because it is said that all theory is autobiography, it will not surprise you that I bewail the old days.

Wilhelm Pauck's time was a different day and age, when scholars tended to publish if they had something to say, as opposed to today, when tenure or promotion committees force their hand. Pauck did not easily put pen to paper, and cogent reasons have been given. Yet the point is not so much what might be advanced by way of explanation as it is that his wisdom and expertise were recognized even though he did not publish much, a striking characteristic that incidentally also applies to his contemporary Roland H. Bainton at Yale. Profound ideas and stories are not necessarily confined to the printed page. This is, of course, where Marion Pauck comes in, for Pauck's mature and insightful publications of the 1960s and 1970s surely show how her professionalism as a former editor of the Oxford University Press facilitated the transfer of Pauck's erudition onto the printed page.

I fear that unless my musings take on the format of a funeral oration, I must turn to the occasion that has brought us together: the past, to be sure, but even more so the present and the future. For the Marion and Wilhelm Pauck Manuscript Collection here at Princeton is meant, above all, to preserve a part of the past for the present and the future. Both the occasion and our presence signify the meaning of the past and of memory.

What once was can well be ignored, or neglected—Henry Ford famously said, after all, that history is bunk—but it does reach into each present. It is the past that established for us that we should use knife and fork to eat, and not chopsticks, even as the past determined our driving on the right side of the road. Sometimes this past can be challenged, as, for example, when new tastes develop in popular music, but sometimes it cannot. Change or petrification, then, carries the day.

The appropriation of the past is often an ambiguous and complex assignment. Both the actors of history and the reporters of history can be moved as much by the desire for power, for recognition, or for rationalization as by lofty ideals or the claim of only recording "*wie es eigentlich gewesen*" (how it really was). Indeed, in recent times we have been reminded that the straightforward memory of what once was is more complicated than meets the eye. We have autobiographies that have been shown to be works of fiction and we have candidates for political office whose stump speeches offer different accounts of events than do their autobiographies. Even if we had Martin Luther's autobiography, the dispute over the nailing of the ninety-five theses to the church doors in Wittenberg would hardly be settled.

The appropriation of memory is the lifeblood of the historian, for it is memory that turns a past into a present. After all, memory allows us to recall what we had for dinner last night, even as it allows Monarch butterflies to find their way to Mexico. Memory allows relationships, connections, causalities, although with increasing age, some memory—such as last Sunday's sermon or the plot of last week's movie—fades.

Libraries and archives are depositories of memory. They would be empty edifices, empty shelves, if decades, centuries, even millennia ago someone had not decided that this book, that parchment, or that codex held ideas and memories worthy of being passed on. As easy as this sounds, in practice it has been neither easy nor simple, for there are not only the preservers of memory but also those who wish to distort or even destroy it. Often, one fears, the destroyers make as much impact as the preservers. Sometimes memory is destroyed carelessly. When wars and conquest ravish the countryside, libraries and books go up in flames. When efficiency experts appear for solutions of space pressures or personnel costs in libraries, books are not ordered. John Calvin's sermons were sold as scrap paper two hundred years ago, when space became scarce in Geneva, and some of the Nag Hammadi treasures were used as kindling, while the autograph of Bach's *St. Matthew Passion* had to be rescued from a Leipzig merchant who wanted to use it to wrap cheese.

And so today, we do not have the writings of Marcion or Celsus because the imperial church detested their memory, and we have less than a handful of copies of Michael Servetus's *Restitution* because reformers and inquisitors joined in their determination to obliterate the book and its ideas from human memory. Book burning is a favorite pastime of both the establishment and its critics, and when books are burned and slowly turn into ashes, memory is gone as well. Of course, memory may also be destroyed by simply ignoring that which has gone before, such as when reading lists for humanities courses seem to suggest that the printing press is only a few years old. The destroyers of ideas destroy memory.

Each book, each letter or memo, is a mosaic stone to tell a story and thereby—when added to many others—to create memory. We all have walked down narrow aisles between two stacks, books to our left and books to our right, with the colors and sizes of the books flowing into one another as do hues in a watercolor. We have marveled at the tediously lengthy book and the strangely brief book, and our imagination has taken us to a lifetime devoted to "the" book or a rush to publish to secure tenure. In each case, the book on the shelf has told us how the author wished to record insights, facts, concerns.

And we, the readers, are the last judgment, so to speak, since in retrieving the book, we retrieve memory and adjudicate significance. Libraries do an exit poll each time a book is checked out. In the olden days, the book on the shelf had a little card that told when and by whom it had been checked out. In some instances, this showed it never happened, meaning memory was lost and with it, the author's determination, persistence, and sacrifice.

Collections are a special form of such preservation of memory. They harbor personalized memory: intimate, blunt, personal, formalistic, artificial, or distorted. They also tell stories. I recently came across a piece of paper on the attic floor of our house after one of our grandchildren had received permission to look for "treasures" and had left the attic in a state of advanced chaos. Picking it up, I saw that it was a memo from 1968, addressed to me and written by my then dean. I do not recall the facts behind the memo (sometimes the loss of memory is a blessing), but evidently I had requested a travel subsidy to read a paper at the San Francisco meeting of the American Society of Church History; in those days there were no institutional travel subsidies to conferences even when reading a paper. I was already a full professor. "What were you thinking when you agreed to give a paper in San Francisco?" the memo began. "The next time you had better inquire of your travel agent as to cost of travel … I have no funds for such behavior. … As an exception, I will authorize $50." I suggest that this innocuous memo tells more about the culture of the Duke Divinity School at the time than the dean's annual reports to the Duke University administration.

Libraries and collections thus are also the depositories of human folly, along with insight and wisdom. The reformer Huldrych Zwingli's notebook in the Zurich archives tells us about the chronic mistakes he made when he conjugated Greek verbs. A scholar's find of Zwingli's letter confessing to an affair with a barber's daughter in Einsiedeln is a testimony of affirming memory even when painful. The baptismal records of Johann Sebastian Bach's children tell us of the parents' mourning over their infants who lived but a few days. The transcripts of Luther's pontifications across the dinner table demonstrate that even then students did not always get it.

The memory of Wilhelm Pauck, expressed in his papers, and also Marion Pauck's memories have now found a depository here at Princeton Theological Seminary. On the face of things, Princeton Seminary, citadel of the Calvinist-Reformed tradition, seems a dubious choice for the papers of a man nurtured on the mother's milk of Luther and the Lutheran tradition, not to mention on liberal theology. After all, the rich library of this Seminary houses the American Presbyterian Collection, the Karl Barth Collection, and the Abraham Kuyper Collection. It is now also committed to bringing out a digital edition of Barth's *Church Dogmatics*, about which Pauck observed, back in 1931, that it revealed an "unintelligible complexity of thought." I imagine him chuckling and saying, in paraphrase of Galileo's famous utterance, "it IS unintelligible." But it is worthwhile to recall that his first monograph was on that ecumenist of the Reformation Martin Bucer and on his program for a Christian commonwealth, *De Regno Christi*. Judging from his essay on "the prospects for ecumenical theology today," he would have approved—sharing a Calvin anecdote that none of us had ever heard.

The Marion and Wilhelm Pauck manuscript collection will open a window of memory to a most exciting time in the history of American church historical scholarship and American Protestantism. The collection invites us to awareness of Wilhelm Pauck's role and stature as an individual and as a scholar. But as we celebrate memory and the past, we must also reflect on the present. Even more importantly, even as we celebrate Wilhelm Pauck's memory, we must be aware there surely is a new Wilhelm Pauck somewhere, young, energetic, insightful, gifted, and ready to make her mark, even as Wilhelm made his mark—because the story and the memory continue.

Over 200 years ago, a stone mason working in the cemetery of the memorial church of Jamestown, Virginia, chiseled a couple of sentences onto the tombstone of a Virginia gentleman by the name of John Amber. He wrote: "He was early distinguished by his love of letters and well knew how to adorn a manly sense with all the eloquence of language. To the extensive knowledge of man and things he joined the noblest sense of liberty, and in his own example held up to the world the most striking picture of the amiableness of religion."

It is almost as if our anonymous stonemason had known Wilhelm Pauck—and to these strangely timeless words there is thus really nothing that can be added. ■

Essay

Biblical Theology Revisited: An Internal Debate

by C. Clifton Black

Dr. C. Clifton Black is Princeton Theological Seminary's Otto A. Piper Professor of Biblical Theology. His most recent book is The Eighth Day of Creation: An Anthology of Christian Scripture *(2008).*

The author is grateful to the editor and readers of the Princeton Seminary Bulletin *for indulging this essay's unconventional presentation.*[1] *Its style accurately reflects a conversation, at times heated, within the essayist himself, a debate that ends in these pages without complete resolution. This peculiar approach further attacks the preponderance of contemporary theological literature at its most impoverished point: its sense of humor. Good Friday, the liturgical year's most sober observance, is forever followed by joyous resurrection on Easter. Of all disciplines, therefore, Christian theology addresses issues in deadly earnest with what should be the lightest, most mirthful touch. Theologians take their subject matter with utmost seriousness; by now, however, we scribes and Pharisees should have learned not to take ourselves seriously at all. At the last is God's laugh.*[2]

Woody Allen: "The curtain rises on a vast primitive wasteland, not unlike certain parts of New Jersey."[3]

Bold-Faced Black: *So it's come to this. You're talking to yourself in public. Even worse: in print.*

[1] My sincere thanks extend to fellow members in residence at Princeton's Center of Theological Inquiry, to whom an earlier draft was presented on January 30, 2008.
[2] See "Basic Christian Existence as 'a Laugh,' " in Daniel W. Hardy and David F. Ford, *Praising and Knowing God* (Philadelphia: Westminster, 1985), 71–73.
[3] Woody Allen, "A Guide to Some of the Lesser Ballets," in Woody Allen, *Without Feathers* (New York: Random House, 1975), 16.

DOI:10.3754/1937-8386.2008.29.1.10

Bald–Faced Black: There are worse things than schizophrenia. It beats dining alone.

BFB: *You call this doggerel an essay?*
BFB: No. That would be an insult to the entire canine world. This I call a "work in progress."

Offering something this cockamamie will render you ridiculous before your readers.
If by now my readers haven't figured me out, what they make of this article will neither add to nor subtract from their estimate. Besides, the venerable Q & A/*videtur–sed contra* style served St. Thomas rather well.

In your dreams: If you thought half as lucidly as Aquinas, you'd stick your quill back in your goose. Let's get down to cases: You claim to have "revisited biblical theology." What has your revisit taught you to this point?
I've learned that in academic scholarship, precious little of it is either "biblical" or "theological." G. L. Bauer (1705–1806) disjoined Old Testament theology from New Testament theology more than two centuries ago.[4] Since then a mere handful—among others, Paul Minear (1906–2007),[5] Brevard Childs (1923–2007),[6] Paul Hanson (1939–),[7] and Walter Moberly (1952–)[8]—have encompassed both testaments. Most sincerely do we thank them.

My most jarring discovery, or confirmation of a hunch, is that some among even those who have attempted biblical theology—a coherent, comprehensive description and assessment of religious views expressed in both testaments—are not actually doing theology, at least not in the first instance. Usually they are executing *historical* reconstructions of what, as William Wrede memorably said over a century ago, was "believed, thought, taught, hoped, required, and striven for" in ancient Israel, earliest Judaism, and the earliest era of Christianity.[9]

---

[4] Georg Lorenz Bauer, *Theologie des Alten Testaments, oder, Abriss der religiösen Begriffe der alten Hebraïer* (Leipzig: Weygand, 1796).
[5] Paul S. Minear, *Eyes of Faith: A Study in the Biblical Point of View* (Philadelphia: Westminster, 1946).
[6] Brevard S. Childs, *Biblical Theology of the Old and New Testaments: Theological Reflection on the Christian Bible* (Minneapolis: Fortress, 1993).
[7] Paul D. Hanson, *The People Called: The Growth of Community in the Bible* (San Francisco: Harper & Row, 1986).
[8] R. W. L. Moberly, *The Bible, Theology, and Faith: A Study of Abraham and Jesus*, Cambridge Studies in Christian Doctrine (Cambridge: Cambridge University Press, 2000).
[9] William Wrede, "The Task and Methods of 'New Testament Theology,'" in *The Nature of New Testament Theology*, ed. and trans. Robert Morgan (London: SCM, 1973), 84 (italicized in the original).

Do you agree with that grouchy buzzard Wrede?
No, not for the most part. Wrede's answer triumphed—and that's no solution for us. It is, instead, part of our problem.

Wrede (1859–1906) rent asunder the conceptual marriage that Johann Philipp Gabler (1753–1826) had attempted to broker in 1787.[10] For Wrede, German liberal theology's "method of doctrinal concepts"—grouping thoughts expressed by the New Testament in alignment with dogmatic topics—betrays "scientific criticism" and provokes caricature of New Testament writers as systematicians in the modern sense. That method's default setting on canonical documents is likewise misguided: a document's canonization makes no difference for either the Protestant theologian or historical investigator. New Testament theology is, or should be, the attempt to understand the development of primitive Christian religion in its historical situation: the earliest Christians' beliefs and aspirations, not how their literary artifacts may be plundered for our reconstructions of "faith," "hope," or whatever. Wrede believed that the responsible procedure is to begin with Jesus as he was increasingly "dogmatized" by early Christian adherents, then move to the primitive church (of which "we should have to know more than we in fact do know"), Paul ("the creator of a Christian theology"), Gentile Christianity, John (who "made the picture of Jesus' life entirely into a mirror of his own ideas"), and Ignatius (who typifies and embodies "personal Christianity at the beginning of the second century").[11] "New Testament Theology" is, for Wrede, a double misnomer. First, none of its subject matter was born canonical. Second, it is less with *theology* than with *religion* that we should be concerned, specifically "the history of early Christian religion and theology."[12] Wrede conceptually disjoined what Gabler had only differentiated: religion and theology.

You conclude, then, that Wrede was altogether wrong?
No. He got some things right. First, hindsight teaches us that there is genuine gain to be attained by interpreting loaded terms in both the Old and New Testaments within a conceptual framework larger than the canon. No fair-minded exegete fails to learn important nuances of, say, *ṣedek* ("rightness," "justice" [Hebrew]) or *pistis* ("trust," "faith" [Greek]) by consulting Botterweck and Ringgren's *Theologisches Wörterbuch zum Alten Testament* (1973–1995) or Kittel and Friedrich's

[10] Johann Philipp Gabler, "On the Proper Distinction between Biblical and Dogmatic Theology and the Specific Objectives of Each," in J. Sandys-Wunsch and L. Eldredge, "J. P. Gabler and the Distinction Between Biblical and Dogmatic Theology," *Scottish Journal of Theology* 33 (1980): 133–58.
[11] Wrede, "The Task and Methods," 104, 106, 113, and 89.
[12] Ibid., 116.

Theologisches Wörterbuch zum Neuen Testament (1933–74), encyclopedias that expand our intellectual horizons into the ancient Near East and Mediterranean antiquity.[13] Second, Wrede's impulse to differentiate modern dogmatic categories from less systematized, ancient formulations was sound in two respects. First, the prophets and the apostles functioned at least as preachers, at most what we would call practical theologians, rather than as systematicians. Like Gabler before him, Wrede asserted that theology is *a dimension of* religious experience though *not coterminous with and therefore interchangeable* with it. Second, even if he himself did not frame the matter theologically, Wrede's proposal creates space for biblical authors to stand apart from modern readers, the better to critique, rather than to mirror or otherwise to confirm, their theological assumptions. From the beginning, that is one of the capital things historical criticism has claimed as a positive contribution for the church.

Then why do you consider that Wrede contributed to the problem, not to its solution?

Because Wrede's understanding of history and, therefore, of historical criticism was naive; his take on constructive theology was at best indifferent, at worst hostile; and his position has prevailed in biblical scholarship to the church's detriment.

Wrede writes as though historical research were neutral, to protect biblical interpretation from its practitioners' "religious commitments." We didn't have to wait for postmodernism to expose the illusion of objectivity. Another great modernist, Adolf Schlatter (1852–1938), spotted this in 1909: "a historical sketch can only take shape in the mind of a historian, and … in this process the historian himself, with all his intellectual furniture, is involved. If this fact is lost sight of, then it is no longer science in which we are involved, but crazy illusions."[14] Schlatter put his (historian's!) finger on an even deeper problem with Wrede's position: "As soon as the historian sets aside or brackets the question of faith, he is making his concern with the New Testament and his presentation of it into a radical and total polemic against it."[15] In effect, Schlatter turned Wrede's fundamental critique against himself: if the New

[13] G. Johannes Botterweck and Helmer Ringgren, *Theologisches Wörterbuch zum Alten Testament* (Stuttgart: W. Kohlhammer, 1970); Gerhard Kittel, Otto Bauernfeind, and Gerhard Friedrich, *Theologisches Wörterbuch zum Neuen Testament* (Stuttgart: W. Kohlhammer, 1932).
[14] Adolf Schlatter, "The Theology of the New Testament and Dogmatics," in *The Nature of New Testament Theology,* 125–26.
[15] Ibid., 122.

Testament's authors had been illegitimately "modernized" into dogmaticians, then neither should they be modernized as Troeltschian historians. All biblical authors, without exception, wrote "from faith for faith"—as no responsible historical critic in 2009 would deny.

Furthermore, for Wrede, the historian as such is not competent to serve today's church, whenever "today" might be. Unlike Gabler, Wrede is indifferent to modern dogmatics: "Like every other real science, New Testament theology has its goal simply in itself, and is totally indifferent to all dogma and systematic theology. How the systematic theologian gets on with its results and deals with them—that is his own affair."[16]

And why was Wrede so persuaded?

Because, as a dutiful child of the Enlightenment, he assumed that "historical facts" and "religious values" could and should be cleanly separated. In his own words: "Could dogmatics teach New Testament theology to see the facts correctly? At most it could color them. Could it correct the facts that were found? To correct facts is absurd. Could it legitimize them? Facts need no legitimation."[17]

At best this overreaches what historians, so operating, can retrieve; at worst it's nonsense. Whether we speak of Habakkuk or Paul, "The righteous shall live by faith" is not a "fact" like the mathematical idea described by the Pythagorean theorem. As a matter of fact—or, if you prefer, common sense—dogmatics, *pace* Wrede, might very well help biblical exegetes to understand the *theological* claims made in that literature. Whilst anxious Lutherans might rejoice to sing his chorus, "Facts need no legitimation"—that is, the truth of the gospel depends on no historical criticism—Wrede's magisterial dictum obscures rather than clarifies the task of New Testament *theology*.

Hold on. You just said that Wrede, like Gabler, differentiated "religion" from "theology."

He did—and then immediately confused the issue by asserting that what New Testament *theologians* should really be studying is "early Christian *history of religion*."[18] Those two disciplines are kindred but not identical. Put it this way: the historian of ancient Israel or of earliest Christianity may or may not be able to verify that Habakkuk and Paul made the claim "The righteous shall

[16] Wrede, "The Task and Methods," 69. In the original these two sentences appear in reverse order.
[17] Ibid., 69–70.
[18] Ibid., 116 (my emphasis).

live by faith." The historian of religious ideas may be able to fill in enough gaps to render terms such as "righteousness" and "faith" more intelligible in semantic settings remote from our own. It takes someone other than a historian, however, to explain what is intended by that claim. To be precise, it takes a theologian—not merely a phenomenologist of religion, of its adherents, and of their ideas.

Then why did Wrede's position, not Schlatter's, carry the day in biblical interpretation?

Schlatter's views conceded too little to the historical-critical *Zeitgeist*, and his own historical reconstructions were suspect because of their consistent alignment with conservative Christianity. For hard-nosed historical critics, the game was up the moment Schlatter claimed that even historians hold religious values, transmitted through "the large communities in which we live and on which we depend."[19] Wrede's project, on the other hand, was immediately appropriable by *religionsgeschichtlich* scholars such as Hermann Gunkel (1862–1932) and Wilhelm Bousset (1854–1920) and their form-critical progeny, such as Martin Noth (1902–1968) and Rudolf Bultmann (1884–1976). These, in turn, begat contemporary social-scientific criticism, from Gerstenberger and Theissen, et al., most of whom would rather check all religious claims at the door before getting on with their work.[20]

Well, what's wrong with that?

In itself, nothing. Scholars are free to study whatever they like, however their hearts so move them. The best of their work is insightful and incisive; the rest, pedestrian and usually harmless. But not everything scholars want to do, and how they want to do it, is profitable for the church and the world in which it serves. "All things are lawful; but not all things build up" (1 Cor. 6:12). Moreover, scholars are *not* free to dictate to biblical theologians what they will do and how they will do it.

Watch it. Your rhetoric is simmering to a boil.

Is it? Here's what one of the most talented of those social-scientific exegetes, Wayne Meeks, declared three years ago in his presidential address to *Studiorum Novi Testamenti Societas*:

---

[19] Schlatter, "The Theology of the New Testament," 152.

[20] Erhard Gerstenberger, *Theologien im Alten Testament: Pluralität und Synkretismus alttestamentlichen Gottesglaubens* (Stuttgart: Kohlhammer, 2001); Gerd Theissen, *Die Religion der ersten Christen: eine Theorie des Urchristentums* (Gütersloh: Kaiser/Gütersloher, 2000).

> We should start by erasing from our vocabulary the terms "biblical theology" and, even more urgently, "New Testament theology." Whatever positive contributions these concepts may have made in the conversation since Gabler, we have come to a time when they can only blinker our understanding. First, the notion "biblical theology," despite all the qualifications we have learned to make regarding it, in practice tends always to smuggle in a cognitivist model of religion … privileging doctrine at the expense of life. Second, "biblical theology" implicitly claims textual and historical warrants for propositions that in truth arise only out of continuing transactions between text and reader through many times and places, and it invites our complicity as historians in this masking of the source of authority. Whenever we hear the phrase, "The Bible clearly teaches," in contemporary debates, we may be sure that this covert relocation of the warrant is taking place. Third, "biblical theology" has functioned ideologically in the attempt to secure our own positions in the theological hierarchy, as the teachers of the teachers of the church. We have not done very well in that role, and we should give it up.[21]

Professor Meeks is as entitled to his scholarly preferences as anyone, but his reasons for denying even an *option* for biblical theology in our day are remarkable rubbish for an analyst otherwise so discerning. Yes, there's a necessarily cognitive dimension in biblical theology, for the simple reason that the Christian religion has a cognitive or theological component embedded *within* its life, not "*at the expense of* life": "Always be prepared to make a defense to anyone who calls you to account for the hope that is in you" (1 Pet. 3:15b). Christianity is not thereby *reduced* to cognitivism—an obscurantist reductionism that Meeks himself is smuggling in. (Since few methods of current historical exegesis are more cognitivist than social-scientific criticism, thick with Geertzian description, Meeks, its expert practitioner, should beware of the pot's calling the kettle black.) Second, I've no idea who in Meeks's hearing is pompously thumping "The Bible clearly teaches," but it's a safe bet they do not teach at Yale or at Princeton. Third, some biblical scholars indeed recognize as their vocation "teaching the church's teachers"; I can honestly say that none I know makes such a claim to shore up their credibility in some imagined theological hierarchy. In most of the schools represented by the S.N.T.S. (Society for New Testament Studies), that idea is laughably

---

[21] Wayne A. Meeks, "Why Study the New Testament?" *New Testament Studies* 51 (2005): 167–68.

incredible. Finally, "not doing very well" in a historically recognized role—biblical theology has, after all, a longer lineage than historical criticism—is no reason "to give it up." It may well be a reason to do it better. Studying scripture in the Ivy League is like learning about women at the Mayo Clinic.

Cheap shots aside, I'm glad you got those small potatoes off your chest.
I feel better for it. *Cogito ergo* spud: I think, therefore I yam.

Spare us, please. May we return to Wrede's triumph over Schlatter?
Well, I never said that it was unmitigated.

Where's the evidence that Schlatter's confessional approach to biblical theology bore fruit?
Two heavyweights come to mind: Bultmann and Karl Barth (1886–1968).[22] Bultmann's *Theology of the New Testament* (1951 and 1955) is universally acknowledged as the twentieth century's most important experiment in New Testament theology.[23] Though remembered for many things, his own self-assessment of that attempt is sometimes forgotten: "The presentation of New Testament theology offered in this book stands, on the one hand, within the tradition of the historical-critical and the history-of-religion schools and seeks, on the other hand, to avoid their mistake, which consists of the tearing apart of the act of thinking from the act of living and hence of a failure to recognize the intent of theological utterances."[24] The one hand takes from Wrede: "a … really historical grasp and reflection that is truly history of *religion*."[25] The other hand receives from Schlatter: "There is no need to associate the concept of 'theology' with an artificial separation of thought and existence."[26] In short, Bultmann tried to hybridize Wrede and Schlatter's equally stubborn, seemingly contradictory positions. That's what makes his *Theology* so fascinating and, possibly, influential: no matter which set of modernist assumptions the reader adopted, in Bultmann one might find a home—up to a point.

---

[22] For further comparison of Bultmann and Barth's respective projects, see my forthcoming article, "Theology, New Testament," in *The New Interpreter's Dictionary of the Bible*, vol. 5, ed. Katharine Doob Sakenfeld (Nashville: Abingdon, 2009).
[23] Rudolf Karl Bultmann, *Theology of the New Testament,* 2 vols., trans. Kendrick Grobel (New York: Scribner, 1951, 1955). Originally published as *Theologie des Neuen Testaments* (Tübingen: Mohr, 1953).
[24] Bultmann, *Theology of the New Testament*, 2, 250–51.
[25] Ibid., 2, 251.
[26] Ibid., 2, 246.

I know where you're hedging—up to the point that the reader accepts Bultmann's assumption that the "heroes" of New Testament theology, Paul and John, could be existentially demythologized.

Well, yes. Another problem is Bultmann's less than auspicious view of the Old Testament: "[F]aith requires the backward glance into Old Testament history as a history of failure, and so of promise, in order to know that the situation of the justified man arises only on the basis of this miscarriage."[27] The Old Testament as an abortion, the New as faith's pregnancy carried to full term: somewhere Marcion smiles.

Why on earth bring Barth into the picture? He's not a New Testament theologian as such, much less a biblical specialist.

So what? Who invited Derrida or Levinas to the Mad Hatter's tea party? Barth belongs here. In his second *Römerbrief* preface (1921) he acknowledged "feel[ing him]self most closely related to Schlatter."[28] Where Barth really cut loose, however, was in his *Church Dogmatics*.[29] There he broke with Enlightenment epistemology by regarding all humans as living nowhere other than within a God-centered history, the sphere of God's self-communicative action.

Are you claiming such a view basic to the theological perspectives adopted in the Old and New Testaments?

I'd say that it is conceptually closer to the Bible's own witness than Bultmann's call to a decision for authentic human existence. As theories go, that's only marginally better than Mark Russell's hypothesis that Saturn's rings are composed entirely of lost airline baggage. Remember, too, that Barth's aspiration was nothing but *Nachdenken*: a faithful listening to the biblical narratives in both testaments, "after-pondering" their testimonies to God as "the One who loves in freedom" and then thinking through all the implications of God's self-revelation for the church's faith and life.

Time out. Do you realize you've spent eight pages on a history of biblical interpretation? This essay is as boring as Fred Allen's hamlet in Maine: "the town so dull that when the tide went out it refused to come back."[30]

---

[27] Rudolf Karl Bultmann, "Prophecy and Fulfillment," in *Essays on Old Testament Hermeneutics*, ed. Claus Westermann; trans. James Luther Mays and James C. G. Greig (Richmond: John Knox, 1964), 75.

[28] Karl Barth, *The Epistle to the Romans*, trans. E. C. Hoskyns (Oxford: Oxford University Press, 1933), 7.

[29] Karl Barth, *Die kirchliche Dogmatik,* 14 vols. (Zürich: Theologischer, 1932–70); English translation G. T. Thomson and Geoffrey W. Bromiley, et al.; ed. Geoffrey W. Bromiley and Thomas F. Torrance (Edinburgh: T&T Clark, 1936–77).

[30] Fred Allen, "The Cape Codder," in *Fred Allen's Letters*, ed. John J. McCarthy (New York: Doubleday, 1965).

What do you expect? I was trained as *a historian.* Old habits die hard. Besides, why else study history than to recognize your mistakes when you make them again?

Do any of these natterings move us to a positive point you'd care to register?
I think so, though its simplicity is terribly embarrassing.

You're beyond embarrassment, flirting with professional humiliation. Why stop now?
I think it boils down to this: if biblical theology has a productive future in our day, then biblical scholars are going to have to be trained to think not only historically but theologically, from stem to stern, with all that implies both philosophically and confessionally.

Wait, wait. Are you suggesting that all biblical scholars must be required to study theology?
No. Only those who care about the church, its faith, and its theology. For those with such a vocation, historical and systematic theology will have to be as much a part of their curriculum as Hellenistic Greek and papyrology. Arguably more so, for in every era theology is as informed by its own discipline and philosophical assumptions as is historical investigation and the tools of its trade.

Are you giving up on historical criticism?
Of course not. Historical thinking is inescapable for the contemporary church, the academy, and the larger world in which they all live. Were it not so, there would be no cable History Channel, and *The Da Vinci Code* moonshine, tricked out as suppressed history, could never have purchased Dan Brown a villa on the Adriatic. First-rate historical investigation, like first-rate philosophical inquiry, still has its place. What I'm saying, at least, is that Gotthold Lessing was right but needn't have feared his conclusions. To paraphrase: the truth about God and ourselves, to which scripture bears witness, is not directly accessible by or contingent upon historical inquiry. But unless we are hell-bent to view it as such, there is no "ugly ditch" between the "accidental truths of history" and the "necessary truths of reason"—only different intellectual procedures properly suited to different objectives.[31]

[31] Gotthold Ephraim Lessing, "On the Proof of the Spirit and of Power" (1777), in *Lessing's Theological Writings*, ed. and trans. Henry Chadwick (London: Adam & Charles Black, 1956), 18.

You said that was the least you'd claim about history and its investigation. What's the most?
That Barth—though certainly not he alone—got it right. From the view of faith and of theology that attempts to interpret faith, history does not belong to us. We just live there. History is a realm of the created order, and creation belongs to God. And so do we, along with everything that we do. Regarded *sub specie aeternitatis*, "All history is the history of grace."[32]

That's a theological claim about history that historical inquiry cannot verify.
That's right. Now you're catching on.

I have here a list that you've compiled: "Six Suggestions for Remapping Biblical Theology." Our readers would appreciate your commenting on them, beginning with:

***Thesis #1:* For theologically invested biblical interpreters, let a moratorium be declared on New Testament theology as generally practiced for the past two centuries. Let us instead reconsider biblical theology of both testaments as a scriptural theology, a discipline both normative and descriptive.**
My impression is that New Testament theology as practiced in the modern era may be wheezing to the end of its current usefulness. During the past decade alone we have received massive "New Testament theologies" from the Continent, structured as historical-genetic reconstructions,[33] systematic-conceptual surveys,[34] or some procedural combination thereof.[35] The historical-genetic accounts plow Wrede's well-worn furrows. The systematic-conceptual analyses carry us not far beyond Bultmann, occasionally flirting with the sort of "method of doctrinal concepts"—historically cast, to be sure—that Wrede excoriated in nineteenth-century liberal Protestantism. If we are to progress, rather than merely to rehearse, a fresh approach is invited.

A second observation: if New Testament theology is to nourish the church again, it must take the Old Testament more seriously than it lately has.

---

[32] Nicholas Lash, "How Do We Know Where We Are?" in Nicholas Lash, *Theology on the Way to Emmaus* (London: SCM, 1986), 67.
[33] Georg Strecker, *Theologie des Neuen Testaments* (Berlin and New York: de Gruyter, 1996).
[34] François Vouga, *Une Théologie du Nouveau Testament* (Geneva: Labor et Fides, 2001).
[35] Ferdinand Hahn, *Theologie des Neuen Testaments*, 2 vols. (Tübingen: Mohr/Siebeck, 2002); Ulrich Wilckens, *Theologie des Neuen Testaments* (Neukirchen-Vluyn: Neukirchener, 2002–2005).

***Don't tell me. We must lay sacrifice at the altar of* Intertextualität.**
No, the reasons are much deeper than clamoring to be *au courant*. The New Testament's authors themselves found it practically impossible to think theologically apart from the Old Testament, as C. H. Dodd taught us many decades ago.[36] Their basic concepts were not original with Christianity but derivative from the synagogue's Bible.

You are essentially propounding Childs's canonical approach. Correct?
There's an obvious overlap. Death may have prevented Childs from going as far as he might have—a possibility that will surprise biblical scholars who think he'd already gone much too far. But that's for another debate.

For an unabashedly theological approach to scripture, Childs deserves our thanks, even though some problems attended his project. Especially in the 1970s and '80s, it proved hard for him to breathe freely under the historical-critical mantle, even when on his own terms its *magisterium* was no longer apt for his endeavor. This, in turn, made him fair if frustrating game for critics who chastised him for inadequate clarity about the canon itself: Whose canon? The Septuagintal? The Masoretic? Roman Catholic? Eastern Orthodox? The Protestant? All overlap but none is identical to the others. Yet in the last decade of his vast publications, Childs was commendably moving beyond *sola scriptura*: the Bible as the single canonical guide for Christian thought and practice.[37]

Isn't it?
Certainly not. An unfortunate hangover of the Reformation is an implied delimitation of "canon" to a body of literature regarded as scriptural.[38] Yet there are many canonical, or regulative, resources and practices that overlap but are not equivalent to the Christian Bible: the church's liturgy and sacraments, orders of ministry (lay and ordained), art and music, and many other traditional distillates.[39] *Sola scriptura* is nowhere claimed *within the Bible*;

[36] C. H. Dodd, *According to the Scriptures: The Sub–structure of New Testament Theology* (New York: Scribner, 1953).
[37] See, for instance, Brevard S. Childs, "Toward Recovering Theological Exegesis," *Pro Ecclesia* 6 (1997): 16–26. Dennis T. Olson, "Seeking 'The Inexpressible Texture of Thy Word': A Practical Guide to Brevard Childs' Canonical Approach to Theological Exegesis," *The Princeton Theological Review* 14 (2008): 53–68, offers a splendid conspectus of Childs's comprehensive process of exegesis.
[38] See David Brown, *Trinity and Imagination: Revelation and Change* (Oxford: Oxford University Press, 1999).
[39] Thus, William J. Abraham, *Canon and Criterion in Christian Theology: From the Fathers to Feminism* (Oxford and New York: Clarendon/Oxford University Press, 1998).

it is itself a hermeneutical principle arising from a particular construal of *tradition*. A truly "canonical approach to scripture" would invite this entire range of canonical resources and practices to bear on interpretation of the church's scripture.

You say "biblical theology" should be reconsidered as "Christian scriptural theology." What's the difference?

The Christian "Bible," consisting of Testaments Old and New, is a neutral designation, like TANAK, the Qur'an, or the Upanishads. One can study any of those books without regarding them as scriptural. In a secular university's department of religious studies it is appropriate for Christians to read the Qur'an, for Muslims to read the Vedas, for Hindus to read the Hebrew Bible, for Jews to read the New Testament, for agnostics to read any or all of them, without prior conversion to the religious body for whom each of those works occupies a central place. In today's religiously suspicious and volatile world, it would be a very good thing if more of that happened. That experience would be even richer if students were led into those books by, respectively, imams and satgurus and rabbis and priests: well-trained "native speakers" of their religions who could help sympathetic outsiders to appreciate the nuances and subtleties muffled on the printed page, obscured even more when translated.

For Christians, however, the Bible in two testaments occupies a place different from the primary writings of other religious bodies. Simply put, for Christians, that Bible is scriptural: it reveals to them a particular God, whose life elicits from theirs peculiar responsibilities within and beyond the church. Wrede was wrong: Christians should not be *required* to sacrifice either their confession or their intellect when studying those works that for them are scriptural. And while Gerhard Ebeling (1912–2001) correctly diagnosed the internal contradictions within eighteenth-century biblical theology—its ambivalence toward dogmatics and its predisposition to identify the Bible's internal *Mitte*—I am suggesting responses, if not solutions, to both intellectual contretemps.[40]

That seems to lead us to Thesis #2: **"Scriptural theology" interprets the Christian Bible as scripture. That is to say, the endeavor acknowledges the sacramental character of the church's charter documents. As with baptism and the Eucharist, scripture is a homely place where God has promised to meet us, to reveal himself to us, and to sanctify us.**

---

[40] Gerhard Ebeling, *Wort und Glaube* (Tübingen: Mohr [Siebeck]), 1960; English translation James W. Leitch, *Word and Faith* (London: SCM, 1963).

Consonant with orthodox doctrines related to the Incarnation, it is important to recognize both the truly human and truly divine character of scripture. Water may be subjected to spectroscopic analysis. Bread may be broken down into its chemical elements. Biblical literature may be considered historico-critically. Routine gatherings of religious adherents may themselves be studied social-scientifically. Provided that the mode of investigation suits the analytical aim, each of these has its proper place. None of them, however, is adequate as a *theological* account of what happens when the worshipping church receives the gifts of Sacrament and of Word. The Triune God, self-communicated to us as Father-Son-Holy Spirit, has pledged regularly to meet and to support the church in special ways through divinely selected, ordinary media: water, bread, wine, texts.

And what of sanctification?
Through God's freely chosen means, humanity matures in its knowledge, reverence, and love of God above all things, to the end that God may better adapt the church to participate in his consummate redemption of the world through Jesus Christ.

Thesis #3: **The practice of "scriptural theology" assumes the same subliminal, proto-Trinitarian pattern that sets the agenda for articulation and continued development of all dimensions of the church's life, trust, and practice.**

Why stipulate this?
If not, then other, less orthodox assumptions will quickly move in to occupy its place.

Orthodox twenty-first-century Christians stand in the same position as those in the first: for them it is no longer possible to identify Israel's God without reference to Jesus any more than they can identify Jesus without reference to Israel's God. The theological explanation of that epistemic reality is that the one Spirit through whom God the Father relates to God the Son, and vice-versa, is the same Spirit through whom the Father relates through the Son to the Body of Christ, the church—and the self-same Spirit through whom the church relates through the Son to the Father. That Trinitarian hermeneutic integrates, silently or expressly, every practice of the church—including scriptural interpretation—that actualizes humanity's created destiny to live in full communion with the God whose will is love.[41]

[41] I explore such a Trinitarian hermeneutic in "Trinity and Exegesis," forthcoming in *Pro Ecclesia*.

Do you really intend to foist Nicea and Chalcedon onto the Book of Psalms?

No, if by your question-begging "foist" you're implying an *equalization* of claims in the Psalms with the resolutions of patristic Trinitarian debate. I suggest only several simple things. First: without the Psalms a good deal of the New Testament's theology and its subsequent creedal formulations could never have been articulated. In this respect Robert Jenson is surely right: "The Hebrew Scriptures [are] the Root of Trinitarianism."[42] Thus there is consanguinity between the hermeneutic here suggested and the texts being interpreted—a deeper affinity than the Bible's mere historicality, assumed by historical criticism. Second: the Psalms may—for Christians, should—be read *in the light of* God-inspired, scripturally consonant, ecclesially recognized traditional distillates. It happens all the time: every Sunday in most churches and, in a materially different though formally similar way, every Saturday in most synagogues. Within the church catholic it has been so from the start, as David Yeago has persuasively demonstrated.[43] All I ask is that we be clear and honest about what most of the church's teachers and preachers are already and quite properly doing; to do it more acutely, more joyfully, and without embarrassment; and to honor it with privilege over the ephemeral prestige of anecclesial biblical scholarship and its covert worship of what John Webster perceptively nails as "the sublimity of reason."[44] To paraphrase Oscar Wilde on Henry James's fiction: some exegetes produce commentaries as if it were a painful duty.

You sound like a true child of Schlatter.

At heart I am, though ironically closer to Wrede at the point of many *strictly historical* judgments.[45] But Schlatter got one very important thing right: biblical scholars whose vocation entails service within the church cannot be mandated to divest themselves of "the truth of the gospel" for the sake of a specious historical neutrality. That, truly, would amount to "the rending of the act of thinking from the act of living."[46] That Bultmann learned from

---

[42] Robert W. Jenson, "Second Locus: The Triune God," in *Christian Dogmatics*, ed. Carl E. Braaten and Robert W. Jenson (Philadelphia: Fortress, 1984), 102–5.

[43] David S. Yeago, "The New Testament and the Nicene Dogma: A Contribution to the Recovery of Theological Exegesis," *Pro Ecclesia* 3 (1994): 152–64.

[44] John Webster, *Holy Scripture: A Dogmatic Sketch*, Current Issues in Theology (Cambridge: Cambridge University Press, 2003), 104.

[45] William Wrede, *Das Messiasgeheimnis in den Evangelien* (Göttingen: Vandenhoeck & Ruprecht, 1901). Although Wrede was mistaken to reduce all divine mystery in the gospels to a narrow "Messianic secret," subsequent redaction criticism has proved correct his more fundamental historical assessment of the Evangelists' theological proclivities.

[46] Bultmann, *Theology of the New Testament*, 2, 246–51.

Schlatter, even if much of his own career as New Testament exegete towed Wrede's *religionsgeschichtlich* line.

Beyond its severance from the Old Testament, the problem with Bultmann's *Theology* is that, in an attempt to render the New Testament accessible to modern thinking, it was beguiled, at points distorted, by Martin Heidegger's existentialism, which was canonical nowhere except maybe within a few square miles of Marburg.[47]

What philosophical orientation would you substitute in its place?

None, as such. That was David Friedrich Strauss's solution, and it won't wash.[48] Mind you, every Christian era has been carried by philosophical winds in its day, whether Stoicism (the New Testament period), Neoplatonism (Augustine and Maximus Confessor), Aristotelianism (Aquinas and Luther), and today's modernist and postmodernist options. That is a part of the Christian interpreter's own historical contingency. Some current philosophical options (those, say, of Gadamer[49] and Ricoeur[50]) seem to me more compatible with the church's gospel than others (Rorty[51] and, in his more rambunctious moments, Derrida[52]). But philosophy, like history and even like theology, are finally *ancilla* of the gospel, not a substitute for it (1 Cor 2:1–16). For Strauss, orthodoxy was an overbearing monster to be fled or slain. Perhaps for some, in that context, it had become such. In our rather different day, Trinitarian dogma may be pure oxygen for a suffocating church. To state the issue contrariwise: if classical resources of Trinitarian and incarnational faith no longer hold epistemic purchase in a world riddled with dangerously misplaced trusts and murderous self-deception, then Christian theologians might as well pack it in and drop what they must concede as a charade.[53]

***Thesis #4:* "Scriptural theology" is not a method. More accurately, it is a penitent, self-critically Christian attitude or approach to biblical exegesis.**

---

[47] Martin Heidegger, *Sein und Zeit* (Halle: Niemeyer, 1927).
[48] David Friedrich Strauss, *Das Leben Jesu,* 2 vols. (Tübingen: Osiander, 1838–9).
[49] Hans-Georg Gadamer, *Wahrheit und Methode: Grundzuläge einer philosophischen Hermeneutik* (Tübingen: Mohr, 1960).
[50] Paul Ricouer, *Interpretation Theory: Discourse and the Surplus of Meaning* (Fort Worth: Texas Christian University Press, 1976).
[51] Richard Rorty, *Objectivity, Relativism, and Truth* (Cambridge: Cambridge University Press, 1991).
[52] Jacques Derrida, *De la grammatologie* (Paris: Les Éditions de Minuit, 1967).
[53] For a scrupulous examination of the epistemological purchase of Trinitarian thought, consult Bruce D. Marshall, *Trinity and Truth,* Cambridge Studies in Christian Doctrine (Cambridge: Cambridge University Press, 2000).

It is, specifically, a theological context within which interpretation occurs, potentially embracing a variety of methods that collectively endeavor to describe and to assess the Bible's intracanonical interpretations of God's relationship to humanity and the world, especially as that engagement is revealed in Jesus Christ.

Would you care to make all that even more opaque?

Well, I hold no brief for adoption of a particular method or cluster of methods. I've been eclectic, or confused, all my life. Choose the simplest exegetical tool that, in your judgment, is most responsive to the questions raised by the text in front of you. Only remember that if you operate as a scriptural theologian, your ultimate responsibility is to expose scripture's express or tacit gospel for the church's edification—which is not the same as sanctioning everything the church may say and do.

Say more.

Lenny Bruce: "Every day people are straying away from the church and going back to God."[54]

Say still more, less epigrammatically.

Like sacramental theology, scriptural theology stands in dialectical tension with the real-world worshipping community with whom it is perpetually conversant. When that community—*in sich realiserende Auslösung*—strays from the gospel or rejects its gift and its demand from a God who inspires love and requires obedience, then scriptural theology's task is to call the church to account. Whether it is a church or a bridge being constructed, the crew must assess stress factors and when necessary, discard substandard materials. That is why scriptural interpretation within the church should renounce sin, the devil, and all his works, even as do baptisands and communicants. This, moreover, is why scriptural theology must never be neoplatonically reified in isolation from true-to-life injustices to creation's welfare, human being, morality, and intellect. If Almighty God deemed it fitting to dwell fully within history in all its social and historical contingencies for the benefit of their redemption, then our interpretive practices can do no less. Thus, we return to the proper role of historical study within biblical and all theological scholarship: to quote Rowan Williams, "[Christian language] grows out of a particular set of communal and individual histories, and its images and idioms are fundamentally shaped by this fact."[55]

---

[54] Precise source unknown.
[55] Rowan Williams, "The Discipline of Scripture," in Rowan Williams, *On Christian Theology*, Challenges in Contemporary Theology (Oxford: Blackwell, 2000), 49.

What about "the Bible's intracanonical interpretations"?
Here I use the adjective "canonical" in its customary sense, referring to that literature held by the church as regulative. The compound "intra-" acknowledges the reality that Christian scripture comprises a choir of voices, harmonious and discordant, in ongoing conversation not just with the church, but also amongst one another. The same conditions obtain within scripture as within the church, Christ's many-membered body, as with the Triune God: being is always relational, because relationship is eternally rooted in God's being. Accordingly, scriptural theology regards the Bible's polyphony as a gift to be celebrated and a mystery to confound, not a mess to be puréed.[56]

But how does the church, or the scriptural theologian in the church's service, arbitrate those disparate voices in cases where a practical decision must be reached?
A small but necessary clarification: the scriptural theologian's service is first to God's gospel, which has called the church into being but is never a substitute for it.

Another caveat: not every disagreement within scripture is of equal weight, all touching on God's salvation. Premodern interpreters were clearer about that than we often given them credit for. St. Thomas: "Nothing is contained under the spiritual sense that is necessary for faith that scripture does not hand down *openly elsewhere* through the literal sense" (*Summa Theologiae* 1a.1.10). The emphasis is mine, because, when used with brilliance, adverbs are important.

Pace Luther and other worthies, by now we should know there's no center within scripture itself. As Frances Young observes, "Scripture does not offer its own key to its own interpretation."[57] If there exists a point of concentration, invariably the interpreter brings it to the Bible: the Lutheran "canon within the canon," Eichrodt's "covenant,"[58] Bultmann's anthropocentricism, Cullmann's *Heilsgeschichte*.[59]

So which of these is correct?
While each throws some light, none is satisfying; nor is it for a single interpreter to decide *die Mitte*.

---

[56] Andrew Louth, *Discerning the Mystery: An Essay on the Nature of Theology* (Oxford: Clarendon, 1983).
[57] Frances Young, *The Art of Performance: Towards a Theology of Holy Scripture* (London: Darton, Longman and Todd, 1990), 61.
[58] Walther Eichrodt, *Theologie des Alten Testaments,* 3 vols. (Berlin: Evangelische Verlagsanstalt, 1948).
[59] Oscar Cullmann, *Heil als Geschichte: heilsgeschichtliche Existenz im Neuen Testament* (Tübingen: Mohr, 1965).

Who decides? And by what criteria?
That's what Thesis #5 intends to address.

***Thesis #5:* In practical cases of theological dispute within scripture, the supreme court of interpretive appeal is the *regula fidei* of the church catholic.**
The "rule of faith"—a traditional distillate of scripture itself, comprising the pith of classical creeds and their sacramental implications—has survived for two millennia and may be the only thing that yet holds together a fractious Christianity. It is the property of neither Christian fundamentalism nor liberalism, those intellectual twins separated at birth. It belongs to no sect or denomination, no individual or party. The canon of faith is a birthright bequeathed to all Christians at their baptism, the fortification of all in the Eucharist. In the face of real doctrinal differences, the rule of faith may be the only comprehensive, delimiting ecclesial consensus on what constitutes the church's true self.[60]

What constitutes "the rule of faith"?
We might put that question to our ecclesially minded readers, if they're still awake. For now, taking our lead from Irenaeus: the truth of God's gospel, the divine economy revealed and given to the church by God, is that God eternally operates through "two hands," the Son and the Spirit, to relate himself to the church for the saving redemption of the world (*Adversus Haereses* 4.20.1). Please note the consistency: the church's hermeneutical *regula fidei*, like scripture itself, bears a proto-Trinitarian structure.

I detect little sympathy in this position, lately reclaimed in some postmodern projects, for the Renaissance ideal of an individual genius standing against tradition.
You're right. The only "genius"—the Enlightenment's facile term, not mine—who was and remains in position to assail human tradition, religious and otherwise, is Jesus Christ (Mark 7:1–23). If Christ is none other than what the church's creed professes, then in him inheres, to say the least, considerable advantage over the rest of us. Yet the performance of scriptural theology via *regula fidei* does not—hey, presto!—banish all historical ambiguities. If anything, it is more likely to reveal faithful interpreters' vulnerability and the gospel's tensile strength.

[60] See Ebeling, *Word and Faith*, 162–90.

Thesis #6: **The genuine aim of scriptural theology—in line with the patristic and monastic tradition, and more recently with such interpreters as Barth and Bonhoeffer—is to assist the church in perceiving and then activating, at the Spirit's behest and with more faithful acuity, God's self-presentation in scripture through the indispensable lens of the gospel of Christ.**

Here what I'm driving at—rather, find myself being driven to—is akin to what Barth and especially Dietrich Bonhoeffer (1906–1945) described as *Vergegenwärtigung*: the gospel's "making itself present" in, before, and in confrontation with what a yet-unredeemed world regards as truth.[61] Unlike Barth, I am amused but unperturbed by the "almost indefinable odour," as he wrote Bonhoeffer, "of a monastic ethos and pathos ... [that] disturbs me."[62] To sharpen a point with which I think Bonhoeffer would have agreed: this *Vergegenwärtigung* happens in the Old Testament as well as the New because the Triune God underwrites all of scripture, which the attentive church takes as its doctrinal reference point. In line with the church's *regula fidei*, I, beside Bonhoeffer, disavow the benighted attempt of a would-be autonomous interpreter who, by dint of self-delusion, would judge scripture before the tribunal of modernity's reason or postmodernity's solipsism. "*That* 'making present' of the Christian message leads directly into paganism."[63] I part with Bonhoeffer at a few points. "Wherever Christ comes to speech in the word of the New Testament," he asserts, "there is 'making present.'"[64] I would prefer to say that genuine *Vergegenwärtigung* occurs when the Triune God expresses himself to the receptive church in word and in sacrament. Whereas Bonhoeffer claims, "God is with us today only as long as we are there ... taken back to the holy history of God on earth,"[65] I would rather say that God is *always* with us, whether or not we are there with God. The self-actualization of God's own presence does not depend on

---

[61] Dietrich Bonhoeffer, "Vergegnwärtigung neutestamentlicher Texte" (1935), in Dietrich Bonhoeffer, *Gesammelte Schriften*, vol. 3: *Theologie–Gemeinde: Vorlesungen, Briefe, Gespräche*, ed. Eberhard Bethge (Munich: Kaiser, 1960), 303–24.

[62] Letter of Barth to Bonhoeffer (Bergli, Oberrieden, October 14, 1936) in *The Way to Freedom: Letters, Lectures and Notes 1935–1939 from the Collected Works of Dietrich Bonhoeffer*, vol. 2, ed. and trans. Edwin H. Robertson and John Bowden (London: Collins, 1966), 121.

[63] Bonhoeffer, "Vergegnwärtigung neutestamentlicher Texte," 305 ("*Diese Vergegnwärtigung* der christlichen Botschaft führt direkt ins Heidentum" [emphasis in original]).

[64] Ibid., 307 ("Wo Christus im Wort des Neuen Testaments zu Worte kommt, dort is Vergegnwärtigung").

[65] Dietrich Bonhoeffer, *Life Together* (Dietrich Bonhoeffer Works 5; ed. Gerhard Ludwig Müller, Albrecht Schönherr, and Geffrey B. Kelly; trans. Daniel W. Bloesch; Minneapolis: Fortress, 1996), 62. In fairness to Bonhoeffer, we should note that the context of this and kindred claims is often in refutation of the claim that God supported *Nationalsozialismus* (see, e.g., "Vergegnwärtigung neutestamentlicher Texte," 313).

our being attentive to God. Through Spirit, sacrament, and word, God has promised never to abandon the church to its own pitiful resources. It is the church that too routinely absents itself from God.

Your counterpoint—"What a yet-unredeemed world regards as truth"—sounds like a straw man.
I quote a senior adviser to President Bush, twenty months after the United States' invasion of Iraq (2003):

> [Our critics live] in what we [in the White House] call the reality-based community … those who believe that solutions emerge from your judicious study of discernible reality. That's not the way the world works anymore. We're an empire now, and when we act, we create our own reality. And while you're studying that reality—judiciously, as you will—we'll act again, creating other new realities, which you can study too, and that's how things will sort out. We're history's actors … and you, all of you, will be left to just study what we do.[66]

No. "The earth is *the* LORD'*s* and the fullness thereof" (Ps. 24:1). Only a messianic American Calvinist and his equally self-deluded retinue would claim "creation of our own reality" and a *laissez-faire* imperialism to force it upon the rest of the world. The ones left to study what they have done may be grateful only that they are not among those of all nations who lost their lives to an illusion so bloody.

Thus spake the prophet Adlai Stevenson: "Your public servants serve you right."[67] Might we test your theses? What might a "scripturally theological" interpretation of John 8:31–59 look like?
Speaking of vulnerability, thank you for selecting such an amenable text.

A pudding's proof lies in its less digestible portions.
A quick-and-dirty account would touch at least on the following.

Most important, this text epitomizes what is true for all scripture—on it we must patiently ruminate. We dare not nibble and spit it out any more than we receive the Lord's Supper at a salad bar. Scriptural theology depends on an

---
[66] Ron Suskind, "Without a Doubt: Faith, Certainty, and the Presidency of George W. Bush," *The New York Times Magazine* (October 17, 2004): 51.
[67] Adlai Stevenson, "The Mike Wallace Interview," June 1, 1958. © Mike Wallace.

attitude toward exegesis that proceeds from and returns to prayer, expressed in the classical tradition of *lectio divina*.[68]

This text also points up in the sharpest possible way what is at stake in scriptural theology as presented here: either scripture such as John 8 is little more than an embarrassment and travesty for contemporary sensibilities, or it is truly God's salvation *extra nos*, "from outside ourselves." The effective proof of the latter is that not a single contributor to the *Princeton Seminary Bulletin* would have the gall to present his or her peers a statement as polemical as what we find here—nor, in all likelihood, would this journal's editor allow it.

In addition, the Jesus we encounter in John's Gospel is the Christ of the Holy Catholic Church's confession: the one and only Son who was with God from the beginning (1:1–3), who comes down from above (3:31; 8:23), reveals the Father who sent him (14:8–11), saves those born from above who believe in him (3:1–17), sends the Spirit who is one with the Father and the Son (16:12–25) to counsel those who trust in him (14:14–17, 25–31) and to confront those who do not (16:7–11; cf. 3:18–21). Johannine theology authorizes the Great Church's ecumenical confession. While John does not articulate the Nicene-Chalcedonian Creed, the deep structure of the Fourth Gospel's theology is proto-Trinitarian. The same could arguably be said of 1 Corinthians 8:6, Philippians 2:5–11, and Colossians 1:15–20, which, in turn, appear to be quasi-creedal and hymnic expressions of early Christian rumination on such texts as Deuteronomy 4:35–39 and 6:4, Malachi 2:10, and Isaiah 45:21–24.

Lastly, by Jesus's own testimony, "Salvation is of the Jews" (John 4:22). Interpreters who fully recognize themselves as "Abraham's offspring [an heir], according to [the] promise" embedded in the gospel's divine economy (see Gal. 3:29)— interpreters, in short, who embrace the merciful gift of inclusion among God's people Israel (see Eph. 2:11–22; 1 Pet. 2:9–10)—will recognize in John 8 "the Jews" not as an "other" to be tormented but *their own race*, in the Spirit if not in the flesh. Within John 8 are authentic children of Abraham (vv. 39b–40), "the Jews who have believed in" Jesus (v. 31), as well as Jews in whom his word finds no place (v. 37), who think Jesus a bastard (v. 41) and mean to kill him (vv. 37, 40). That division within Israel is akin to congregants at Nazareth who aim to murder Jesus when he reminds them of scripture that offends their sensibilities (Luke 4:23–30). Jerusalem has always done away with its prophets (Matt 23:29–39; see 2 Chron. 24:20–22). The historical fact that John 8 has been suborned to justify Christian persecution

[68] Mariano Magrassi, *Bibbia e preghiera: La* lectio divina (Milan: Editrice Àngora, 1990); English translation *Praying the Bible: An Introduction to* Lectio Divina, trans. Edward Hagman (Collegeville: Liturgical, 1998).

of Jews—siblings' murder of siblings—is *an indictment of such Christians' own parentage*. By their murder they have proved *themselves* to be children of the devil: a murderer and liar through and through (John 8:44). To paraphrase Walt Kelly's Pogo: We have met the Jews, and they is us. And if that seems to some an exegetical sleight of hand, then they might reread 1 John 3:11–18, which reasons similarly about hateful, murderous fraud *within the church*.

How does this interpretation of John 8 differ from that of conventional historical criticism?
Naturally there are intersections, even as premodern exegetes insisted on intersections of readings literal and spiritual. Reasonably sound historical imaginations, such as Lou Martyn's,[69] have helped us clarify things we might easily have forgotten, such as Christianity's origin in Judaism and, before those ways parted, the gospel's promise of "a fall and rising for many in Israel" (Luke 2:34). Give Stevie Smith (1902–1971) full marks for candor: "If I had been the Virgin Mary, I would have said 'No.'"

Still, many historical critics, apart from Martyn's intention, have by now so deep-frozen the Fourth Gospel in its alleged original setting—a hostile controversy between Jewish Christianity and proto-rabbinic Judaism—that thawing the text for the church's preaching and teaching has proved extraordinarily difficult. Exhibit A is the Revised Common Lectionary (1992), which expurgates everything in John 5, 7–8, save twelve verses (5:1–9, 7:37–39) designated as "alternative texts." However well-intentioned, such a bowdlerized Bible—protecting Christians from their own scripture—always misguides, leaving the church a patsy for its own darkest temptations to hubris, triumphalism, and all other "sinful desires of the flesh." Disregard of John 8:31–59 is a case in point—all the more dangerous when the consensus results of historical criticism are claimed to sanction that dismissal.

My, all these words you've spent. Reading them is like staring at a cow for an hour.
My readers join with me in thanks for your questions, while waiting for the first shoe to drop.

I'm sure they'll agree this paper fills a much-needed gap.
Every professional exegete has a theological essay in him. That's the best place for it.

CURTAIN ■

[69] J. Louis Martyn, *History and Theology in the Fourth Gospel*, 3rd ed. (Louisville: Westminster John Knox, 2003).

Book Excerpt

The Theology of John Calvin

by Charles Partee

Charles Partee is P.C. Rossin Professor of Church History at Pittsburgh Theological Seminary. He earned his doctorate in theology, with a concentration in the history of doctrine, from Princeton Theological Seminary under Prof. Edward Dowey. His dissertation, supervised by Dowey, was published in 1977 as Calvin and Classical Philosophy. *He also wrote* Adventure in Africa: The Story of Don McClure *(1990) and cowrote, with Andrew Purves,* Encountering God: Christian Faith in Turbulent Times (2000). *This article is abstracted from* The Theology of John Calvin, *published by Westminster John Knox Press (Louisville, Kentucky, 2008), and reprinted with permission from the author.*

Introduction to Book II of the *Institutes of the Christian Religion*: God the Redeemer

Book II involves two of the most important and interlocking and ineffable Christian doctrines: Trinity and Christology. Trinitarian doctrine combines the concept of one substance (or essence) and three persons, claiming a unity that is tri-unity. This relation addresses the mystery of God in terms of the proper *unity of essence* (ὁμοουσία, περιχώρησις) (*consubstantialitas*, or *coessentialitas*) and also the proper *distinction of persons* (οἰκονομία, ἰδιοποίησις)

NOTE: References in parentheses are to the book, chapter, and paragraph in the *Institutes of the Christian Religion*, 2 volumes, in the Library of Christian Classics edition (LCC), edited by John T. McNeill and translated by Ford Lewis Battles (Philadelphia: Westminster Press, 1960). Citations of Calvin's biblical commentaries are by book, chapter, and verse in the latest available English translation. For the Old Testament: *Commentaries of John Calvin*, various translators, 46 vols. (Edinburgh: The Calvin Translation Society, 1843–55). For the New Testament: *Calvin's New Testament Commentaries* edited by David W. Torrance and Thomas F. Torrance, various translators, 12 vols. (Grand Rapids: Wm B. Eerdmans, 1959–72). When no English translation was available, reference is made to *Ioannais Calvani opera quae supersunt omnia (CO)*, edited by G. Baum, E, Cunitz, and E. Reuss, 59 vols. (Brunsvigae: C. A. Schwetschke, 1863–1900).

Throughout this excerpt, the titles of Calvin□s commentaries are cited in abbreviated form in parentheses, e.g., Com. Jn. refers to *Commentary on John.*

DOI: 10.3754/1937–8386.2008.29.1.11

(*persona*, or *dis-crimen*). Christological doctrine combines the concept of one person and two complete natures—a real unity in real duality. The debate led through the heresies of the Ebionites, the Gnostics, Origen, the Monarchians, the Adoptionists, Arius, Apollinaris, Nestorius, and Eutyches until the orthodox formula adopted at the Council of Nicaea (325), which was supplemented at the Council of Chalcedon (451). This formulation is not an explanation but a confession. Its lasting purpose is not to satisfy the mind, but to protect the heart of the central mystery that in Jesus Christ God was reconciling the world to himself (2 Cor. 5:19).[1]

The knowledge of God the Redeemer is the main subject of the *Institutes* Book II. Calvin's exposition begins with a reflection on the fact of sin from which much of the caricature of Calvin and Calvinism derive. Major topics thereafter include the gospel and the law, the one person and two natures of Christ, and the work of Christ discussed in three offices: prophet, king, and priest. Following Calvin's exposition of the person and work of Christ is the best place to consider the issues of mysticism and deification in Calvin, followed by the narrative of faith using the Apostles' Creed as an outline.

That the fact of sin forms no part of the actual knowledge of the Redeemer is obvious. Sin is the reality from which human beings require redemption, but the reality of the Mediator is not exhausted in the work of the Redeemer. In a historical sense, sin is preliminary to redemption, but in a theological sense, sin is a foreign body. The fact that Calvin begins his exposition of God the Redeemer by discussing human sin in five chapters is noteworthy. Among theologians, the fall is most often treated as the human distortion of divine creation rather than as a prologue to divine redemption. Traditionally the fall is assigned meaning, even if negative meaning, as the occasion that brings redemption. Calvin does not make these common connections.

Among the sections contributing directly to the knowledge of God the Redeemer, Calvin teaches that the gospel precedes the law, asserting that God's grace is extended to human beings *before* they are instructed how to behave. This

---

[1] Three post-Calvin revolutions continue to influence modern culture in powerful ways. The historical revolution raises fundamental questions about the nature and proper authority of the Bible. The social revolution raises fundamental questions about sexual nature and proper roles and proper language for men and women. The christological revolution raises fundamental questions about the nature(s) and role(s) of Jesus Christ. Essentially this revolution is an attack on the adequacy of the Chalcedonian formulation. Barth recognizes this formulation as confessional. "The statement that Jesus Christ is the One who is of divine and human essence dates to unite that which by definition cannot be united" (*Church Dogmatics* 4.2.61). For a discussion of the hypostatic union, see *CD* 4.2.60–69.

conviction reverses the central Lutheran view that law precedes grace. Second, while Calvin explains the orthodox view of Jesus Christ as one person in two complete natures, he places a distinctive emphasis on the humanity of Christ. Third, with the three offices, Calvin offers a dynamic and functional account of the work of Christ in connection with the previous section, which was focused on the person of Christ. As prophet, Christ brings an end to all prophesies by his perfect teaching; as king, Christ rules over death, the devil, and the world; and as priest, Christ reconciles us to God by his holy obedience. In the fourth section Calvin explains atonement within the narrative of the Apostles' Creed.

Calvin insists that the created order was such "that the frame of the universe should be the school in which we were to learn piety, and from it pass over to eternal life and felicity." However, "after the fall of the first man no knowledge of God apart from the mediator has had power unto salvation" (II.6.1). Therefore, God is comprehended in Christ alone (II.6.4) until such time as we shall see God as he is (II.14.3).

Early in Book I Calvin asserted that the knowledge of God is twofold: the Lord who shows himself as Creator is also seen as Redeemer in the face of Christ (I.2.1). In Book II, following the description of sin, Calvin turns to the second fold dealing with what God has done for us in Jesus Christ. This exposition of the knowledge of God the Redeemer also begins the exposition of ourselves as redeemed, to which the remainder of the *Institutes* is devoted. Calvin's "anthropology" thus includes a threefold knowledge of ourselves: as created, as corrupted, and as redeemed. Importantly, the knowledge of our corruption is treated existentially but is denied ontological reality.

A Personal Note

For many years I thought Calvin's exposition of Christ was one among many doctrines rather than the basic conviction on which his entire theology rests. With nodding acceptance I had read past statements like we know God clearly in the person of Christ.[2] That Jesus was more than the mightiest of the prophets (Mark 1:7) had been affirmed from childhood, as was some kind of vague notion of two natures later located more technically in the fundamental

[2] The complete citation reads, "For how can any mortal man ascend to the height of God unless he is raised on high by his hand? God in Christ descended to the lowliness of men to stretch out his hand to them. . . . Whoever aspires to know God without beginning at Christ must wander in a labyrinth . . . because everyone is deprived of all right knowledge of God who leaves Christ [but] whoever directs his mind and all his senses to Christ will be led straight to the Father. We clearly behold God in the person of Christ" (Com. Jn. 8.19).

mystery of hypostatic union (*unio hypostatica*). The text that finally exploded in my mind was Calvin's declaration that "Christ was the true Jehovah" (I.13.9). He continues:

> Moreover, if apart from God there is no salvation, no righteousness, no life, yet Christ contains all these in himself, God is certainly revealed. And let no one object to me that life and salvation have been infused with Christ by God for Christ is not said to have received salvation, but to be salvation itself. ... The name of Christ is invoked for salvation; therefore it follows that he is Jehovah. ... And to have it more plainly understood that "the whole fullness of divinity dwells bodily" in Christ [Col. 2:9], the apostle confesses that he introduced no other doctrine among the Corinthians than knowledge of him, and that he has preached nothing but this [I Cor. 2:2]. (I.13.13)

I had read these statements a number of times, but I remember vividly the first time I felt the full force of their stupendous claim. In spite of what I understood and accepted as the orthodox view of Trinity and Incarnation, I realized that I still maintained some kind of vestigial subordination of the Son to the Father. As a response to these passages in Calvin, I spent considerable time reflecting on whether my own theology allowed me to make so brief and bold a declaration as "Christ is Jehovah." I decided that the confession "Jesus Christ is Lord" (Phil. 2:11; 1 Cor 12:3) (which I did accept) was in fact equivalent to "Jesus Christ is Jehovah" (which I now accept). I concluded that I agreed with Calvin in believing "God is comprehended in Christ alone" (II.6.4), meaning God is like Christ, not that Christ is like God. Perhaps the simplest and clearest evidence of identification is prayer addressed to Christ which is only appropriately directed to God (I.13.13). Calvin is not being hyperbolic when he interprets the phrase, "They shall look to me whom they have pierced" to demonstrate that the essence of the Father and the Son is the same. This denies the blasphemy that the Father is the only true God and Christ is some kind of God, too. The Father and the Son are one and the same God (Com. Zech. 12:10).

This conclusion is neither obvious nor easy. Even so careful a scholar as J. K. S. Reid, while recognizing Calvin's Christocentrism, still maintains that his theology contains a "comprehensive principle." He writes, "It is wrong to represent Calvin as exalting the sovereignty of God at the expense of a real interest in Jesus Christ. The comprehensive principle of his theology is, of course, God's sovereignty; but when one asks concerning the content of which this is the framework, he is led by Calvin straight to Christ. Calvin's theology is theocentric in no sense that precludes Christocentricity."[3] Reid is certainly correct that no intellectual principle can replace Christ in Calvin's theology, but interpreting Calvin through a comprehensively abstract intellectual principle like the sovereignty of God runs the great risk of substituting the abstract principle for the concrete person of Jesus Christ the Lord.

The Christian faith begins in God's presence with us (Matt. 1:23). God is revealed in and as Jesus Christ (2 Cor. 5:19). That is, God is fully revealed in Christ (Col. 1:19). Thus, Calvin writes, "Christ is the one and only foundation of the Church" (Com. 1 Cor. 3:11, cf. IV.2.1), "hence all thinking about God without Christ is a vast abyss which immediately swallows up all our thoughts" (Com. 1 Pet. 1:20). Emil Brunner makes this confession:

> The Christian Faith is not other than (*nichts anderes als*) faith in Jesus Christ. Therefore the whole of Christian theology is not other than (*nichts anderes als*) the explication of faith in Christ. Hence faith in Jesus Christ is not simply part of this faith, and Jesus Christ is not one "subject" among other subjects in the Christian Creed. The doctrine of God, of His Nature and of His Will, of the Creation and the Divine government of the world, of man as created in the Image of God and as sinner, of the Old Covenant as promise and the preparation for the New—all these doctrines are various moments in the one faith in Jesus Christ.[4]

Such statements on the centrality of Jesus Christ are not to be understood as expressions of an essential tenet, not even as the most essential tenet. Confessing Jesus Christ as Lord is not the first item on a list of essential beliefs. Rather, God's revelation in Jesus Christ is the foundational reality of essential faith.

---

[3] Reid, *Authority of Scripture*, 52. [John K. S. Reid, *The Authority of the Scripture: A Study of the Reformation and Post-Reformation Understanding of the Bible* (New York: Harper and Brothers, 1957).]

[4] Emil Brunner, *The Christian Doctrine of Creation and Redemption*, trans. Olive Wyon (Philadelphia: Westminster Press, 1952), 2:239. The same point is made by Thomas F. Torrance. "In Jesus Christ we meet the very embodiment of the majestic Sovereignty of God breaking into the world to claim it for himself, the coming of *Immanuel* (עמנואל), God himself to be with us and one of us, and specifically *Yeshua* (ישוע), meaning *Yahweh-Savior*, for, 'he shall save his people from their sins.' He is the *Lord Jesus*, the divine Savior of mankind, [who is not] a kind of 'double' for God in his absence, but the incarnate presence of *Yahweh*, the Lord God himself. … We come to know Christ today as the Lord and Savior in the same way as the disciples and their converts came to know him at the very beginning, when they called upon Jesus to save them from their sins, worshipped him, and prayed to him, and glorified him, as *Jesous Kyrios* (Ἰήσους κύριος) thereby accepting the designation of him as *Yahweh*, the very name God had given himself in his unique revelation to Israel when he delivered them redemptively out of their bondage in Egypt" (Thomas F. Torrance, *The Christian Doctrine of God, One Being Three Persons* [Edinburgh: T & T Clark, 1996], 51).

He is the basis for, the ground of, and the truth from which all essential tenets derive. In the human realm, fact and interpretation cannot be entirely separated, though they are not the same. Similarly, in theology Christ and Christology are not the same. Reality properly precedes all interpretations of it. While there is no knowledge of Jesus Christ that is not christological, Jesus Christ is never exactly identical with our doctrines concerning him. Even christological doctrine is required to bow the knee before the person of Jesus Christ.

The confession "Jesus Christ is Lord" is at once the most fundamental, most far-reaching, and most remarkable of Christian claims.[5] Ultimately the coalescence of its historical, ontological, epistemological, and behavioral components seems to be a miracle—at least the conviction of its truth remains mysterious. In short, the church's one foundation is Jesus Christ her Lord. Christians worship God revealed in, through, and as Jesus Christ. This is the basic truth from which all doctrines, including the so-called essential tenets, derive. Essential tenets protect the church's confession of her one Lord, but they cannot replace the foundational encounter with him which occurs in experience and issues in service.

With the exposition of Christology, the general, and generally unthreatening, discussion of God's being and works moves to the specific, and specifically demanding, question of God's relation to Jesus of Nazareth.[6] Attempting to understand the experience that "in Christ was God reconciling the world to

---

[5] The scorn the great historian Edward Gibbon pours on the conviction of Christ's Lordship in his impressively rolling prose is nonetheless savage for being lofty. According to Gibbon, "The theologian may indulge the pleasing task of describing Religion as she descended from Heaven, arrayed in her native purity. A more melancholy duty is imposed on the historian. He must discover the inevitable mixture of error and corruption which she contracted in a long residence upon earth, among a weak and degenerate race of beings." Included in the results a historian must recognize that Christian divines in rejecting the observance of the Mosaic law pronounced "with the utmost caution and tenderness a sentence of condemnation so repugnant to the inclination and prejudices of the believing Jews." In reviewing the history of christological reflection, Gibbon deals chiefly with the Gnostics and the Ebionites, expressing some sympathy for the latter. "The unfortunate Ebionites, rejected from one religion as apostates and from the other as heretics … insensibly melted away either into the church or the synagogue" (Edward Gibbon, *Decline and Fall of the Roman Empire*, vol. 1 (Chicago: William Benton, 1952), chap. 15: 179, 182, 183).

[6] In the relative context of the world's religions, the absolute claim, "I am the way, and the truth, and the life" (John 14:6) must be faced. If Christ is Lord, he is more than Kant's example or Hegel's symbol. In his address of July 15, 1838, delivered before the senior class at Harvard Divinity School (from which he had earlier graduated), Ralph Waldo Emerson, *The Spiritual Emerson: Essential Writings*, ed. David M. Robinson (Boston: Beacon Press, 2003), complained that "the first defect of historical Christianity" is its exaggeration of the personal. "It has dwelt, it dwells, with noxious exaggeration about the *person* of Jesus" (71, emphasis in original). On a different subject, "Threnody," Emerson's attempt to console himself on the death of his son, "the deep-eyed boy," demonstrates the thinness of hope in transcendental philosophy and is one of the saddest poems I know.

himself" (2 Cor. 5:19) led to the development of the doctrine of incarnation, which has both natural and supernatural components. As John E. Smith writes, "No one, I believe, will deny that this doctrine is a legitimate and absolutely essential part of Christian theology." Moreover, apart from traditional biblical or devotional language, a restatement of the doctrine looks something like this: "There is an event or series of events within recorded human history which we describe as the appearance of the Christ, and this event is both a legitimate part of the historical process and a unique revelation of the meaning (in the sense of divine purpose) of that process as a whole." Smith observes that the definition contains words like "event," "unique," and "history," which have both ordinary, commonsense meanings as well as more carefully reflective ones. In other words, "We do not and cannot learn, for example, the meaning of a concept like 'unique' from the Bible alone without recourse to an analysis of our general human experience."[7] Granting the importance of ordinary, commonsense meanings, there are also confessions of faith that go beyond ordinary common sense. According to Calvin, Paul calls Christ, "'the image of the invisible God,' meaning by this, that it is through him alone that God, who is otherwise invisible is manifested to us . . . The word 'image' is not used of his essence, but . . . Christ is the image of God because he makes God in a manner visible to us." This is a powerful weapon against the Arians. "The sum is, that God in himself, that is in his naked majesty, is invisible; and that not only to the physical eyes, but also to human understanding; and that he is revealed to us in Christ alone, where we may behold him as in a mirror. For in Christ he shows us his righteousness, goodness, wisdom, power, in short, his entire self. We must, therefore, take care not to seek him elsewhere; for outside Christ everything that claims to represent God will be an idol" (Com. Col. 1:15). Any "supposed knowledge of God outside Christ will be a deadly abyss" (Com. Jn. 6:46).[8]

---

[7] John E. Smith, *Reason and God: Encounters of Philosophy with Religion* (New Haven, CT: Yale University Press, 1961), 153, 154.

[8] Paul van Buren's Basel dissertion written under Karl Barth, *Christ in Our Place: The Substitutionary Character of Calvin's Doctrine of Reconciliation* (Grand Rapids: Eerdmans, 1957), was a helpful contribution to Calvin studies. The main focus is the atonement interpreted by the substitutionary theme of Christ in our place. His emphasis on Christ as substitute is one-sided and the remarks on the "penal substitutionary" doctrine (142) inadequate. Additionally, the Christian narrative is set in motion more by the bad news of human sin than the good news of God's grace. Moreover, in eschewing careful engagement with other scholars, van Buren needlessly deprives himself of challenges from other minds. Nevertheless, the exposition in part 1 of the incarnation as Christ's union with us and part 3 of incorporation as our union with Christ is sound. As is the following testimony of the foreword: "This study in Calvin has strengthened my conviction that as Christ is the center of our faith, so Christology is the *determining* center of all theology." The most far-reaching and disturbing question reads, "Is the work of Christ to be understood as having gained the *reality* of salvation, or only as having opened up its *possibility*?" (32, emphasis in original). In response, van Buren sets aside Calvin's doctrine of predestination and concludes, "Christ's work, in itself, remains for Calvin

A. Sin: How Total Is Depravity?

In the popular mind Calvin and Calvinism are associated with predestination and total depravity. For that reason, any proper understanding must address the question in some detail: "Just how total is depravity and what does it mean?" The correct and short answer is that Calvin's "doctrine of total depravity" is neither total nor a doctrine. The crucial distinction is that by "total" Calvin means totally susceptible to sinfulness but not totally situated in sin. In addition and equally surprising, sin is declared to be accidental. Calvin believes in free will, although he prefers not to use the term. Moreover, while original sin is affirmed, actual sin is also emphasized. Calvin's teaching about sin is here examined under four headings. First, by following our noses we take a quick sniff at the T.U.L.I.P. and the question of total depravity. Second, Calvin offers the remarkable insistence that sin is adventitious. Third, Calvin's view of the freedom and bondage of the will is briefly examined. Fourth, the role of original and actual sin is considered.

1. Total and Partial Depravity

John Calvin's doctrine of sin is often regarded as so severe that "Calvinism" can be used as a synonym for the gloomiest possible evaluation of the human condition and its most dreary prospects. Robinson writes both correctly and ironically, "We speak as though John Calvin invented the Fall of Man, when that was an article of faith universal in Christian culture."[9] Based on the conviction that Calvin taught the total depravity of all human beings, this view of sin is represented by the framework of the famous (or infamous) acrostic T.U.L.I.P., a device used by both friend and foe as a faithful summary of Calvin's theology. For example, Gary Scott Smith writes, "For the purposes of this study, we will define a Calvinist as one who adheres to the theology of John Calvin primarily as set forth in his *Institutes of the Christian Religion*." At this point Smith and I are on the same page, but then he turns over a new leaf: "This theology is popularly summarized in five points often referred to by the acronym TULIP—Total depravity, Unconditional election, Limited (or definite) atonement, Irresistible grace, and Perseverance of the saints." Smith recognizes, "These points were not formulated by Calvin but by the Synod of Dort in 1619 about fifty years after his death, in response to the challenges of Jacob Arminius to his teachings." Never-

an unfilled possibility" (143). The former is impossible; the latter is implausible. Not long after his Calvin book, van Buren wrote *The Secular Meaning of the Gospel* (New York: Macmillan, 1963), which associated him with the death-of-God theology of the 1960s. See Charles N. Bent, *The Death-of-God Movement* (New York: Paulist Press, 1967).

[9] Marilynne Robinson, *The Death of Adam: Essays on Modern Thought* (New York: Houghton Mifflin Company, 1998), 151.

theless, Smith accepts this popular summary as an accurate and adequate summary.[10] Even those who argue that TULIP is useful are not likely to insist that so short a summary is an adequate reflection of the range and nuance of Calvin's theology. Moreover, those who think the acronym is accurate must admit that the interpretive importance of order and context does not and cannot come to full bloom in this TULIP.[11]

On the other hand, the TULIP summary commends itself for several reasons. First, many people already know and accept it. Second, as a mnemonic device it is clever and easy to remember. Third, an important synod in the Netherlands produced the five Canons of Dort which, by a slight rearrangement of sequence, can be made to assert each of the points of TULIP. Fourth, tulips today remind us of Holland although they were introduced into Europe by the Turks.[12] Fifth,

[10] Gary Scott Smith, *The Seeds of Secularism: Calvinism, Culture, and Pluralism in America, 1870–1915* (Grand Rapids: Christian University Press, 1985), 4. Obviously the TULIP mnemonic was created by an English-speaking person.

[11] Among the more interesting expositions of TULIP Calvinism is Richard J. Mouw's *Calvinism in the Las Vegas Airport* (Grand Rapids: Zondervan, 2004). The opening chapter entitled "*Hardcore* TULIP" describes a scene in the movie *Hardcore*, set in the Las Vegas airport, where George C. Scott, playing an agonized Calvinist named Jake Van Dorn, explains the theology of TULIP to a teenage prostitute named Niki, played by Season Hubley. While Mouw defends each of the doctrines represented by TULIP, he admits "that, when stated bluntly, they have a harsh feel about them. To articulate them 'with gentleness and respect' takes some effort" (14). He is especially hesitant about limited atonement. Not so Paul Helm, "The Logic of Limited Atonement," in *Scottish Bulletin of Evangelical Theology* 3, no. 2 (Autumn 1985): 47–54, who, defending logic and reason, sees doctrine as argument, not confession. See also Jonathan H. Rainbow, *The Will of God and the Cross: An Historical and Theological Study of John Calvin's Doctrine of Limited Redemption* (Allison Park, PA: Pickwick Publications, 1990). Gentle respect leads Mouw to keep his powder dry with the Heidelberg Catechism rather than firing away with the Canons of Dort. The movie *Hardcore* was written and directed by Paul Schrader, a graduate of Calvin College, where Richard Mouw taught for seventeen years. Schrader also wrote *Taxi Driver* and both wrote and directed *American Gigolo*. Another well-known Calvin College alumnus who satirized his Calvinistic background was the great humorist Peter De Vries. See his "TULIP" in *No, But I Saw the Movie* (Boston: Little, Brown & Company, 1946), 1–16. His Rev. Andrew Mackerel claims, "[The Dutch Calvinists] were hair-splitters the like of which an ordinary human being in our time is totally unlikely to hear. 'One Dutchman, a Christian; two Dutchmen, a congregation; three Dutchmen, heresy'" (*The Mackerel Plaza* [Boston: Little, Brown and Company, 1958], 31). Growing up among Dutch Calvinists Reverend Mackerel moves away from that background to become pastor of the "People's Liberal" church, and his story begins with an angry telephone call to the zoning board objecting to a newly installed sign which he can see from his study window.The sign read, "Jesus Saves." In contrast, in the profoundly moving *The Blood of the Lamb* (New York: Penguin Books, 1961 [1985]), written as his only daughter, Emily, died of leukemia, De Vries wrote, "I came to understand a few things about what people believe. What people believe is a measure of what they suffer" (25). See also Roderick Jellema, *Peter De Vries: A Critical Essay* (Grand Rapids: Wm. B. Eerdmans, 1966). Cruelly jesting at the reality of pain, Lord Byron writes, "As I suffer from the shocks / Of illness, I grow much more orthodox" (*Don Juan*, Canto 11, 5).

[12] As an exotic footnote, this information on the tulip is provided by Lord Kinross. Sultan Ahmed's

> S*eraglio* during the winter was regaled with *helva fêtes*, social gatherings in which

Dutch Calvinists accept the Canons of Dort, indicating the existence of a living community more disposed to affirm than to deny—or even to question—the validity of the TULIP acrostic.[13]

That TULIP represents the Calvinistic theology of the Synod of Dort can scarcely be doubted. Additionally, if one assumes that the historical development of Calvinism was in the main an enhancement of Calvin's theology, rather than a distortion of it, there is no need to review the adequacy of the Canons of Dort or the later Westminster Confession as faithful expressions of Calvinistic theology. Furthermore, since a goodly number of the godly people interested in Calvin's theology (and thus in this book) are also loyal to either Dort or Westminster or both, some tiptoeing around the TULIP might be appropriate.

While crucial to the history of Calvinism, a detailed analysis of the Synod of Dort (1618) or the Assembly at Westminster (1644) is clearly outside the scope of a study of the *Institutes* of Calvin (1560). The extremely important question whether, and in what ways, later Calvinism improved or distorted Calvin's theology is addressed in the introduction and need not be treated here. The

> philosophical symposia, together with poetry recitals, dancing, Chinese shadow plays, and prayers were accompanied by the distribution of sweets, otherwise helva. But when the winter was over there was now introduced for the Sultan's delectation a spring fête which developed largely into a festival of tulips. Ahmed had a great love for flowers—for the rose, the carnation (which his moustache was said to resemble), the lilac, the jasmine. But it was eventually the tulip that captured his fancy above all the rest. Its name in Turkish was *lale*, held to have a sacred significance from its resemblance to "Allah," and the reign of Ahmed III became known to posterity as *Lale Devri*, or the Reign of the Tulip. The tulip was a wild flower of the Asiatic steppes which had strewn the path of the Turks throughout their centuries of westward migration. It was Busbecq, the Austrian imperial ambassador of the sixteenth century, who as a keen botanist first introduced the tulip to the West, taking tulip bulbs back to Flanders on his journey home. Its European name was derived from the nickname the Turks gave it: *tulbend*, or "turban" in the Persian language. Not long afterward the tulip was imported by European merchants and propagated in large quantities in Holland, where in time some twelve hundred varieties of it were known. This gave rise in the seventeenth century to a craze of tulipomania among the Ottoman elite, in the course of which fortunes were made and lost from rare tulip bulbs, and the tulip became known as "the gold of Europe."

From Lord Kinross, *The Ottoman Centuries: The Rise and Fall of the Turkish Empire* (London: Jonathan Cape, 1977), 378–79. Jack Goody, *The Culture of Flowers* (Cambridge: Cambridge University Press, 1993), 188–89, under the title "tulipomania," deals with commercial and theological aspects of flowers.

[13] R. B. Kuiper, *As to Being Reformed* (Grand Rapids: Wm. B. Eerdmans, 1926). In his chapter on "Christianity and Calvinism" Kuiper claims the five points of Calvinism were sponsored by the Genevan Reformer. He concludes, "Calvinism is the most nearly perfect interpretation of Christianity. In the final analysis, Calvinism and Christianity are practically synonymous. It follows that he who departs from Calvinism is taking a step away from Christianity. . . . For in the last instance the fundamentals of Calvinism are also the fundamentals of the Christian religion" (88, 91).

present purpose only requires the observation with which both sides would agree. Calvin's theology does not start with total depravity. Since Calvin locates his discussion of sin at the beginning of Book II, clearly he does not begin the *Institutes* with it.

Calvin can, and certainly does, paint his portrait of human beings in the darkest colors, giving some credence to the emphasis on the power of the vice grip. For example, he writes, "I have said that *all parts* of the soul were possessed by sin after Adam deserted the fountain of righteousness." Again the soul's "*entire nature* is opposed to supernatural grace." Yet again, no part of mankind "is immune from sin and *all that proceeds* from him is to be imputed to sin" (II.1.9, emphases added). On the other hand, Calvin also says, "We grant that God's image was *not totally annihilated and destroyed* in [Adam], yet it was so corrupted that whatever remains is frightful deformity" (I.15.4).

As usual Thomas Aquinas has an elegant solution to the issue of total and partial depravity. The fall destroyed the supernatural virtues: faith, hope, and love, which are restored by God's grace alone. The natural virtues: wisdom, courage, moderation, and justice were seriously damaged, but not totally destroyed. They remain as essential natural components of human being. By the exercise of free will, the natural virtues can, and should, be improved. Carlos Eire reads Calvin in a Thomistic direction. Sinful humanity's "natural gifts have been corrupted and his spiritual gifts have been completely taken away."[14] Calvin's remarks lend some plausibility to this understanding. For example, Calvin says sin destroyed the supernatural gifts of faith and love and damaged the natural gifts, which means "something of understanding and judgment remains as a residue along with the will." The fall did not totally wipe out reason, nor did the will perish (II.2.12). The remaining residue includes vestiges of truth, equity, and order. However, when Calvin is describing the fall directly rather than defending God's mercy to the fallen creature, he carefully avoids placing even relatively sound capacities in the natural human apart from God's special grace. In other words, for Calvin, unlike Thomas, grace does not perfect created nature but restores fallen nature. The proper resolution of this dilemma is not a doctrine of operating and cooperating grace as in Thomas (*ST*, I.2.111ff.). Rather, by total depravity Calvin means totally susceptible to sin but he says, "I grant that not all these wicked traits appear in every man"; therefore he continues, "Yet one cannot deny that [all these wicked traits lurk] in the breast of each" (II.3.2).

---

[14] Carlos M. N. Eire, *War against the Idols: The Reformation of Worship from Erasmus to Calvin* (Cambridge: Cambridge University Press, 1986), 203.

2. Sin: A Fact without Meaning

Remarkably, for Calvin sin is defined as an accident. Sin "is an adventitious quality which comes upon man rather than a substantial property which has been implanted from the beginning" (II.1.11). This definition owes something to Aristotle's distinction between reality and actuality (substance) on the one hand and contingency and possibility (accident) on the other.[15] Sin is a fact for Calvin, but an inexplicable fact. Since sin is defined as an accident, it cannot become a substantial doctrine. Human depravity cannot be regarded as a central dogma in John Calvin's Calvinism. Sin has devastating consequences, but no positive meaning.

The threefold outline of much popular theology assigns an important meaning to sin. That is, (1) God created everything good, but (2) man and woman abused the good gift of free will, thereby falling into sin.[16] (3) In response to sin God sent Jesus Christ to redeem the world. According to this scheme, sin is the pivotal event between creation and redemption that both requires and explains the incarnation. Calvin takes the fact of sin with absolute seriousness, but sin as accident does not have meaning. The popular three-step theology which moves from God's creation to sin's destruction to Christ's restoration understands human sin as a logically necessary part of salvation history. In contrast, Calvin's five small chapters on sin are not essential to the relation between Creator and Mediator. Rather the discussion of sin is inserted between the knowledge of the Creator (Book I) and Redeemer (Book II). For Calvin sin is a terrible reality, but it is not a major division of his theology. Calvin should be understood as a theologian of God's grace, not of human sin.

The setting of Calvin's main account of sin is not as a pivotal discussion between creation and redemption, but rather a bracketed discussion between the knowledge of God the Creator and the knowledge of God the Redeemer. The fact of sin affects both kinds of knowledge, but sin is not part of either. Sin is treated as a strange or foreign object in the body of Calvin's theology, having no necessary connection to Creator or Mediator although the Mediator is the Redeemer.

If sin were meaning-full it would not be sin. The presence of sin and evil in a world created by an omnipotent, omniscient, and loving God is incomprehensible.[17] Calvin refuses to give sin an ontological grounding or justification. "[The

---

[15] This distinction is employed often against Pighius in *The Bondage and Liberation of the Will* [by John Calvin]. Human corruption is accidental, not substantial (Book II, 263).

[16] Usually not addressed is the difficulty of a physical transmission of a moral failure or the legitimacy of guilt transferred to a person for actions occurring centuries before.

[17] In a chapter entitled "The Riddle of Sin," G. C. Berkouwer agrees. He writes, "Sin, for the Christian, is unreasonable, idiotic, and incomprehensible in the light of God's love *as now*

orthodox faith] does not admit that any evil nature exists in the whole universe. For the depravity and malice both of man and of the devil, or the sins that arise therefrom, do not spring from nature, but rather from the corruption of nature" (I.14.3). Calvin passionately refuses to make the logical inference from God's omnipotence to God's responsibility for sin. Without being able to challenge the premises, he denies the conclusion insisting that it is impious to think of the sovereign God as the author of evil, but he cannot claim it is illogical. In some sense, then, Calvin's view of sin is both accidental and unreasonable. Calvin insists that "all things take place by God's determination" (III.23.6), meaning that "God foreknew what end man was to have before he created him, and consequently foreknew because he so ordained by his decree" (III.23.7). "Accordingly, man falls as God's providence ordains, but he falls by his own fault" (III.23.8). Calvin can criticize the unbridled use of reason in theology (II.2.18) and asserts the will of God as the final standard (III.22.11). However, most of the time he assumes that God has "reasons" even if we do not know what they are. "It would be claiming too much for ourselves not to concede to God that he may have reasons for his plan that are hidden from us" (II.11.14). In connection with the reality of sin, Calvin simply refuses to carry his reflection to its logical conclusion. Sin is a fact, but it is an accidental fact, which means it has no ultimate meaning.[18] Additionally, while Calvin takes sin with utmost seriousness,

revealed." "Sin itself, in its source and cause, can never be explained." "One can only affirm that there is no *reason* and no sensible motive for man's sin. . . . One cannot find sense in the senseless and meaning in the meaningless" (G. C. Berkouwer, *Sin* [Grand Rapids: Wm. B. Eerdmans, 1971], 144, 131, 134). Utilizing Gabriel Marcel's distinction between "problem" and "mystery," George Dennis O'Brien suggests the *problem* of the justification of suffering cannot properly be raised because of the primacy of the *mystery* of "the existential relation of God and man" which "cannot be avoided or transcended" and blocks "any literal meaning to the qualitative characteristics of power and goodness which are used to generate the dilemma [of justification]." O'Brien declares, "The final answer is what God *is* in Christ" (emphasis in original) (George Dennis O'Brien, "Prologomena to a Dissolution to the Problem of Suffering," *Harvard Theological Review* 57, no. 4 [October 1964]: 322, 316, 323). I take the term "existential relation" to be equivalent to "union with Christ." For a more recent theological/philosophical reflection on Christology, sin, and horrendous evils as a *distinct* category, see Marilyn McCord Adams, *Horrendous Evils and the Goodness of God* (Ithaca, NY: Cornell University Press, 1999), and *Christ and Horrors: The Coherence of Christology* (Cambridge: Cambridge University Press, 2006).

[18] Among the famous cries of the heart is Dorigen's agonized question concerning evil and God's providence in "The Franklin's Tale" of Chaucer's *Canterbury Tales*. As she waits anxiously for the return of her seagoing husband, Arveragus, whom she loved more than her own life, Dorigen cannot understand why a loving, perfect, and omniscient God would allow "grisly, fiendish, black rocks" in his world on which have perished "a hundred thousand bodies of mankind." To her mind those rocks do not benefit man, nor bird, nor beast. Among other similar outcries that immediately come to mind are Ivan's challenge to Alyosha in the chapter "Rebellion" of *The Brothers Karamazov*. See also Nicholas Wolterstorff, *Lament for a Son* (Grand Rapids: Eerdmans, 1987); and chap. 10, "The Accident of Sin," in Andrew Purves and Charles Partee, *Encountering God: Christian Faith in Turbulent Times* (Louisville, KY: Westminster John Knox Press, 2000).

the victory over sin is absolute. In that context, his teaching of "total depravity" properly understood can be considered a cheerful doctrine.

3. Freedom and Bondage of Will

In the sixteenth century among early Protestants, bondage of the will to sin was considered a liberating doctrine. Any kind of confidence in human free will led to questions about its proper exercise and immediately to uncertainty and therefore anxiety about one's salvation. Assurance of faith meant understanding redemption can only be found in God's grace and not at all in human merit. Sin did not totally deprive human beings of will but of soundness of will (II.3.5). Since the fall of Adam all are alienated from God by sin. "I readily allow that a certain remnant of life remains in man's soul. For understanding and judgment and will and all the senses are so many parts of life. But since there is no part which aspires to the heavenly life, it is not surprising if the whole man is accounted dead so far as the Kingdom of God is concerned" (Com. Jn. 5.25). God's grace is not extended on the basis of our merit. On the contrary, "The first part of a good work is will; the other, a strong effort to accomplish it; the author of both is God" (II.3.9). Freedom can be an intolerable burden, as famously argued by the Grand Inquisitor in Fyodor Dostoevsky's *The Brothers Karamazov*. When the notion of freely choosing and faithfully following God's way becomes a frightening responsibility, the proclamation that God's grace rescues men and women from an impossible situation is comforting good news. The issue, of course, is the relation between divine sovereignty and human freedom. Two perils must be avoided. If divine sovereignty is overemphasized, the result is complete resignation. If human freedom is overemphasized, the result is brazen confidence or abject fear. Calvin's astounding conclusion is that we should accept our freedom but not boast of it. He observes that some theologians teach there is no freedom to choose between good and evil, but we are free to act wickedly. Others "teach that man, despoiled of the powers of free will, takes refuge in grace alone. At another time they provide, or seem to provide, him with his own armor" (II.2.9). Calvin thinks the danger of all discussion of free will leads to celebrating human achievement and robbing divine honor.

According to Calvin, pride was the beginning of all evils and disobedience was the beginning of the fall. In this section of the *Institutes*, Calvin contrasts pride with humility. The great danger of a discussion of free will is that it fosters pride. In contrast, "The foundation of our philosophy is humility . . . so if you ask me concerning the precepts of the Christian religion, first, second, third, and always I would answer, 'Humility'" (II.2.11).[19] Bondage of will in Calvin does not obviate responsibility and accountability: "Obviously, man's ruin is to be ascribed to man alone; for he, having acquired righteousness by God's kindness, has by his own folly sunk into vanity" (II.1.10).[20]

The topic of free will was famously and historically addressed by Augustine and Pelagius in the fifth century. During the Reformation Martin Luther responded to Erasmus with a powerful attack entitled *Bondage of the Will* (1524). Until then many thought Erasmus was supportive of Luther's challenges to Rome. By some Erasmus was thought to lay the egg that Luther hatched. Erasmus came out of his shell and cracked the egg by writing *The Freedom of the Will* in order to distance himself from the Lutheran movement. In his teaching on total depravity and bondage of the will Calvin is essentially following Augustine and Luther and not creating a so-called Calvinistic doctrine. At the end of the Reformation period the issue returned in the Arminian controversy, which led in the next century to the charge that John Wesley was "Arminian." [21] John Calvin's absolutely pessimistic view of total depravity was taken to deny the possibility of human perfection in this life, while John Wesley's resolutely optimistic view was taken to encourage Christian perfection in this life. It is not really clear whether Wesley thought of Christian perfection as a possession or a process. But, whatever the degree of expectation, it was a hope. [22]

---

[19] The Greek idea of hubris includes the intoxication of mind found in those most certain it does not apply to them.

[20] In a powerful contemporary vindication of Calvin's position, Robinson writes, "the belief that we are all sinners gives us excellent grounds for forgiveness and self-forgiveness, and is kindlier than any expectation that we might be saints, even while it affirms the standards all of us fail to attain." Modernity has replaced this vision "with an unsystematic, uncritical and in fact unconscious perfectionism, which may have taken root among us while Stalinism still seemed full of promise, and to have been refreshed by the palmy days of National Socialism in Germany, by Castro and by Mao . . . Gross error survives every attempt at perfection and flourishes. No Calvinist could be surprised. No reader of history could be surprised" (Robinson, *Death of Adam*, 156).

[21] On Arminianism, see Herbert Darling Foster, "Liberal Calvinism: The Remonstrants at the Synod of Dort in 1618," *Harvard Theological Review* 16, no. 1 (January 1923): 1–37.

[22] Benjamin B. Warfield wrote a thousand pages attacking perfectionism and defending the Reformers' "miserable-sinner Christianity." According to Warfield, the Roman Catholics, Arminians, Wesleyans, Quakers, and others join in this assault on the Reformers' doctrine of sin and grace (Benjamin Breckinridge Warfield, *Perfectionism*, 2 vols. [New York: Oxford University Press, 1931–32]). In 1958 Samuel G. Craig edited and shortened Warfield's work (Grand Rapids: Baker Book House), adding a summary talk to students entitled "Entire Sanctification." Warfield believed in entire sanctification but not that it could occur in this life. Although despising Wesleyanism, Albrecht Ritschl championed Christian perfection (*Die christliche Vollkommenheit*). English translation in *Bibliotheca Savra* 35:140 (October 1878), 656–80. As a boy I always wondered whether I was totally depraved as my father suspected or on the way to perfection as my mother hoped.

Calvin's most important practical, as opposed to theoretical, discussion of the behaviors expected of Christian life is found in his exposition of sanctification and justification in Book III. The general conclusion is that sanctification is a lifelong process and cannot be completed on this earth. However, in this "Wesleyan moment" of Calvin's theology he suggests the possibility of a perfection before death. Citing Augustine, Calvin writes, "The grace of persisting in good . . . is given to us in order that we may will, and by will may overcome concupiscence. . . . The original freedom was to be able not to sin; but ours is much greater, not to be able to sin." This is *not* "a perfection to come after immortality," but connected with human will and God's grace. "Surely the will of the saints is so much aroused by the Holy Spirit that they are able because they so will, and that they will because God brings it about that they so will" (II.3.13). In this discussion Calvin seems to suggest (against the I [Irresistible grace] of T.U.L.I.P.) that grace is resistible! Grace is "offered by the Lord, which by anyone's free choice may be accepted or rejected." However, Calvin continues, "It is [God's] grace which forms both choice and will in the heart, so that whatever good works then follow are the fruit and effect of grace." In Calvin's theology, good works come not by our choice or by our nature, but by God's grace (II.5.8).

In summary, because the idea of even restricted freedom produces a foolish assurance, Calvin says that to designate our wicked acts as "freedom of the will" is to label a slight thing with a proud name (*superbus titulus*) (II.2.7). The notion of freedom of the will is always in danger of robbing God of his honor. Calvin admits it is possible to speak of freedom of will without misunderstanding, but he prefers not to use the idea (II.2.8).

4. Original and Actual Sin

The primary purpose of Calvin's doctrine of original sin is to reaffirm the bondage of the will. The purpose of the doctrine of the unfree will is, as we have seen, to demonstrate that human beings can recover what they have lost by sin only through God's grace revealed in Jesus Christ. Calvin refers to his earlier affirmation that nearly all wisdom consists of the knowledge of God and ourselves (I.1.1) in order to point out the knowledge of ourselves has a two-part dialectic. First, we must consider our original nature and the natural excellence which comes from God's creation and involves the purpose of our creation and the good gifts bestowed on us. This reflection leads to meditation on divine worship and the future life. Second, we must also recognize our fallen nature and the misery of our condition, which should bring us humility and shame. In this connection Calvin cites the classical recommendation to "know thyself," which too often leads to pride since the philosophers contemplate only our best qualities. Philosophers are aware of human evil, but they "hold as certain that virtues and vices are in our power [thus] we seem to do what we do, and to shun what we shun, by free choice." Some of these philosophers even accept life as a gift of the gods, but regard the way humans live as their responsibility. "This is the sum of the opinion of all philosophers: reason which abides in human understanding is a sufficient guide for right conduct; the will, being subject to it, is indeed incited by the senses to evil things; but since the will has free choice, it cannot be hindered from following reason as its leader in all things" (II.2.3).

According to Calvin, the philosophers "locate the will midway between reason and sense" (II.2.2). Reason is defined as the guide for a good life, while sense is a lower impulse that leads to error and baseness. The will is free to follow either the reason or the appetites. The philosophers are aware that living according to reason is not easy, but they insist it is possible. Right reason leads to right conduct if the will follows, but the will is too often tempted toward evil by the senses. Nevertheless the will can freely choose to follow reason. Free will entails that both virtue and vice are within our power. In contrast to the philosophers, theologians recognize that the original state no longer obtains because sin has damaged both reason and will, but theologians have been misled not only by their desire to receive the approval of philosophers but also by their fear that asserting an unfree will would lead to slothfulness. Calvin objects that too many theologians agree with or waffle in the house of the philosophers. In fact, "all the ancients, except Augustine, so differ, waver or speak confusedly on [free will], that almost nothing certain can be derived from their writings" (II.2.4).

Calvin thinks "blind self-love is innate in all mortals" (II.1.2), and for that reason, "There is, indeed, nothing that man's nature seeks more eagerly than to be flattered" (II.1.2). Nevertheless, "Since in the person of the first man we have fallen from our original condition, [we must remember] that primal worthiness cannot come to mind without the sorry spectacle of our foulness and dishonor presenting itself by way of contrast" (II.1.1). Calvin recognizes that the ancient doctors taught obscurely about original sin (II.1.5), and there was much debate surrounding the doctrine. "For all to be made guilty by the guilt of one" is not easy to accept. Nevertheless Adam's sin caused his own death, consigned all people to ruin, and even "perverted the whole order of nature" (II.1.5). Some modern theologians disagree with Calvin about the extension of sinfulness to nonhuman nature. Calvin thinks the disobedience of Adam led not simply to the ruin of the human race but means that all creatures are subject to corruption (Rom. 8) because "they are bearing part of the punishment deserved by man, for whose use they were created" (II.1.5).

Calvin offers this definition: "Original sin, therefore, seems to be a hereditary depravity and corruption of our nature, diffused into all parts of the soul, which first makes us liable to God's wrath, then also brings forth in us those works which Scripture calls 'works of the flesh' [Gal. 5:19]" (II.1.8). Due to original sin, human nature cannot be extolled in such a way as to make us satisfied with ourselves and forgetful that in God we "may recover those things which we have utterly and completely lost" (I.1.1). "Here, then, is the course that we must follow if we are to avoid crashing upon these rocks: when man has been taught that no good thing remains in his power, and that he is hedged about on all sides by most miserable necessity, in spite of this he should nevertheless be instructed to aspire to a good of which he is empty, to a freedom of which he has been deprived" (II.2.1). At this point Calvin once again pushes beyond the limits of logic by declaring both that no good thing remains in our power and that we should aspire to a good which is not present with a freedom which we do not possess.[23] Such assertions without obvious rational coherence may be called paradoxical or contradictory. In either case, as affirmations they are integral parts of Calvin's theology. This situation applies most dramatically in the relation between completed justification and continuing sanctification, defined as twin graces, as we shall discuss in Book III.

Dealing with Adam's fall in the exposition of predestination and addressing the relation of God's decree and God's permission, Calvin confesses with Augustine that "the will of God is the necessity of things." This means "the first man fell because the Lord had judged it to be expedient; why he so judged is hidden from us. Yet it is certain that he so judged because he saw that thereby the glory of his name is duly revealed." The human race falls as God's providence ordains but falls by their own fault. According to Calvin we are wasting our time and God's patience in seeking the cause of God's decree when we should contemplate our corruption. On this question, "The craving to know [is] a kind of madness" (III.23.8). Calvin is aware that this answer does not satisfy the impious who still "growl and mutter." Nevertheless, Calvin continues to insist that the calamities decreed for some are the results of their faults (III.23.9).

[23] In his classic *The New England Mind: The Seventeenth Century* (Cambridge: Harvard University Press, 1954 [1939]), 367, Perry Miller sees both American "Arminianism" and "Antinomianism" as a reaction against Calvin's perceived ethical absolutism, which "seemed to these critics devoid of any grounds for moral obligation: what duties could be exacted from ordinary men when everything depended upon a mysterious decree of election." By 1600, American divines felt obligated to answer the question, "If I am not elected, I can do nothing and why should I try?" Miller observes that "Calvin himself had simply brushed aside such frivolous cavils, magisterially declaring, '"Man, being taught that he has nothing good left in his possession, and being surrounded on every side with the most miserable necessity, should nevertheless, be instructed to aspire to the good of which he is destitute.'"

Without doubt Calvin teaches a strong doctrine of original sin. However, he also sounds a cautionary note—perhaps especially useful for preachers and pastors. We are not to understand that human beings are guiltless and do not deserve the curse that falls upon them. It is true that Adam's sin infected all of us, but we are all sick in ourselves. There is considerable danger that a too-forceful presentation of original sin will allow Adam and Eve to be blamed for the original sin in a way that excuses all others from their actual sin. The delicate balance between justification and sanctification, bondage and freedom of the will, also applies to original and actual sin. Calvin suggests that contemplating the doctrine of original sin so overwhelms us that we are forced to throw ourselves entirely upon the mercy of God. However, Calvin also insists that we "are guilty *not* of another's fault but of our own" (II.1.8). This comment indicates that humans cannot blame only Adam and Eve for *original sin*. Everyone must accept personal responsibility for *actual sin*.

The main issue for Calvin is how Christ's righteousness and life are restored to us. Those who deny original sin think our actual sin has not been transmitted from Adam but occurs only in imitation of Adam. If that were true, Christ's righteousness would be ours by imitation, not communication. Calvin exclaims, "who can bear such sacrilege!" The proper relationship is this: "Adam, implicating us in his ruin, destroyed us with himself; but Christ restores us to salvation by his grace" (II.1.6). Calvin recognizes the depth of sin, but he does not rejoice in it, as some of his critics suggest. His major point is not human depravity but divine grace.

B. The Gospel and the Law

After five chapters on sin, Calvin turns in the next six to gospel and law. Educated as a lawyer, Calvin has an insider's appreciation of the crucial role of law in human society, especially with regard to equity and order, both extremely high values for him. However, Niesel rightly claims, "If with the usual prejudices about the legalism of Calvin we come to his writings and really read them, it is just here [in Book II] that we shall find what a lot we have to unlearn."[24] The main and specific point Calvin makes in this section of the *Institutes* is that grace takes precedence over law. The first caution to readers is to resist the temptation to focus on the topic of gospel and law to the neglect of their basis, unity, and purpose, which is the knowledge of God

[24] Wilhelm Niesel, *The Theology of Calvin*, 1st ed., trans. Harold Knight (Philadelphia: Westminster Press, 1956), 92.

the Redeemer. Christ alone is the end of the law and prophets (Com. Mt. 17:3). Every doctrine of the law, every command, every promise points to Christ (Com. Rom. 10:4). The gospel does not supplant the law but ratifies it (II.9.4). The law guides our life like a candle, but Christ is the sun of righteousness dispelling the darkness (Com. Dan. 9:25; Com. Mal. 4:2). This discussion of gospel and law is most emphatically part of Calvin's Christology. The focus is not on Scripture itself but the role of the gracious gospel and the gracious law in the revelation of the Mediator and Redeemer. The second caution requires the recognition that the subject of gospel and law is not equivalent to New and Old Testaments. Calvin finds gospel in the Old Testament and law in the New Testament.[25] The third caution points out that the central dynamic between gospel and law in Calvin's theology does not allow an analysis of law even relatively separate from grace using categories like eternal, divine, natural, and positive law in the way Thomas Aquinas does.[26] Niesel and Wendel each treat this subject in two chapters. The first deals with the law of God, the second with the Old and New Testaments, but dual analysis obscures the christological unity of Calvin's exposition. Moses and the prophets are, he thinks, true teachers because "the law is nothing but a preparation for the Gospel" (Com. Jn. 10:8).

The central theological point of these chapters is that God's grace is the result of God's love and is extended to humanity before instruction in behavior is given.[27] Even more important is Calvin's focus on Jesus Christ as the promise of the law and the fulfillment of the gospel. Martin Luther wrote, "Nearly the entire Scripture and the knowledge of all theology depends upon the correct understanding of law and gospel."[28] However, Luther emphasizes more strongly than Calvin both the sequence of law to gospel and the role of law as demand rather than promise. In early editions Calvin began this part of the *Institutes* with the Old Testament, observing the historical pattern of treating the Old and then the

---

[25] On the unity of the Old and New Testaments, see Hans Heinrich Wolf, *Die Einheit des Bun-des: des Verhältnis von Alten und Neuen Testament bei Calvin* (Neukirchen: Kr. Moers, 1958). Whenever the word "covenant" appears, Calvin affirms that we should think "grace" (Com. Is. 55:3).

[26] See Karl Barth, "Gospel and Law," in *God, Grace and Gospel*, trans. James Strathearn McNab (London: Oliver and Boyd, 1959), 1–27. Also, John T. McNeill, "Natural Law in the Teaching of the Reformers," *Journal of Religion*, 26 (1946): 168–82. Gessert asserts that Calvin's real mentors are the Hebrew prophets, not the statesmen of Greece and Rome. While Calvin occasionally implies one of Thomas's four kinds of law, his primary concern is the divine law (Robert A. Gessert, "The Integrity of Faith: An Inquiry into the Meaning of Law in the Thought of John Calvin," in *Scottish Journal of Theology* 13 [1960], 247–61).

[27] See I. John Hesselink, "Law and Gospel or Gospel and Law? Calvin's Understanding of the Relationship," in *Calviniana: Ideas and Influence of Jean Calvin*, ed. Robert V. Schnucker (Ann Arbor, MI: Sixteenth-Century Essays and Studies, 1988), 13–32.

[28] Weimarer Ausgabe of *Luther's Works*, 7:505.

New Testament. In the final edition, he changed the order from historical to theological to emphasize more strongly the common witness of law and gospel to Christ. Historically the law precedes and prepares for the gospel, but the gracious law is God's promise of salvation and the gracious gospel is God's fulfillment of that promise. In his earlier writings Calvin followed Luther's emphasis on and order of "law before gospel," but later, Calvin teaches that grace precedes law. This sequence contains another flashpoint for Calvin interpretation. By careful scholars Calvin's so-called legalism was never considered graceless. The law and the gospel are both grace-full but in different ways. The issue remains priority and emphasis, which is distorted in the Westminster Confession's distinction between the covenant of works and the covenant of grace as discussed in the section on Calvin and the Calvinists. The role of law in the covenant of works is a post-Calvin topic.

In Book I Calvin discussed the knowledge of God the Creator, but because of sin this knowledge is useless without the gift of faith "setting forth for us God our Father in Christ" (II.6.1). In Book II Calvin declares his purpose is not yet to discuss faith in Christ in detail (II.6.1.4). God calls us to faith in Christ because "we cannot by contemplating the universe infer that [God] is Father." After "the fall of the first man no knowledge of God apart from the Mediator has had power unto salvation." According to Calvin, the electing grace of God revealed in the Old Covenant "taught believers to seek salvation nowhere else than in the atonement that Christ alone carries out" (II.6.2). The new covenant is a confirmation of the old covenant (Com. Mt. 5:17). Since Christ is the central content of both the Old and New Covenants, Calvin devotes an entire chapter (II.10) to explaining, "The covenant made with all the patriarchs is so much like ours in substance and reality that the two are actually one and the same. Yet they differ in the mode of dispensation" (II.10.2). The difference between the two covenants is discussed in II.11, but the conclusion is, "The Old Testament fathers (1) had Christ as pledge of their covenant, and (2) put in him all trust of future blessedness" (II.10.23).

On this Christocentric focus David Puckett writes, "[Calvin] believed Christian exegetes, in their eagerness to relate the Old Testament to Christian doctrine, were often guilty of twisting the text to an unnatural interpretation." Nevertheless while Calvin was concerned to respect the literary and historical context of the Old Testament, "He insists that Christ is the true substance of the Old Testament."[29] Calvin admits the christological center was not clearly

[29] David L. Puckett, *John Calvin's Exegesis of the Old Testament* (Louisville, KY: Westminster John Knox Press, 1995), 6, 140–41.

taught in Moses. Still in the messianic lineage of David it was clearly evident that God willed to be propitious to the human race through the Mediator. Citing Habakkuk 3:13; 2 Kings 8:19; Isaiah 7:14; 55:3–4; Ezekiel 34:23–25; 37:24, 26; Hosea 1:11; 3:5; Micah 2:13; Amos 9:11; Zechariah 9:9; and Psalm 28:8–9 Calvin states, "Here I am gathering a few passages of many because I merely want to remind my readers that the hope of all the godly has ever reposed in Christ alone" (II.6.3). Scripture teaches that faith in God is faith in Christ. "Believe in God, believe also in me" (John 14:1). Calvin comments that faith properly mounts up from Christ to the Father, but "although faith rests in God, it will gradually disappear unless he who retains it in perfect firmness intercedes as Mediator." God is the object of faith but "unless God confronts us in Christ we cannot come to know that we are saved." In comparison with the immensity of God's glory, human beings are like grubs crawling on earth, which means that "apart from Christ the saving knowledge of God does not stand" (II.6.4).

Having emphasized the primacy and priority of God's grace revealed in Jesus Christ, Calvin turns to the role of law. As Calvin reads the Old Testament, the law was added some four hundred years later to the covenant made by God with Abraham. The purpose of this addition was not "to lead the chosen people away from Christ; but rather to hold their minds in readiness until his coming" (II.7.1). According to the apostle, Christ is the end of the law unto salvation to every believer (Rom. 10:4) which means that even the ceremonial laws, vain exercises in themselves, and now "abrogated not in effect but only in use" (II.7.16), were designed to lift the minds of the Jewish people to Christ.

Turning from the law's purpose to its effects, Calvin suggests that the moral law would produce eternal salvation if it could be completely observed (II.7.3). In this line Calvin veers closest to the Westminster Confession's concept of a once-valid-but-now-rejected covenant of works. However, Calvin's comment is directed to the gracious purpose of the law in the context of his insistence that the teaching of the moral law, which includes the Decalogue and Jesus' summary, by being so far above human capacity makes its fulfillment impossible. Calvin defines "impossible" as "what has never been and what God's ordination and decree prevents from ever being" (II.7.4). Calvin returns to the praise of the gracious law in describing the Christian life in Book III. "The law of God contains in itself that newness by which his image can be restored in us [but] our slowness needs many goads and helps" (III.6.1). Again, "The law of the Lord provides the finest and best disposed method of ordering a man's life" (III.7.1).

Calvin insists that while the law cannot be perfectly obeyed, it serves three functions: punitive, protective, and pedagogical. The first function of the law is to punish sinners. The second function is to protect society. The third and principal function of law is to teach believers how to live.[30] This subject is continued in the discussion of sanctification—the doctrine of the holy life in Book III (3–10).

The first use of the law is to warn, inform, convict, condemn, and finally to destroy sinners. For believers this punitive function of the law produces a misery that teaches humility. Through this use of the law, believers come to recognize "they are not fit to receive Christ's grace unless they first be emptied" (II.7.11). Second, the law restrains evil people from enacting with their hands what their minds have conceived. The dread of the law's punishment does not change the hearts of these evildoers, but restraining them is necessary for public tranquility. Because of the folly of the flesh, believers too need the restraining function of the law. "For all who have at any time groped about in ignorance of God will admit that it happened to them in such a way that the bridle of the law restrained them in some fear and reverence toward God until, regenerated by the Spirit, they began wholeheartedly to love him" (II.7.11). The third use of the law is pedagogical. That is, the law teaches believers what the will of God is and encourages them to follow it. Among sinners the law threatens and condemns, but among saints the law guides by its precepts and comforts by its promise of grace. The law guides the faithful toward salvation (Com. Ps. 19:7). Strangely, Wendel looks askance at this exposition of God's gracious law guiding believers. Unaccountably he writes, "It is here that the author of the *Institutes* has laid himself the most widely open to the reproach of legalism so often laid against him."[31] On the contrary, John Hesselink in his thorough study insists, "For Calvin, as we have seen, the law is a dynamic entity primarily expressive of the gracious will of God for the benefit of his people." Hesselink focuses primarily on the third use of the law but provides a fine discussion of natural law and conscience.[32] In addition, he affirms the centrality of Christ in the covenant of grace

[30] Luther clearly explicated two uses of the law, but Calvin and Melanchthon employed three. Gerhard Ebeling's "On the Doctrine of the *Triplex Usus Legis* in the Theology of the Reformation," in *Word and Faith*, trans. James W. Leitch (Philadelphia: Fortress Press, 1963), 62–78, deals only with Luther and Melanchthon.

[31] François Wendel, *Calvin: The Origins and Development of His Religious Thought*, trans. Philip Mairet (New York: Harper and Row, 1963), 200.

[32] In her chap. 4 Susan Schreiner also treats natural law and conscience in connection with the vestiges of the image of God remaining after the fall and their role in society. Especially valuable is the historical review of natural law and the conclusion, "Calvin was not interested in natural law in and of itself. He did not develop a 'theology of natural law' but rather, used the principle of natural law as an extension of his doctrine of providence" (*The Theatre of His Glory: Nature and the Natural Order in the Thought of John Calvin* [Durham, NC: Labyrinth Press, 1991], 94).

and denies the so-called covenant of works. "There is, moreover, ultimately only one covenant and that covenant is the covenant of grace. In this regard, there is an important difference between Calvin and later Reformed theology which also taught a covenant of works."[33]

One of the most warmly debated topics in theology generally and in Calvin studies particularly is the doctrine of natural law.[34] The subject is framed in large measure by the Stoic confidence in nature as guide. Another part of the problem in Calvin is discerning the precise meaning and distinction between created and fallen nature. Calvin equates the natural law and the moral law when he asserts, "The Lord has provided us with a written law to give us a clearer witness of what was too obscure in the natural law" (II.8.2). Since the inward or natural law is the same as the moral law, Calvin devotes one of his longest expositions to the Ten Commandments. The goal of the law is to mold human life to outward honesty and to inward righteousness (II.8.6). "Whatever he requires of us … we must obey out of natural obligation. But what we cannot do is our own fault. If our lust in which sin reigns so holds us bound that we are not free to obey our

[33] I. John Hesselink, *Calvin's Concept of the Law* (Allison Park, PA: Pickwick Publications, 1992), 277, 88. Hesselink concludes his study by quoting Calvin to the effect that we must set reason aside and submit to the Holy Spirit in order to hear Christ living and reigning in us (III.7.1). This summary includes the correct observation, "The law is not the gospel, but it serves the gospel; it is an indispensible part of the gospel." And this puzzling one: "In a sense, [the law] is prior to and more comprehensive than the gospel, for it was the mode of God's relationship to humanity prior to and apart from sin" (285). In two overlapping essays, "Calvin's Doctrine of the Covenant of Grace," *Reformed Review* 15, no. 4 (May 1962): 1–12, and "The Covenant of Grace in Calvin's Teaching," in *Calvin Theological Journal* 2, no. 2 (November 1967): 133–61, Anthony A. Hoekema agrees with Hesselink that Calvin does not teach the covenant of works directly but thinks "the spiritual truths underlying this doctrine are found in Calvin." Disagreeing with Perry Miller's conclusions about the covenant of grace in Calvin and Calvinism, Hoekema insists "Calvin was as much concerned about the responsibility of man as about the sovereignty of God" (134). Hoekema judges that the covenant is unilateral in origin but bilateral in fulfillment. "The covenant of grace has its origin wholly in the undeserved grace of God, but, when once established, that covenant imposes mutual obligations on both God and man" (140). This affirmation of "mutual obligations" and the view of God's promises as conditional undervalues the reality of union with Christ, the unconditional gift of grace, and the work of the Holy Spirit in the Christian life.

[34] In his classic survey of political theory George H. Sabine devotes three chapters to natural law but does not discuss the subject in connection with the early Protestant Reformers. Hugo Grotius gave this definition of natural law: "The law of nature is a dictate of right reason, which points out that an act, according as it is or is not in conformity with rational nature, has in it a quality of moral baseness or moral necessity; and that in consequence, such an act is either forbidden or enjoined by the author of nature, God" (George H. Sabine, *A History of Political Theory*, 3rd ed. [New York: Holt, Rinehart and Winston, 1961], 424). Even though Grotius himself appeals to God, in the seventeenth century naturalism and rationalism begin to detach from theology. See the excursus for remarks on "right reason." See also Kai Nielsen, "The Myth of Natural Law," *Law and Philosophy*, ed. Sidney Hook (New York: New York University Press, 1964), 122–43.

Father, there is no reason why we should claim necessity as a defense, for the evil of that necessity is both within us and to be imputed to us" (II.8.2).

Josef Bohatec's magisterial study *Calvin und das Recht* was published in 1934 as Adolf Hitler was coming to power in Germany.[35] Additionally, Karl Barth and Emil Brunner were debating the broad topic of natural theology and the narrower topic of natural law within it, as previously discussed. Among the conclusions now to be drawn is that the political situation in the Third Reich and the theological responses to it overrode the clear evidence of Calvin's text. For example, Arthur Cochrane expresses his allegiance to Barth's view of natural law[36] but admits the force of McNeill's criticism to this effect: "The assumption of some contemporary theologians that natural law has no place in the company of Reformation theology cannot be allowed to govern historical inquiry or to lead us to ignore, minimize, or evacuate of reality, the positive utterances on natural law scattered through the works of the Reformers."[37]

Returning to the topic a couple of years after Cochrane, David Little offers both an unsatisfactory compliment and analysis. Calvin is praised for not overdoing his natural law theory but also for not rejecting or neglecting the idea altogether. Little's interest appears to be not so much in Calvin as on prospects for natural law theory among Christians, which he thinks will require (1) empirical generalizations about human nature applied cross-culturally and historically, (2) movement from these generalizations to behavioral prescriptions, (3) an understanding of the moral reliability of human nature corrupted by sin, and (4) a relation between natural moral obligation and Christian moral obligation.[38]

Following his exposition of the three uses of the law, Calvin discusses its two results. He declares, "In our discussion of the knowledge of ourselves we have set forth this chief point: that empty of all opinion of our own virtue, and shorn of all assurance of our own righteousness . . . we may learn [(1)] genuine humility and [(2)] self-abasement. Both of these the Lord accomplishes in his law" (II.8.1). Calvin's strong conviction about the need for humility before God and his abhorrence of pride is clear, but this summary of the law in two results

---

[35] Josef Bohatec, *Calvin und das Recht* (Feudigen: Buchdruckereri u. Verlagsanstalt, 1934).
[36] Arthur C. Cochrane, "Natural Law in the Teachings of John Calvin," *Church-State Relatons in Ecumenical Perspective*, ed. Elwyn A. Smith (Louvain: Duquesne University Press, 1966), 180.
[37] McNeill, "Natural Law," 168.
[38] David Little, "Calvin and the Prospects for a Christian Theory of Natural Law," in *Norm and Context in Christian Ethics* ed. Gene H. Outka and Paul Ramsey (New York: Charles Scribner's Sons, 1968), 175–97.

appears to be only one. That is, humility and self-abasement seem to be two names for the same virtue.

In the final edition of the *Institutes*, Calvin added a chapter affirming again that while Christ was known to the Jews under the Law, he was clearly revealed only in the gospel (II.9). This chapter emphasizes further the role of both law and gospel in pointing to Christ. Calvin also expresses a wide hope for God's ancient chosen people. John's statement, "'No one has ever seen God; the only begotten Son, who is in the bosom of the Father, has made him known' [John 1:18] does not exclude the pious who died before Christ from the fellowship of the understanding and light that shine in the person of Christ" (II.9.1). Calvin declares that "the word 'gospel,' taken in the broad sense, includes those testimonies of his mercy and fatherly favor which God gave to the patriarchs of old" (II.9.2).

The chief and often-neglected subject of Calvin's discussion of law and gospel in Book II is Jesus Christ. The point Calvin makes is that Christ is the content of both law and gospel but in different ways. Christ is revealed as promise in the law and as fulfillment in the gospel. However, even in Christ's fulfillment there remains a promise. While Christ has entirely accomplished our salvation, "the enjoyment thereof ever lies hidden under the guardianship of hope, until, having put off corruptible flesh, we be transfigured in the glory of him who goes before us" (II.9.3). On this "already" and "not yet," Calvin comments, "These two things agree rather well with each other: we possess in Christ all that pertains to the perfection of heavenly life, and yet faith is the vision of good things not seen" (II.9.3).

C. The Person of Christ

The full title of Book II is "The Knowledge of God the Redeemer in Christ, First Disclosed to the Fathers under the Law and Then to us in the Gospel." After the bracketed five chapters on sin, Calvin begins his Christology proper with an explication of the revelation of Christ in the gospel and the law, as we have just seen. In the present section Calvin expounds the doctrine of Christ with the more traditional topics of the person (II.12–13) and work (II.14) of Christ. In the former Calvin affirms the orthodox Chalcedonian doctrine that Christ is one person in two natures. In the second Calvin explains the three offices of Christ: the prophetic, the kingly, and the priestly. These two sections represent the usual distinction between the person and work of Christ. The former is a more static reflection on Christ's being—who Christ is. The latter is a more dynamic reflection on Christ's ministry—what Christ accomplishes. This distinction is only for convenience in teaching. As Jansen observes, "Christian theology must ever insist that Jesus' person and work interpret each other in indissoluble unity."[39] The interpretative problem is that the orthodox formula of "one person and two natures" is an intractable mystery, and as it is impossible to imagine that Christ's personal being can be explained with precision, so it is impossible to think his personal action can be explained adequately within human categories. This mystery leads to reflection on Calvin's doctrine of accommodation usually considered in connection with Scripture, but even more pertinent to Christology.

In the introduction to his recent book on Calvin's Christology, Stephen Edmondson necessarily notes and predictably claims that all previous studies of this topic are incomplete.[40] He then declares, "For Calvin, Christ's person and office are two sides of the same coin, so that, just as we must understand Christ's person functionally, so, too, must we understand his office personally. That is what it means to say that Christ is the Mediator: it is to tie person and office inextricably together."[41] Nevertheless, Edmondson in making a distinction between the substantial self and the functional self tilts toward emphasizing work over person, asserting, "The central pattern of Calvin's Christology [is] that Christ mediates the covenant in history through the threefold office of priest, king and prophet."[42] His interpretation insists the office of mediator is the center of Calvin's Christology because Calvin privileges Christ's work over his person.[43] Being mediator seems a function of the person rather than a function attached to a person. The key to understanding is that things "which apply to the office of the mediator are not spoken simply either of the divine nature or of the human." Nevertheless, Christ's mediatorial functions requiring his human nature were exerted *before* the incarnation (II.14.3). Commenting on Hosea 12:4, Calvin writes, "Christ, the eternal wisdom of God, did put on the character of a mediator, before he put on our flesh. He was therefore then a mediator and in that capacity he was also an angel. He was at the same time Jehovah, who is now God manifested in the flesh" (see also Com. Zech. 1:18). Calvin believes Christ's divinity was silent

---

[39] John Jansen, *Calvin's Doctrine of the Work of Christ* (London: J. Clark, 1956), 13.
[40] Stephen Edmondson, *Calvin's Christology* (Cambridge: Cambridge University Press, 2004), 3.
[41] Ibid.
[42] Ibid., 41. Jill Raitt, "Calvin's Use of Persona," in *Calvinus Ecclesiae Genevensis Custos*, ed. Wilhelm H. Neuser (New York: Verlag Peter Lang, 1984), employs three broad categories: person as office, person as "somebody," and person in reference to Trinity. Nevertheless, she asserts their inaccuracy because Calvin never used the word "person" to refer to a static mode of being. "Rather than begin with ontology and proceed to derived activity, Calvin preferred to begin with activity and proceed to the relations such activity indicated" (286).
[43] Edmondson writes, "I take as the center of Calvin's Christology his repeated titular definition in the 1559 *Institutes* of Christ as the Mediator and articulate the form and content of Calvin's teaching around this central focus. . . . A variety of implications are entailed by Calvin's choice of this central moniker for Christ [including that for] Calvin, a focus on Christ as Mediator makes the doctrine of Christ's office in its relation to Christ's work the fundamental organizing principle in his Christology" (*Calvin's Christology*, 5).

"whenever it was the business of the human nature to act alone in its own terms in fulfillment of the office of mediator" (Com. Mt. 24:36). Moreover, Jesus' growth in wisdom and God's favor refers to his human nature (Com. Lk. 2:40) as does his manifestation in the form of a servant (Com. Phil. 2:7). In this emphasis Calvin follows Augustine and Thomas (*ST* III.26.2), who assert that Christ is mediator as he is a human being. Augustine declares that God having become a partaker of our humanity affords us access to participation in his divinity (*City of God* 9:15).

Edmondson's emphasis on the work of the Mediator raises two immediate questions. First, does the strong focus on the role of Mediator, which is presumably prior to sin, lead inevitably to some diminution of the role of Redeemer, which is responsive to sin? After all, Redeemer is the term employed in the title of Book II. Second, and of potentially surpassing seriousness, to privilege Christ's work over his person can lead to an instrumental Christology in which Christ's work of salvation replaces his person as mediator and savior. This dangerous view was held by Friedrich Schleiermacher in the nineteenth century and John Hick in the twentieth. Surely union in Christ is not to be understood as union with Christ's work. In any case, Calvin exposits person before work. Edmondson affirms person this way: "Though our primary interest may be in what Christ has done for us, we cannot properly conceive of this activity if we do not also understand who Christ is."[44] At the same time he insists, "[Calvin's] Christology turns not on questions of who Jesus was, but rather around the axes of what Christ has done to save."[45] A more felicitous expression of the relation between person and work and the roles of Mediator and Redeemer is offered by David Willis, who asserts Calvin uses the word "Mediator" in a twofold sense, identifying "the Redeeming Mediator in the flesh with the Mediator who is the Eternal Son of God."[46] In other words, God the Mediator is apprehended in God the Redeemer (I.2.1). The person-and-work sequence need not be crucial for interpretation, but it can be. For example, in his 1927 book, *The Mediator*,[47] Emil Brunner employed the more traditional pattern of treating person, then work. In volume 2 of his 1949 Dogmatics, Brunner treats first the work of Christ and then his person.[48] Beginning with the work of Christ can improperly focus on the benefits of

[44] Ibid., 88.
[45] Ibid., 42.
[46] Willis, *Calvin's Catholic Christology, The Function of the So-called Extra Calvinisticum in Calvin's Theology* (Leiden: E. J. Brill, 1966), 99.
[47] Emil Brunner, *The Mediator: A Study of the Central Doctrine of the Christian Faith*, translated by Olive Wyon (New York: The Macmillan Company, 1934).
[48] Emil Brunner, *The Christian Doctrine of Creation and Redemption*, trans. Olive Wyon (Philadelphia: Westminster Press, 1952).

Christ to the neglect of his person, indicating interest selfishly concentrated on what Christ does for us without properly reverent attention to Christ in himself.[49]

The Protestant Reformers did not set out to reform the doctrine of Christ *as such*; they reaffirmed the christological decisions of the patristic period. Wendel is correct that "[Calvin] adopts in full the dogma of the two natures of Christ and the current explanations of the relation between the two natures."[50] The doctrine of "Scripture alone" did not imply the rejection of the historical development of doctrine (the Trinity, the two natures of Christ, etc.) because the Reformers believed that these developments faithfully served the truth of Scripture. In this essential way the Reformers accepted "tradition." The topics cannot be finally separated, but the primary focus of the Protestant Reformation was soteriological rather than christological. The question was not "Who is Jesus Christ?" because this question was regarded as correctly answered in the patristic period. The question was, "How does he save us?"

Calvin affirms Jesus Christ is both fully God, fully a man, and entirely one person. Each of these assertions is an ineffable mystery but altogether a necessary confession of the Lordship of Christ. In explanation of this confession Calvin rejects the overemphasis of Christ's divinity expounded by Andreas Osiander (discussed in the section on justification) as well as the overemphasis on Christ's humanity of Francesco Stancaro. "Stancarism," as Joseph Tylenda points out, "was neither a system of theology nor a new confession of faith, but a single idea." Accepting the Father, Son, and Holy Spirit as "the only one and true God, of one essence, of one will and of one operation," Stancaro concluded that our Lord Jesus Christ, true God and true man, is mediator according to his humanity alone. To the contrary Calvin insisted Christ is the Son of God in respect to both natures and therefore mediator in both natures.[51]

Although he affirms traditional Chalcedonian orthodoxy, Calvin's exposition of the person and natures of Christ is probably the most difficult part of the *Institutes* to understand and evaluate in terms of the text itself because so much depends on Calvin's emphases, which, in turn, involve what he does not say and in relation to views he does not discuss. In other words, understanding what Calvin is affirming requires knowing what he is tacitly denying. The three

---

[49] See Barth's note criticizing Melanchthon on the benefits of Christ (*CD* 1.1.28, 259).
[50] Wendel, *Calvin, the Origins and Development*, 215.
[51] See the two articles by Joseph Tylenda, "Christ the Mediator: Calvin versus Stancaro," *Calvin Theological Journal* 8, no. 1 (April 1973): 5; and "The Controversy on Christ the Mediator: Calvin's Second Reply to Stancaro," *Calvin Theological Journal* 8, no. 2 (November 1973): 137.

most notable features of Calvin's Christology are first the brevity of his discussion of the Trinity, including the doctrine of incarnation. The second is Calvin's emphasis on the continuing integrity of Christ's human nature. The third is the problem of accommodation. While Calvin affirms the orthodox one-person-in-two-natures formulation of Chalcedon, his emphasis on the humanity of Christ is remarkable. A crucial part of this doctrine of the humanity of Christ is expounded in Book IV in the chapter on the Eucharist. The result is that although both Luther and Calvin affirmed the orthodox doctrine, their different emphases led to fierce controversies over Christology.

These disagreements became obvious when Joachim Westphal attacked the Zurich Consensus, which Calvin and Bullinger had worked out. Calvin replied to Westphal in three treatises and then gave up continuation of the debate as unprofitable. According to Wendel, "Calvin and Westphal helped to envenom the controversy by the way they conducted it [but it was their] enthusiastic and often blundering allies who gave the lamentable quarrel its vast extension and its irresoluble character."[52] The lasting result of the debate appears in Article VIII of the Lutheran Formula of Concord (1577), which mentions the Eucharistic controversy between "the sincere theologians of the Augsburg Confession and the Calvinists, who had, moreover, perturbed other theologians." This controversy extends to the person of Christ and differing positions on the subtleties of the communication of attributes, which involves the proper understanding of the relation between Christ's human and divine natures. The *Concordia* charges Calvinists with a defective view of the hypostatic union, teaching "the combination that takes place when two boards are glued together, where neither confers any thing on the other nor receives any thing from the other." According to the Lutherans, the proper union and communion of the two natures can be illustrated by the similitude of a blade glowing in a fire. Such a knife will both cut and burn. According to Calvin there is an irreducible duality between Christ's divinity and humanity. Thus, "We hold that Christ, as he is God and man, consists of two natures united but not mingled" (II.14.4). Again, Calvin writes, "For we affirm his divinity so joined and united with his humanity that each retains its distinctive nature unimpaired, and yet these two natures constitute one Christ" (II.14.1). Rejecting both the metaphors of the two boards and the fiery blade, Calvin substitutes our two eyes. Our left and right eyes are each real and each visionary, but they are not the same. Nevertheless, almost always they bring to us a single sight (Sermon on I Tim. 3:16; *CO* 53:326).[53]

---

[52] Wendel, Calvin, *The Origins and Development*, 104.
[53] The christological debate between Lutherans and Calvinists continues today. The subjects of "ubiquity" and "local presence" are more fully considered in Book IV as part of the Supper Strife.

In sum, Lutheran theology sees an unacceptable duality in Calvinistic Christology; Calvinistic theology sees an unacceptable unity in Lutheran Christology.[54] Since acceptable Christology maintains the unity of person and the duality of natures, the fine tuning of the distinctions is more confessional than analytic. Edmondson asserts, "The *communicatio idiomatum*, in other words, is a means to express Christ's unity, not to explain it."[55] In his fine study of this doctrine, Willis writes that Calvin's discussion of the communication of attributes indicates "Calvin's awe before the mystery and his distaste for speculation set limits to his inquiry into what, in retrospect, may be called the ontological foundation of the Incarnation." Willis concludes, "For Calvin, the *communicatio idiomatum* is primarily a hermeneutical tool to keep in balance the varied Scriptural witness to the One Person, but it rests upon and presupposes the hypostatic union."[56]

The present reflection on Calvin's view of the person of Christ is treated under three headings: (a) the Eternal and Incarnate Son, (b) the One Person and Two Natures, and (c) the Body and the Head. However, before proceeding, a note on language is necessary.

Prior to the widespread adoption of inclusive language, the phrase "fully God and fully man" was the traditional expression of christological doctrine. It was then assumed that the term "man" did not exclude women. This view has recently changed.[57] However, the older language had a theological advantage in that the word "man" is usefully ambiguous referring both (1) to mankind in general (or humankind as some now prefer) and (2) to a specific human being. The newer language affirming Jesus Christ as fully divine and fully human (or God-human) can be theologically confusing, if not heretical. Concerning the manhood, Jesus Christ is, of course, to be understood in full identity with general humanity, but he was also a single and real person. Replacing "man" with the term "human," whatever its contemporary linguistic comfort value to some

---

[54] In discussing this mystery Joseph N. Tylenda, "Calvin's Understanding of the Communication of Properties," *Westminster Theological Journal* (Fall 1975), concludes, "For Calvin, an attribute of one nature is *assigned* to the person of Christ, though designated by his other nature; for Luther the attribute of one nature is *granted* to the other nature" (64–65, emphasis added).

[55] Edmondson, *Calvin's Christology*, 216. Edmondson offers a helpful short summary of this doctrine (214) which is the subject of Willis's important study.

[56] Willis, *Calvin's Catholic Christology*, 67.

[57] See Brian Wren, *What Language Shall I Borrow? God-Talk in Worship: A Male Response to Feminist Theology* (New York: Crossroad, 1989). I learned a great deal about my own unexamined assumptions from Ursula K. LeGuin, *The Left Hand of Darkness* (New York: Ace Books, 1969). Her Gethenians do not see each other as male or female. They may choose to be either and during their lifetime both. When the mother of several children may be the father of several more, my comfortable categories collapse.

and awkwardness to others, is theologically inferior because it does not prevent a purely symbolic or idealistic understanding of Christ's humanity. In other words, in the new linguistic situation the humanity of Christ can be understood as pointing to an ideal example rather than a real individual.

Concerning the Godhead, the orthodox view insists Jesus Christ is not divine in the adjectival sense that he is *like* God, rather in the substantial sense he is the *same* as God or equal to God. Even the noun phrase "the divinity of Christ" can be understood to refer to Christ's likeness to God rather than his equality with God (Phil. 2:6). A more accurate term is the Deity of Christ, but to declare either Jesus Christ is fully deity and fully human in one person or fully deity and fully a human in one person is still stilted for some and can be misleading. For some English speakers the noun "deity" is not yet clearly parallel to the adjective "human," although "human" is now used often as a noun replacing "man," and will doubtless in time, if not already, connote both humanity in general and a single human being. The point is the orthodox formula confesses the full Deity of Jesus Christ and the full humanity of Jesus Christ, the latter meaning that he was a single real human being and that he represented all human beings when he took the sins of the world upon himself. ■

Sermon

In-Between Places

by Janice Smith Ammon

Genesis 28:10–17

Janice Smith Ammon is the Bryant M. Kirkland Minister of the Chapel of the Princeton Theological Seminary. She preached this sermon on February 1, 2008, in Miller Chapel. Following the sermon, the congregation was led by Martin Tel, C. F. Seabrook Director of Music, Princeton Theological Seminary, in the singing of the hymn "Sometimes a Light Surprises," which is reprinted below.

When I first met my husband, Greg, now sixteen years ago, there was only one trip that he asked we take. And that was a trip to Wyoming, to Yellowstone National Park, in the wintertime. For you see, Greg worked at Yellowstone Park one summer many years before we met, and he always wanted to go back in the winter season. Matter of fact, we talked about this trip for many years, until December of 2001. The week after Christmas, we traveled with our dear friends to Wyoming. We then spent three glorious days, traveling with a guide, over 250 miles through Yellowstone National Park on snowmobiles! Perhaps some of you did not expect this side of your Minister of the Chapel!

Now, let me say that before we went on our trip, I was certain that Yellowstone Park would be beautiful. For I had seen photographs, and I had heard others speak of the magnificent scenery. But what I did not expect was that not only was Yellowstone Park beautiful, but, somehow, I found it to be sacred—to be holy. It's hard for me to even capture this in words, but as we rode over the glorious mountains and through never-ending stretches of meadows—covered with snow, scattered with bison and coyotes and eagles—I felt the deep, profound presence of our Creator God in an unexpected way. I will even confess to you that as we rode along, I often found myself singing hymns out loud—"For the Beauty of the

DOI: 10.3754/1937–8386.2008.29.1.12

Earth," "Great Is Thy Faithfulness," "How Great Thou Art." (A good thing about snowmobiles for my traveling companions is that you can indeed sing at the top of your lungs without being heard!)

Have you ever had an experience like this? An experience of a place becoming a sacred place? An experience of a place becoming a holy place? For that is what happened to me in Yellowstone. And that is what happened to Jacob in our scripture passage for this morning. For here, Jacob encounters God at an unexpected time, at an unexpected place in his life. At this point in our story, Jacob was not exactly a model of faith like his forebears, Abraham and Isaac. Actually, the words that commentators use to describe him are words such as schemer, scoundrel, liar, and cheat, especially when it comes to his older twin brother, Esau, whom he had just tricked out of his birthright.

So this is the Jacob we encounter in our scripture passage for this morning, a man on the run from the wrath of his own brother, who is out to kill him. There had been little time to plan. Jacob departed in haste to save his hide. And as we read in our passage, "He came to a certain place and stayed there for the night." It was not any particular place. It just happened to be where Jacob was when the sun went down. An in-between place. Walter Brueggemann calls it a "non-place." It is here—in this in-between place, in this non-place—that Jacob stops, takes a stone, and puts it under his head to sleep for the night.

It is fascinating to me that the writer of Genesis tells us that he puts a stone under his head for the night. It is fascinating and revealing. For have you ever been camping and tried to sleep on a stone? Or, perhaps even more familiar, have you ever tried to sleep at night with a stone in your soul? I imagine, that night, Jacob felt the weight of a lot of stones in his soul—fear, jealousy, remorse, resentment, alienation, isolation. Stones in his soul.

What are the stones in your soul these days? What weighs you down? What keeps you up at night or what wakes you up early in the morning? Is it preparing for new classes? Sending out dossiers? Sending in applications? Waiting for interviews? Or perhaps a relationship is strained. Your heart is broken. Your heart is lonely. Do you yearn for loved ones who live far away? Are there loved ones who are ill? Or loved ones you have lost? Are there financial pressures? Is it the turmoil in so many of our neighborhoods, in our country, and around our globe? Stones in our souls. Well, friends, the good news is that like Jacob, when we are in the most difficult places—when the weight of life feels the most unbearable—when seminary begins to feel like an in-between place, an uncertain place—it is then that we often find that God breaks in with promises and hope.

Indeed, God breaks into Jacob's life at this unexpected time, in this in-between place, with a dream. A dream where the Lord, the God of Abraham and Isaac, comes and stands right beside Jacob and promises land and offspring. More than that, God promises to be with Jacob wherever he goes. God promises to keep him and bring him back to this land.

When Jacob awoke from his dream, he took the stone that was under his head, turned it up on its end as a pillar, and poured oil on it. Through God's transforming presence, God can take the stones in our souls and transform them into something holy and whole—even at unexpected times and in in-between places of our lives.

You know, there was something else holy that happened while I was in Yellowstone Park that winter. And actually, I did not even realize it until after I returned home. A week or so after we were back, I said to my husband, "My spirit feels so much lighter." If you recall, the fall season of 2001 brought much sadness and sorrow as we dealt with September 11, 2001, and its aftermath, especially in Manhattan, where we were living and where I was serving at the time. Many of us lost loved ones, colleagues, and friends that day. Many of us saw horrific events unfold before our eyes. Many of us lost our feeling of safety and security. And as I led funerals and services and prayers over the next months, I had gathered more stones in my soul than I ever realized.

But there was something about being in Yellowstone. It was so big. It was so vast. It was a place where I could leave behind some of the September stones of my soul. As my wise husband put it, "You could leave them at the altar of Yellowstone." You know, what was so amazing to me about this was that it was something that just *happened*. It was not intentional on my part—perhaps like Jacob's dream—though I should have been suspicious when I found myself singing "For the Beauty of the Earth," "Great Is Thy Faithfulness," "How Great Thou Art." Surely the Lord was in this place and I did not know it.

May we, like Jacob, be able to say this in all the places and in all the in-between places of our lives. Amen!

Sometimes a Light Surprises

Known to biographers as "mad Cowper," William Cowper (1731–1800) is now regarded as one of the finest early Romantic poets. Cowper suffered from severe bouts of depression and spent long periods in asylum. His best-known hymn, "God Moves in a Mysterious Way," demonstrated well the somber and foreboding tone of many of his texts. This text suggests that the ability to sing a song is truly a gift from God. The singing of a song is often a first sign of healing and hope. — *Martin Tel, C. F. Seabrook Director of Music, Princeton Theological Seminary* ■

Sometimes a Light Surprises

William Cowper, 1779

Rutherford

Chrétien Urhan, 1834

History

A Skirmish in the Early Reception of Karl Barth in Scotland: The Exchange between Thomas F. Torrance and Brand Blanshard

edited by Iain R. and Morag Torrance

Thomas F. Torrance served for twenty-seven years as Professor of Christian Dogmatics at New College in the University of Edinburgh. A student of Karl Barth when he attended the University of Basel, he was especially known for his work on theological method and the relationship between theology and science. He was Moderator of the General Assembly of the Church of Scotland from 1976 to 1977 and was awarded the Templeton Prize in 1978. He died on December 2, 2007. Brand Blanshard, an American philosopher of the rationalist school, was influenced by British idealism and known for his defense of reason and for the quality of his writings. He received his doctorate from Harvard University and taught at Swarthmore University and at Yale University, where he served for many years as chairman of the Department of Philosophy.

Iain R. Torrance, the son of Thomas F. Torrance, is President and Professor of Patristics at Princeton Theological Seminary and previously served as Dean of the Faculty of Arts and Divinity at Aberdeen University. He has been coeditor of The Scottish Journal of Theology *since 1982 and coedited, with Bryan Spinks,* To Glorify God: Essays on Modern Reform Liturgy (1999) *and the* Oxford Handbook of Systematic Theology (2007) *with John Webster and Kathryn Tanner. Morag Torrance, President Torrance's wife, was formerly manager of the information technology training unit at the University of Aberdeen. A graduate of St. Andrews in French and psychology, she held tenured positions in computing administration at the universities of Edinburgh and Aberdeen.*

The name of Brand Blanshard may not be as familiar today as it once was. Blanshard was one of the greatest American philosophers of the first half of the twentieth century. Born in Fredericksburg, Ohio, in August 1892, Blanshard was the son of a Congregational minister. He studied first at the University of

DOI:10.3754/1937–8386.2008.29.1.13

Michigan and then won a Rhodes Scholarship to study at Oxford, where he was taught by H. W. B. Joseph and met F. H. Bradley and T. S. Eliot. He gained a doctorate at Harvard and taught at Swarthmore College from 1925 to 1944 and then at Yale until he retired in 1961. He died in 1987. Blanshard is often regarded as the last of the great "absolute idealists," and his study *The Nature of Thought*[1] was recommended to the second-year class in logic and metaphysics at the University of Edinburgh in the 1960s when the set text was F. H. Bradley's *The Principles of Logic*. In 1952, Blanshard delivered the Gifford Lectures at the University of St. Andrews in Scotland.

The Scottish daily newspaper *The Scotsman* reported on the Gifford Lectures and ran a short article noting that Blanshard had indulged in a swipe against Karl Barth. This was too much for Thomas F. Torrance, then Professor of Christian Dogmatics at the University of Edinburgh, to swallow without a response. A theological argument followed, which *The Scotsman* was kind enough to publish in full, day after day, throughout April 1952.[2]

The following is the initial report of Brand Blanshard's comments and then the exchange of letters.

> Professor Blanshard: Gifford Lectures at St. Andrews University.
> Report in *The Scotsman*, April 9, 1952.
>
> "Theology in Crisis"
> Professor Blanshard resumes
> Gifford Lectures

Professor Brand Blanshard, Yale University, resumed his series of Gifford Lectures at St. Andrews University last night with a statement and criticism of the new "theology of crisis." The leaders of the movement are the theologians, Karl Barth and Emil Brunner, both of whom have themselves delivered Gifford lectures in recent years, Barth at Aberdeen and Brunner at St. Andrews.

The new Theology, Professor Blanshard said, owed its attractiveness to its very bold strategy. Faith was not to be achieved by thought or any other sort of effort on our part; it was the result of a "divine encounter," a one-way transaction in which God Himself descended into the human spirit.

---

[1] Brand Blanshard, *The Nature of Thought*, 2 vols. (London: Allen & Unwin, 1939).

[2] In a letter dated December 10, 1991, *The Scotsman* granted me permission to reprint the letters in the context of an article. My father's death, on December 2, 2007, prompted me finally to do this, and I am grateful to my wife Morag (who always got on excellently with my father, one direct person to another), who did most of the work.

Because they were so sure that faith was beyond the reach of reason, Barth and Brunner accepted undisturbed the results of scientific criticism. They could admit that the Scripture was full of errors, and that in the long struggle of theology with science, science had been generally right. They could hold this because they believed that faith provided an insight of its own, different from that of reason, and above it. Unfortunately, when we tried to learn from them what it was that the insight disclosed, we got most unsatisfying answers. Barth and Brunner, like their master, Kierkegaard, reveled in paradoxes. Indeed, they represented God as being so completely "other" that He almost disappeared; we were supposed to believe things about Him that, by our standards, were self-contradictory and ascribe actions to Him that our moral sense could only regard as evil.

Professor Blanshard considered that this attempt to save religious faith by making it irrational was disastrous. The probable effect upon thoughtful men of asking that they believe the incredible would be the repudiation of faith altogether. If revelation occurred, it must come through our human faculties and share the strength and weakness of these faculties.

> "The Theology of Karl Barth." Correspondence between Professor T. F. Torrance of Edinburgh and Professor Brand Blanshard, Gifford Lecturer in St. Andrews University.
>
> Torrance—letter dated April 11, 1952. Published in *The Scotsman*, Edinburgh, April 14, page 4.
>
> Theology of Karl Barth
> New College, University of Edinburgh,
> April 11, 1952

Sir,—I have read with astonishment the account in your columns of the recent Gifford Lecture in St. Andrews, in which Professor Brand Blanshard is reported as describing the theology of Karl Barth and Emil Brunner as the "theology of crisis" and criticising it as "this attempt to save religious faith by making it irrational." It seems difficult to believe that a philosopher as great as Professor Blanshard should still perpetrate this antiquated blunder and be so plainly unaware of the writings of these Swiss theologians.

A more rational and responsible evaluation has recently been given by the Roman Catholic theologian, Hans Urs von Balthasar, who regards Karl Barth as the greatest protagonist of the Protestant Church and who pleads with the Roman Church to take their measure of him in the most serious way.

In his recent work, "Karl Barth, Deutung und Darstellung seiner Theologie," von Balthasar takes careful account of the development of Barth's theology, which falls into three main stages: 1. The early period reaching its climax with the first edition of his "Romans" in 1918 when he was still under the influence of the idealist philosophy: 2. the nineteen-twenties, which saw a thorough revision of his "Romans" and the first volume of his projected "Dogmatics," when Barth had come under the influence of Kierkegaard and his theology became dialectical and realist: 3. at the end of that decade, however, came the really decisive change when, in his study of Anselm, Barth swept aside the language of Kierkegaard and existentialism and emerged, as he said, out of his egg-shells.

Ever since then the theology of Barth has been the theology of analogy in which Christology plays the dominant rôle. It is more than thirty years ago since that important change took place, and all the enormous volumes of his "Kirchliche Dogmatik" have been published since then. These are the volumes in which Barth has taken issue in the most massive way with the theology of Rome, and from which von Balthasar has admittedly learned so much. It is a pitiful tragedy, however, that the American philosopher has not apparently peered beyond the egg-shells of the young Swiss thinker!

One would like to recommend Professor Blanshard at least to read Karl Barth's study of Anselm, "Fides Quaerens Intellectum," published in 1931. In that little volume we are given a clear account of Professor Barth's teaching about the relation between faith and reason which informs the whole of his dogmatic theology. There Barth holds to the basic point that reason is unconditionally bound to its object and determined by it, and that the nature of the object must prescribe the specific mode of the activity of reason. Faith is this reason directed to the knowledge of God, and involves a rational apprehension which answers appropriately to the object given. Here the object is unique and incomparable. What is expected of theology, therefore, is that it should exhibit the kind of rationality which corresponds with this unique object of thought. This is, in fact, the rational objectivity which characterises faith, and which utterly repudiates that *salto mortale*, the sacrifice of the intellect.

That the Gifford lecturer should attribute to Karl Barth a view which all his writings for thirty years have resolutely opposed is particularly surprising to-day when Barth stands out in Europe as the great protagonist against irrationalism, and against existentialism which, particularly in the hands of a new school of interpreters, headed by Professor Rudolf Bultmann, of Marburg, is producing a radical reinterpretation of the Bible that we can only regard as a menace to the Christian Gospel.—I am etc. (Professor) T. F. Torrance

Blanshard—letter dated April 14, 1952. Published in *The Scotsman*, April 16, page 6.

Theology of Karl Barth
The University of St. Andrews,
April 14, 1952

Sir,—Professor Torrance has expressed "astonishment" that in one of my Gifford lectures at St. Andrews I should have described the theology of Karl Barth and Emil Brunner as an irrationalist theology. His astonishment can hardly be greater than mine when I find this description denied.

The best way, of course, is to go to the writings of these men and read their own words. Let me cite a few of them. First a few from various books by Brunner: "Revealed knowledge is poles apart from rational knowledge. These two forms of knowledge are as far apart as heaven is from hell." "Biblical and natural theology will never agree: they are bitterly and fundamentally opposed." ("Revelation and Reason." 16, 65.) "The theological problem as well as the Church problem is this — to deliver modern man and the modernised Church from the illegitimate self-sufficiency of reason . . ." ("The Word and the World." 126.) "Of the truth of God it must ever be said, since it is God's truth, that it is foolishness unto human reason." "This pride, this claim of reason to be the court of last appeal, the superior judge of truth, constitutes sin: it is the heart of sin." ("Theology of Crisis." 43.) Incidentally, Professor Torrance expresses surprise that I should have referred to this school as "the theology of crisis"; the phrase is Brunner's own description, and the title of one of his books. Such expressions as the above could be multiplied many times from Brunner's writings.

Barth is, if anything, more extreme than Brunner. He began his Gifford lectures by repudiating the very possibility of a rational knowledge of God through natural theology. "I certainly see—with astonishment—that such a science as Lord Gifford has in mind does exist, but I do not see how it is possible for it to exist. I am convinced that so far as it has existed, and still exists, it owes its existence to a radical error … it cannot really be the business of a Reformed theologian to raise so much as his little finger to support this undertaking in any positive way" (5–6.) Again, "It is forced down my throat that the Dogmatic theologian is under the obligation to 'justify' himself in his utterances before philosophy. To that my answer is likewise 'No.' … Dogmatics runs counter to every philosophy, no matter what form it may have assumed.… our activities of thinking and speaking … cannot possibly coincide with the truth of God …" ("Credo," 185–86). Professor Torrance will recall that Barth's famous break with Brunner was largely on the ground that Brunner had shown a weakness for natural theology, while he, Barth, thought it should be treated with contempt and scorn. "If you really reject natural theology, you don't stand and stare at the snake while you let it stare you down in return, hypnotise you, and then bite you: when you see it, you take a stick to it and kill it." ("*Nein! Antwart an Brunner*," 13; my translation.)

If statements like this do not justify calling a man an anti-rationalist, it is hard to conceive what would. Professor Torrance suggests that Barth's anti-rationalism belongs to an earlier stage that he has long out-grown, and refers to a work of 1931 as giving his mature opinion. But every quotation I have made from him is subsequent to that date.

When Professor Torrance describes Barth as a defender of reason, he can only be using "reason" with a special meaning and a very different meaning from that of the philosophers. He thinks it enough if he shows that faith for Barth "involves a rational apprehension which answers approximately to the object given." But what if "the object given"—namely, God—is taken as "the absolutely other," which defies all the categories of natural reason? To "answer appropriately" to such an object, reason, as we know it, must simply die and be born again as something else. If one claims to believe in reason, it should surely mean the reason used in commonsense and science, for example, the science of natural theology. Barth maintains that God stands over against such reason as utterly and hopelessly impenetrable. That, to me and, I think, to most philosophers, is what irrationalism means.—I am etc. Brand Blanshard

Greenfield—letter dated April 16, 1952. Published in *The Scotsman*, April 18, page 4.

Theology of Karl Barth
34 Warrender Park Terrace, Edinburgh.
April 16, 1952

Sir,—Kingsley asked on a memorable occasion, "What, then, does Father Newman mean?" The answer was the "Apologia." Barth's reply to such a question would certainly lack that clarity which we associate with the great cardinal, and therefore it is not perhaps surprising that Professor Blanshard and Professor Torrance should have understood him differently. They are not alone in that.

To the uninstructed, however, it may seem that the professors are arguing at cross purposes. Professor Blanshard appears to accuse Barth and his school of "irrationalism"; but by "irrationalism" he means only that Barth denies that a knowledge of God can be obtained by the reason used "in commonsense and science."

But if in this sense Barth is "irrational" he stands in good company. I can think at the moment of no considerable theologian who believed that the whole truth of God could be reached by reason. Even the English deists accepted revelation, and the distinction which St. Thomas Aquinas draws between natural and revealed religion is well known. Barth stands in the succession of all theologians, Reformed and Roman, in his assertion that salvation is of faith.

It is true that Barth in denying that there is any place for "natural religion" goes further than many theologians. Yet the comparative sterility of Gifford lectureships, of which complaint was recently made in your correspondence, seems to show that "commonsense" helps us little towards our knowledge of God. Indeed, all the work of the very distinguished thinkers who have lectured under this foundation amounts to nothing more than a prolegomenon to Christian theology.

We may go further and say that even the scientist and the philosopher, no less than the poet or the artist, are "irrational." As has been often pointed out, most of the greatest discoveries have been due to a *saltus fidei*.

It appears to all come down to a use of terms, and the question would rather appear to be, "Canst thou by searching find out God?"—I am etc. (Rev.) David W. Greenfield

Torrance—letter dated April 18, 1952. Published in *The Scotsman*, April, 19, page 6.

Theology of Karl Barth
New College, University of Edinburgh
April 18, 1952

Sir,—I should like to thank Professor Blanshard for taking the trouble, in the midst of his Gifford Lectures, to reply to my letter.

It is clear that his charge of antirationalism against the theology of Karl Barth involves a particular view of reason, but he cannot claim that it is a view generally accepted by philosophers to-day, by Professor MacKinnon or Professor Ryle, for example. There are, however, three distinct if inseparable issues which should be laid bare.

1. A philosophical issue between an idealist view of reason, and a realist and critical view. Philosophically, Karl Barth stands within the European tradition of critical philosophy, of which his brother Heinrich Barth, Professor of Metaphysics in the University of Basel, is perhaps the most distinguished representative on the Continent. With him Karl Barth is in profound agreement.

   But to come to this university, Professor John Macmurray, like Heinrich and Karl Barth, is concerned to point philosophy and theology away from a substantival to a functional view of reason, and when he says that "reason is the capacity to behave in terms of the nature of the object, that is to say, to behave objectively," he is using language almost identical with that of Karl Barth—and no one would surely wish to call Professor Macmurray an anti-rationalist!

   Against this view Professor Blanshard appears to think of reason as behaving in terms of its own nature, in terms of the categories of its own understanding. It is against that autonomous, self-sufficient reason, reason turned in upon itself, that the citations from Professor Emil Brunner given by Professor Blanshard are directed. That is, they are directed not against reason as such, but against a diseased "rationalism." Professor Karl Barth prefers to call this "heresy" (in the literal Greek sense of the word) as the self-willed reason that chooses to go its own way and refuses to be determined by its object. Far from being anti-rational, this is to champion reason against an irrational subjectivism.

   No doubt it is true, as Mr. Greenfield points out today, that Professor Blanshard and I are arguing at cross purposes, to a certain extent at any rate, though the very citations Professor Blanshard has made from both Barth and Brunner and the use he makes of them indicate a very superficial and indeed a mistaken reading of these theologians.

2. A scientific issue. It is surely an elementary principle of science that the nature of the object must prescribe the specific mode of the activity of reason, and that reason must answer appropriately to the object given. It would be utterly un-scientific and irrational, for example, to transpose into the study of living organisms the specific mode of rational activity that obtains in the study of physics and the particular categories that arise in that connection. That is why Karl Barth insists that the theologian must pursue his theological science without seeking to justify his undertaking before the bar of natural science or philosophy or the so-called natural reason for it would be quite unscientific and irrational in theological science, where we are concerned with God as the object of knowledge, for reason to behave either in terms of its own nature or in terms of some other object alien to that particular field of study.

   What theology demands, therefore, declares Karl Barth, is a ruthless scientific criticism of the activity of reason and of the reasoner himself to ensure that here in theological science he is behaving rationally, that is, that here his reason is conforming properly and obediently to the object given. All science, be it theology or physics, is characterised by humility and a readiness for the most ruthless self-criticism. That is precisely why Barth is so critical of rational activity in theology, in order to be as rational and responsible as possible.

   It is because Karl Barth has carried this ruthless, scientific criticism throughout the whole of his "Kirchliche Dogmatik" that scientists in other fields are showing such increasing interest in and understanding of his work, not least those in the natural sciences—see the letter by an American physicist from the University of Minnesota published in the "Kirchenblatt" (Basel), March 27.

3. A religious issue. The great difference between theological and natural science concerns the difference in the nature of the object. The object of theological knowledge is God infinite and eternal, "always Subject." As Barth puts it, not "the absolutely other" (a notion which Barth cast away many years ago), but the living God who gives Himself to us and reveals Himself in Jesus Christ, and summons us to obedient conformity to Him. In Christian theology, therefore, reason is summoned to behave in terms of Jesus Christ, or as the New Testament puts it, to conform to His image in love.

Here the ruthless criticism, mentioned above, is spoken of as self-denial and taking up of the Cross, and that ruthless criticism is directed toward the theologian and his rational activity to insure that he behaves consciously in terms of the nature of the object, i.e., that he is obedient to the living Christ.

It is here, of course, that the Christian doctrine of sin enters in, for sin is self-will, the attempt of reason to behave in terms of itself and its own norms instead of behaving in terms of the love of Christ. It is understandable that the autonomous reason should here be "offended" at the Cross, and that the preaching of the Cross should be "foolishness" to him.

If that is the real reason why Professor Blanshard calls Karl Barth's view of reason anti-rationalism, then it is clear that the real issue does not lie between Blanshard and Barth, but between Blanshard and the Christian Gospel. But even apart from this offence at the Cross which makes foolish the wisdom of this world, as St. Paul puts it, surely it would be a highly unscientific and irrational way for reason to behave if when directed to know the living God it refused to answer appropriately to His Self-revelation, but insisted instead that God must conform to the categories that reason had acquired elsewhere in "commonsense and science."—I am etc. Thomas F. Torrance

Blanshard—letter dated April 20, 1952. Published in *The Scotsman*, April 22, page 6.

Theology of Karl Barth
University of St. Andrews
April 20, 1952

Sir,—Professor Torrance's courteous letter of April 19 suggests that the issue between us over the "theology of crisis" is a very complex one. It seems to me quite simple.

The question is whether Brunner and Barth are to be called anti-rationalists. I hold that they are, on the ground that both have over and over again, and in the most explicit terms, denied that the standards of natural reason, the reason used by scientists and philosophers, are valid for the knowledge of God. Professor Torrance agrees that they deny this, but thinks this insufficient to justify the name of anti-rationalist. They really believe in reason, he says, if only we take "reason" broadly enough. What is the broader meaning he proposes? It is conformity to the object. Since Barth and Brunner believe that the mind can in some sense conform to God, they may be said to believe in a rational knowledge of Him.

Now with all respect to an able theologian, I think this is juggling with words. That Brunner and Barth do believe in such conformity I agree. But whether it should be called rational or not depends on the nature of the object conformed to. If that object requires that, to conform to it, we must accept both sides of a contradiction, to call such conformity "rational knowledge" seems to me perverse. And yet that is precisely what conformity does require by those authors' explicit admission. Brunner says that at some points the teaching he accepts, "regarded purely from the theological and intellectual point of view, is an irreconcilable contradiction." And Barth insists that our thinking "cannot possibly coincide with the truth of God." Now to describe as "rational" a kind of knowledge that to our natural reason is not only unintelligible but self-contradictory, is to empty the word of all its normal meaning. The reason whose competence Barth and Brunner are here denying is not reason in some technical sense, the reason, for example, of certain schools of philosophy; it is the reason every man does and must use if he is to think coherently at all.

Furthermore, if mere conformity to an object is enough to make our response to it rational, we should have to rewrite the theory of knowledge. We should have to include as rational knowledge the ineffable rapport of the mystic, the Buddhists's absorption in Nirvana, the musician's response to an aria, and, I suppose, the child's response to a command. Even Schopenhauer's irrationalism, since it provided for an adjustment to the irrational Will would, so far, be a form of rationalism. This is stretching a meaning beyond the breaking point.

And what is to be gained by so stretching it? You will never convince the philosopher by these verbal conjurings that Barth and Brunner really believe in reason as he does and you are likely to lose the support of others. The new theology has made its way largely because of its boldness in repudiating reason openly. Instead of trying to meet philosophy and science on their own grounds, as liberal theology did, it has sought to turn the tables on them by rejecting the authority of their rational standards in the field of religion. This was a courageous move which, whether sound or not, did give some hope of keeping the rationalists at bay. But to offer the Barth-Brunner theology to philosophers as a rational account of things is to invite them to swarm down on you like devouring locusts. And Professor Torrance will agree with me that they may be a dreadful pest.—I am &c. Brand Blanshard

Torrance—letter dated April 22, 1952. Published in *The Scotsman*, April 23, 1952, page 6.

Theology of Karl Barth
New College, University of Edinburgh
April 22, 1952

Sir.—It is increasingly clear from Professor Blanshard's good-natured replies to my criticisms that the issue between us is not a simple one, as he maintains, but involves the whole philosophical debate of modern times, particularly since Wilhelm Dilthey, about the relation between knowing and being, thinking and acting, logic and history.

Professor Blanshard still maintains apparently the old idealist view of a natural reason which exists independently of the objectively given world and which bears within itself the condition of understanding the truth (and naïvely assumes that every other philosopher agrees with him!), but this is the very view which has been subjected to such devastating criticism by modern metaphysics and science (as well as by theologians like Barth and Brunner) on the ground that it fails utterly to meet critical metaphysics and science on their own grounds.

The very fact that my criticisms appear to him only like a "juggling with words" shows that Professor Blanshard sits so securely in his idealist parlour that real argument with him is hardly possible, except on his own idealist presuppositions. Otherwise one can only call in question his whole philosophy. That, of course, is not possible to do here, even if it be in the columns of a daily newspaper of the dignity and culture of *The Scotsman*, but there are several points that require further clarification.

Long ago, in Edinburgh University, David Hume, in his "Dialogues Concerning Natural Religion," taught us to observe the distinction between ectypal and archetypal analogy when he protested against projecting into theology the ectypal analogies drawn from the world of nature as though they were archetypal. That is precisely the protest that Karl Barth has raised in the whole field of natural theology. For him the objective revelation of God in the historical Christ is archetypal and governs all our theological analogies, though ectypal analogies may be drawn from the world of nature to articulate faith but not to construct it.

A volume of Hume's "Dialogues" was first thrust into my hands when I was a student by Professor Norman Kemp Smith with the remark that it would destroy a lot of bad theology! If only David Hume could be resurrected and brought back as a Gifford Lecturer!

Further, what does Professor Blanshard mean by "mere conformity to an object"? In his discussion of Anselm's "faith seeking to understand the Truth," Karl Barth points out that the rationality of faith involves a three-fold ratio, in the rational experience of faith, in the rational conformity of faith to its object, and in the ratio of the Truth itself which is fundamental. That is the view which Barth took over from Anselm and it needs no commentary to bring out the radical misinterpretation of Barth's teaching here shown by Professor Blanshard's letters.

The great difficulty about theological knowledge is its bi-polar character: that knowledge of God must be expressed in terms of what it is not. That bi-polar character is nowhere more evident than in the Christian doctrine of the Incarnation, and of the knowledge of God not as He is in Himself but in the form of Man, in Jesus Christ who is both God and Man. It was because they were anxious to face that fact honestly (to behave consciously in terms of the nature of the object!) that Barth and Brunner became dialectical theologians.

That did not mean that "they accepted both sides of a contradiction," as Professor Blanshard mistakenly assumes, but that they recognised the importance and depth of paradox in the human expression of the truth and that they were prepared to say "yes" and "no" at crucial points of an issue where a scholastic distinction would falsify the truth and where a logical synthesis would only force an abortive unity against the facts. As theologians neither was content to remain "dialectical," and it is many years now since that stage was left behind. Brunner moved back in a scholastic direction in the drawing of distinctions, but for Barth progress has been different. His massive mind has refused to allow the distinctions of expression to have the same depth, and depth in being, that they are allowed with Brunner, for they do not correspond to distinctions in reality—e.g., the distinction between revelation in creation and revelation through the Word. Accordingly Karl Barth has sought to evolve a new method of theological exposition in which, while seeking out in Anselmian fashion the full rationality of faith in obedience to the Truth, he tries to formulate and communicate it as a whole. That is why the "Kirchliche Dogmatik" has become so enormous in bulk.

Throughout all this rational theological activity Barth is acutely aware of what Professor Dorothy Emmet has called the "analogical relation to the Transcendent"—the fact that the nature of God is such that He always transcends the concepts and analogies in terms of which we seek to articulate our faith in Him. That is what Anselm called *humilis sapientia*, which he opposed to the *insipiens superbia* of the reason which has never learned to wonder.—I am &c. Thomas F. Torrance

Blanshard—letter dated April 22, 1952. Published in *The Scotsman*, April 30, page 6.

Theology of Crisis
University of St. Andrews, April 28, 1952

Sir,—In several long letters published in your columns, Professor Torrance has taken me to task for calling the theologians Brunner and Barth irrationalists. I offered in reply a series of passages from their own writings in which it was maintained: (1) that our natural reason does and must break down when it seeks a knowledge of God, and (2) that God is so different from the world that His nature is bound to present itself to our reason as "foolishness" and even self-contradiction. To my mind these statements were conclusive. For what could irrationalism mean if not that the real is, to our reason, unintelligible and incoherent? And yet Professor Torrance holds that "Barth stands out in Europe as the great protagonist *against* irrationalism."

What is his ground for this view? This: that if we redefine reason to mean conformity with an object, we can make Barth out to be a kind of rationalist, even if such conformity means the abandonment of the laws and standards of natural reason. To this my answer is that such conformity is merely meaningless: it is not reason, but the suicide of reason. A kind of knowledge which soars so high as to have left mere logic behind has simply evaporated as knowledge.

Professor Torrance tries to convey the idea of what such knowledge might be by references to "archetypal and ectypal analogies," "three-fold ratios," and the distinction between *humilis sapientia* and *insipiens superbia* which suggest that he is trying to cross from reason to non-rational knowledge by a bridge of degrees. But listen to Brunner himself on all this (I take Brunner rather that Barth because he puts the position far more clearly): revelation, he says, is "what no man can know, what is in no kind of continuity with our human ideas, no, not even with the best and highest we possess;" it is "the end of all objectivity … or, rationalism;" it is "something which is distinguished not gradually or quantitatively, but qualitatively, from anything which man can know …" ("The Word and the World." 45, 75, 17.) Could there be a flatter denial of the interpretation Professor Torrance is offering for the theology of crisis?

When I suggest that the issue is simple and clean-cut, he replies that it "involves the whole philosophical debate of modern times," and invokes a series of impressive names running from St. Anselm's day to our own. I should be appalled at the prospect of embroiling myself with this galaxy of saints and sages. And surely it is un-necessary. My argument is one that any reader of this journal can understand and judge, whether he has ever heard of St. Anselm or not. It is this: Whoever says that reality does and must flout our reason is an irrationalist; Barth and Brunner plainly say this; therefore they are irrationalists.

Professor Torrance thinks it dogmatic to hold that the real must conform to the standards of our reason; he suggests that if I say this, it is because I am an idealist, and everyone knows that idealism is dated; Now he is much surer that I am an idealist than I am; it is a name I never claim for myself, however much I owe to this great school. And if he is suggesting that the rationality of the real, in the sense of its self-consistency, is a doctrine peculiar to Idealists, I am nonplussed again; for the doctrine is held as firmly by the arch-enemy of idealism, [G. E.] Moore, as it was by Bradley himself; indeed it is held by all philosophic schools except that of skepticism.

This is significant. It suggests where Barth and Brunner really stand. Their theology, like that of Newman and Pascal, is built on despair of human reason. They hope by renouncing reason to save religion. It is a bad exchange. If you do not accept both, you will end with neither.—I am &c. Brand Blanshard

[This correspondence is closed.—Ed.] ■

Faculty Publications 2007

Diogenes Allen

Philosophy for Understanding Theology, 2nd ed. With Eric Springsted. Louisville: Westminster John Knox, 2007.

Shane Berg

"An Elite Group Within the *Yahad*: Revisiting 1QS 8–9." In *Qumran Studies: New Approaches, New Questions,* B. A. Strawn and M. T. Davis, editors. Grand Rapids: Eerdmans, 2007. Pp. 161–77.

C. Clifton Black

Anatomy of the New Testament: A Guide to Its Structure and Meaning, 6th rev. ed. With Robert A. Spivey and D. Moody Smith. Upper Saddle River: Pearson Prentice Hall, 2007.

"Does Suffering Possess Educational Value in Mark's Gospel?" In *Character Ethics and the New Testament: Moral Dimensions of Scripture,* Robert L. Brawley, editor. Louisville: Westminster John Knox, 2007. Pp. 3–17.

"Piper, Otto Alfred Wilhelm (1891–1982)." In *Dictionary of Major Biblical Interpreters,* Donald K. McKim, editor. Downers Grove: IVP Academic/ InterVarsity, 2007. Pp. 835–40.

"In Memoriam: Paul S. Minear." *Horizons in Biblical Theology* 29 (2007): 57–60.

The Catholic Biblical Quarterly, Associate Editor

Donald Capps

Losers, Loners, and Rebels: The Spiritual Struggles of Boys. With Robert C. Dykstra and Allen Hugh Cole Jr. Louisville: Westminster John Knox, 2007.

"Did King James Have Homosexual Tendencies?" With Nathan Steven Carlin. In *Text and Community: Essays in Memory of Bruce M. Metzger,* vol. 2, New Testament Monographs 20, J. Harold Ellens, editor. Sheffield, England: Sheffield Phoenix, 2007. Pp. 201–43.

DOI: 10.3754/1937–8386.2008.29.1.14

"Preface." In *Special Visions: Poems by and for Pastoral Caregivers*, Orlo C. Strunk Jr., editor. New York: iUniverse, 2007. Pp. xi–xii.

"Augustine's *Confessions*: Self-reproach and the Melancholy Self." *Pastoral Psychology* 55 (2007): 571–91.

"Augustine's *Confessions*: The Story of a Divided Self and the Process of Its Unification." *Pastoral Psychology* 55 (2007): 551–69.

"The Homosexual Tendencies of King James: Should This Matter to Bible Readers Today?" With Nathan Steven Carlin. *Pastoral Psychology* 55 (2007): 667–99.

"Humor and the Rebellious Spirit of the Early Adolescent Boy." *Pastoral Psychology* 55 (2007): 411–30.

"The Making of the Reliably Religious Boy." *Pastoral Psychology* 55 (2007): 253–70.

"Mental Illness Publications in Major Pastoral Care Journals from 1950 to 2003." With Nathan Steven Carlin. *Pastoral Psychology* 55 (2007): 593–617.

"Mother, Melancholia, and Art in Erik H. Erikson's *Toys and Reasons*." *Journal of Religion and Health* 46 (2007): 369–83.

"Mother, Melancholia, and Play in Erik H. Erikson's *Childhood and Society*." *Journal of Religion and Health* 46 (2007): 591–606.

"Shame and the Solitary Way." *Pastoral Psychology* 56 (2007): 3–8.

James H. Charlesworth

"Abraham's Children: Is There a Future for Jews, Christians, and Muslims?" In *From Biblical Criticism to Biblical Faith: Essay in Honor of Lee Martin McDonald,* W. H. Brackney and C. A. Evans, editors. Macon: Mercer University Press, 2007. Pp. 315–40.

"Can We Discern the Composition Date of the Parables of Enoch?" In *Enoch and the Messiah Son of Man: Revisiting the Book of Parables*, G. Boccaccini et al., editors. Grand Rapids: Eerdmans, 2007. Pp. 450–68.

"'God Made Him Powerful in the Holy Spirit': Psalms of Solomon 17.37." In *The Psalms of Solomon: A Critical Edition of the Greek Text,* Jewish and Christian Texts in Contexts and Related Studies, vol. 1, by Robert B. Wright. New York: T&T Clark, 2007. Pp. vii–viii.

"Introducing David Flusser's Jesus." In *The Sage from Galilee: Rediscovering Jesus' Genius*, by David Flusser with R. Steven Notley. Grand Rapids: Eerdmans, 2007. Pp. xiv–xvi.

"The Naming of the Son of Man, the Light, the Son of God: How the *Parables of Enoch* May Have Influenced the *Odes of Solomon*." In "*I Sowed Fruits into Hearts*" *(Odes Sol. 17:13)*: Festschrift for Professor Michael Lattke, Early Christian Studies 12, P. Allen, M. Franzmann, and R. Strelan, editors. Strathfield, NSW: St. Pauls Publication & Centre for Early Christian Studies. Pp. 31–43.

"Return to the Sources in Twenty-first-century Methodist Ecclesiology: John Wesley's Ecclesiology in the Light of New Insights into the New Testament and Its Environment." In *Orthodox and Wesleyan Ecclesiology*, S. T. Kimbrough Jr., editor. Crestwood: St. Vladimir's Seminary Press, 2007. Pp. 65–85.

"The Rotas-Sator Square." In *Text and Community: Essay in Memory of Bruce M. Metzger*, vol. 1, New Testament Monographs 19, J. Harold Ellens, editor. Sheffield, England: Sheffield Phoenix, 2007. Pp. 151–67.

"Bruce Manning Metzger (1914–2007)." *Henoch* 29:2 (2007): 424.

"Dead Sea Scrolls: How They Changed My Life." *Biblical Archaeology Review* (September/October 2007): 60–63.

"Memorial Minute: Bruce Manning Metzger, February 9, 1914, to February 13, 2007." *Princeton Seminary Bulletin* 28:1 (2007): 99–107.

Review of *Emanual: Studies in Hebrew Bible, Septuagint, and Dead Sea Scrolls in Honor of Emanuel Tov*. Supplements to Vetus Testamentum 94, S. M. Paul, R. A. Kraft, L. H. Schiffman, and W. W. Fields, with E. Ben-David, editors. *Princeton Seminary Bulletin* 28:2 (2007): 231–33.

Review of *La Fête de l'Envoyé: La Section Johannique de la fête des Tentes (Jean 7, 1–10, 21) et la christologi,* Études Bibliques, n.s. No. 49, by Luc Devillers. *Princeton Seminary Bulletin* 28:2 (2007): 226–28.

Review of *The Messiah in the Old and New Testaments*, Stanley E. Porter, editor. *Princeton Seminary Bulletin* 28:2 (2007): 228–31.

Review of *Scribal Practices and Approaches Reflected in the Texts Found in the Judean Desert,* by E. Tov. *Catholic Biblical Quarterly* 69 (2007): 134–37.

Stephen D. Crocco

Princeton Seminary Bulletin, Editor.

Kenda Creasy Dean

Youth, Religion and Globalization: New Research in Practical Theology, International Practical Theology, vol. 3, Richard R. Osmer and Kenda Creasy Dean, editors. Zurich: LIT Verlag, 2006/7.

"The Ambiguities of 'Growing up Global': Sowing Hope in an Ambivalent Age," with Tony Jones; and "God Versus Glitz: Globalization, Youth and the Church in the United States." In *Youth, Religion and Globalization: New Research in Practical Theology,* International Practical Theology, vol. 3, Richard R. Osmer and Kenda Creasy Dean, editors. Zurich: LIT Verlag, 2006/7. Pp. 251–72; 87–128.

"Preface," with Ron Foster. In *The God-Hungry Imagination: The Art of Storytelling for Postmodern Youth Ministry,* by Sarah Arthur. Nashville: Upper Room, 2007. Pp. 11–13.

"Transformational Youth Ministry: A Roundtable Discussion." *Network Magazine* (Fall 2007): n.p.
Contributor to *Means of Grace in the Wesleyan Tradition*, DVD, produced by Mark V. Purushotham. Nashville: Discipleship Resources, 2007.
Review of *Branded: Adolescents Converting from Consumer Faith,* by K. Turpin, *Theology Today* 64 (Fall 2007): 403–6.
Theology and Youth Ministry Book Series (Abingdon Press and the Princeton Theological Seminary Institute for Youth Ministry), General Editor

F. W. Dobbs-Allsopp

"Hymns, OT." In *The New Interpreter's Dictionary of the Bible,* vol. 2: D-H, Katherine Doob Sakenfeld, editor. Nashville: Abingdon, 2007.
"(More) Thoughts on Performatives." *Zeitschrift fŸr AlthebrŠistik* 17–20 (2004–7): 36–81.

Robert C. Dykstra

Losers, Loners, and Rebels: The Spiritual Struggles of Boys. With Allan Hugh Cole Jr. and Donald Capps. Louisville: Westminster John Knox, 2007.

Abigail Rian Evans

"Dying Well." In *Health, Christian Reflection: A Series in Faith and Ethics*, vol. 23. Waco: The Center for Christian Ethics at Baylor University, 2007. Pp. 35–43.
Endorsement of *The Toxic Congregation,* by G. Lloyd Rediger. Nashville: Abingdon, 2007. Inside cover.

Beverly Roberts Gaventa

Our Mother Saint Paul. Louisville: Westminster John Knox, 2007.
"Interpreting the Death of Jesus Apocalyptically: Reconsidering Romans 8:32." In *Jesus and Paul Reconnected: Fresh Pathways into an Old Debate,* Todd Still, editor. Grand Rapids: Eerdmans, 2007. Pp. 125–45.
"To Glorify God and Enjoy God Forever: A Place for Joy in Reformed Readings of Scripture." In *Reformed Theology: Identity and Ecumenicity II: Biblical Interpretation in the Reformed Tradition,* Michael Welker and Wallace M. Alston Jr., editors. Grand Rapids: Eerdmans, 2007. Pp. 107–15.
"Take and Read: New Testament." *Christian Century* 127 (2007): 34–35.

Gordon Graham

The Re-Enchantment of the World: Art versus Religion. Oxford and New York: Oxford University Press, 2007.

"Music and Electro-sonic Art." In *Philosophers on Music: Experience, Meaning, and Work,* Kathleen Stock, editor. Oxford and New York: Oxford University Press, 2007. Pp. 209–25.

"Sin and Salvation." In *Routledge Companion to the Philosophy of Religion,* Paul Copan and Chad Meister, editors. London and New York: Routledge, 2007.

"The Ambition of Scottish Philosophy." *The Monist* 90:2 (April 2007): 154–69.

Journal of Scottish Philosophy Volume 5, Editor

Darrell Guder

Exhibition of the Kingdom of Heaven to the World. Louisville: Witherspoon Press, 2007.

Mission i et pluralisk samfund—hvorfor og hvordan? Frederiksberg: Folkekirkens Mission, 2007.

"The Challenge of Evangelization in America: Theological Ambiguities." In *Antioch Agenda: Essays on the Restorative Church in Honor of Orlando E. Costas,* Daniel Jeyaraj et al., editors. New Delhi: Indian Society for the Promotion of Christian Knowledge, 2007. Pp. 163–75.

"The *Missio Dei*: A Mission Theology after Christendom." In *News of Boundless Riches: Interrogating, Comparing, and Reconstructing Mission in a Global Era,* vol. 1, Max L. Stackhouse and Lalsangkima Pachuau, editors. Delhi: Indian Society for Promoting Christian Knowledge (ISPCK), 2007. Pp. 3–25.

"Missional Existence Today," by Michael Welker, translated by Darrell L. Guder. In *News of Boundless Riches: Interrogating, Comparing, and Reconstructing Mission in a Global Era,* vol. 1, Max L. Stackhouse and Lalsangkima Pachuau, editors. Delhi: Indian Society for Promoting Christian Knowledge (ISPCK), 2007. Pp. 45–59.

"Walking Worthily: Missional Leadership After Christendom." *Princeton Seminary Bulletin* 28:3 (2007): 251–91.

Review of *Evangelicals, Ecumenicals, and Anabaptist Missiologies in Conversation,* James R. Krabill, Walter Savatsky, and Charles E. Van Enden, editors. *Mission Focus: Annual Review* 14 (2007): 231–32.

Scott H. Hendrix

"Martin Luther, Reformer." In *Cambridge History of Christianity: Reform and Expansion 1500–1660,* vol. 6, R. Po-chia Hsia, editor. Cambridge, England, and New York: Cambridge University Press, 2007. Pp. 3–19.

Review of *Als Frieden m˘glich war: 450 Jahre Augsburger Religionsfrieden,* Carl A. Hoffmann, Markus Johanns, Annette Kranz, Christof Trepesch, and Oliver Zeidler, editors. *Lutheran Quarterly* 21:4 (2007): 485–86.

Review of *Luther Handbuch,* Albrecht Beutel, editor. *Lutherjahrbuch* 74 (2007): 199–201.

Deborah van Deusen Hunsinger

"Respecting Ourselves as Christian Therapists." *Edification: Journal of the Society for Christian Psychology* 1:2 (2007): 29–31.

Jeremy M. Hutton

"Archer," "Azekah," and "Cuneiform;" and "Hebrew Language," with Aaron D. Rubin. In *The New Interpreter's Dictionary of the Bible*, vol. 1, Katharine Doob Sakenfeld, editor. Nashville: Abingdon, 2007. Pp. 248; 361; 810; and 768–78.

"Isaiah 51:9–11 and the Rhetorical Appropriation and Subversion of Hostile Theologies." *Journal of Biblical Literature* 126 (2007): 271–303.

Review of *Ancient Place Names in the Holy Land*, by Yoel Elitzur. *Maarav* 14 (2007): 77–97.

William Stacy Johnson

"The 'Reality' of Faith: Critical Remarks on Section 63 of *Die Kirchliche Dogmatik*. In *The Reality of Faith in Theology: Studies on Karl Barth, Princeton-Kampen Consultation 2005,* Bruce McCormack and Gerrit Neven, editors. Bern: Peter Lang, 2007. Pp. 205–20.

"Empire and Order: The Gospel and Same-Gender Relationships." *Biblical Theology Bulletin* 37:4 (Winter 2007): 161–73.

"King's Refusal and Ours." In *Perspectives: An Online Publication of the Office of the General Assembly, Presbyterian Church (USA)* (February 2007), http://www.pcusa.org/oga/perspectives/feb07/kings-refusal.pdf (accessed August 12, 2008).

Review of *God vs. the Gavel: Religion and the Rule of Law*, by Marci A. Hamilton. *Journal of Law and Religion* 22:1 (2006–07): 287–90.

James F. Kay

Preaching and Theology. St. Louis: Chalice, 2007.

"Belles Lettres." *Theology Today* 64 (2007): 1–4.

Theology Today, Editor

Jacqueline Lapsley

Character Ethics and the Old Testament: Moral Dimensions of Scripture, Jacqueline Lapsley and M. Daniel Carroll R., editors. Louisville: Westminster John Knox, 2007.

"Alternative Worlds: Reading the Bible as Scripture." In *Engaging Biblical Authority: Perspectives on the Bible as Scripture,* William P. Brown, editor. Louisville: Westminster John Knox, 2007. Pp. 90–97.

"Ezekiel through the Spectacles of Faith." In *Reformed Theology: Identity and Ecumenicity II: Biblical Interpretation in the Reformed Tradition,* Michael Welker and Wallace M. Alston Jr., editors. Grand Rapids: Eerdmans, 2007. Pp. 146–56.

"A Feeling for God: Emotions and Moral Formation in Ezekiel." In *Character Ethics and the Old Testament: Appropriating Scripture for Moral Life,* Jacqueline E. Lapsley and M. Daniel Carroll R., editors. Louisville: Westminster John Knox, 2007.

Review of *Ezekiel,* by Margaret S. Odell. *Theology Today* 63:4 (January 2007): 504–9.

James N. Lapsley

"Charles Ives and the Reformed Tradition: A Musical Pilgrimage." *Theology Today* 64:3 (2007): 305–21.

Elsie A. McKee

"The Character and Significance of John Calvin's Teaching on Social and Economic Issues." In *John Calvin Rediscovered: The Impact of His Social and Economic Thought, Princeton Theological Seminary Studies in Reformed Theology and History,* Edouard Dommen and James Bratt, editors. Louisville: Westminster John Knox, 2007. Pp. 3–24.

"The Emergence of Lay Theologies." In *Reformation Christianity: A People's History of Christianity* vol. 5, Peter Matheson, editor. Minneapolis: Fortress, 2007. Pp. 212–31.

"A Lay Voice in Sixteenth-Century 'Ecumenics': Katharina Schütz Zell in Dialogue with Johannes Brenz, Conrad Pellican, and Caspar Schwenckfeld." In *Adaptations of Calvinism in Reformation Europe: Essays in Honour of Brian G. Armstrong,* Mack P. Holt, editor. Aldershot, England: Ashgate, 2007. Pp. 81–110.

"Teaching Katharina Schütz Zell (1498–1562)." In *Teaching Other Voices: Women and Religion in Early Modern Europe,* Margaret King and Albert Rabil, editors. Chicago: University of Chicago Press, 2007. Pp. 137–53.

Princeton Theological Seminary Studies in Reformed Theology and History, Series Editor

Patrick D. Miller

"Old Testament Exegesis in the Reformed Perspective: The Case of the Commandments." In *Reformed Theology: Identity and Ecumenicity II: Biblical*

Interpretation in the Reformed Tradition, Michael Welker and Wallace M. Alston Jr., editors. Grand Rapids: Eerdmans, 2007. Pp. 217–29.

"'Deinem Namen die Ehre' Die Psalmen und die Theologie des Alten Testaments." *Evangelische Theologie* 67 (2007): 32–42.

Dennis Olson

"Between Humility and Authority: The Interplay of the Judge-Prophet Laws (Deut. 16:18–17:13) and the Judge-Prophet Narratives of Moses." In *Character Ethics and the Old Testament: Appropriating Scripture for Moral Life,* Jacqueline Lapsley and M. Daniel Carroll R., editors. Louisville: Westminster John Knox, 2007. Pp. 51–61.

"Balaam," "Census," "Dathan," "Enrollment," and "Moses." In *The New Interpreter's Dictionary of the Bible,* Katharine Doob Sakenfeld, editor. Nashville: Abingdon, 2006–2008.

Richard Osmer

Youth, Religion and Globalization: New Research in Practical Theology, International Practical Theology, vol. 3, Richard R. Osmer and Kenda Creasy Dean, editors. Zurich: LIT Verlag GmbH & Co., 2006/7.

Luke A. Powery

"Where the Spirit May Be Blowing: The Future of African American Homiletics." *Homiletix E-Forum: An Electronic Journal of the Academy of Homiletics* (September 2007), http://info.wlu.ca/wwwsem/ah/pdfvisitors/homiletixfall2007/homiletix_fall2007_Powery.htm (accessed September 2, 2008).

"Death Threat." *Princeton Seminary Bulletin* 28:3 (2007): 244–50.

Review of *Pastoral Ministry according to Paul: A Biblical Vision,* by James W. Thompson. *Toronto Journal of Theology* 23:2 (2007): 231–33.

Luis N. Rivera-Pagán

God, in Your Grace. ... : Official Report of the Ninth Assembly of the World Council of Churches. Luis N. Rivera-Pagán, editor. Geneva: WCC Publications, 2007.

"Eine Polyzentrische Weltchristenheit – Einführung in Verlauf und Thematik der Vollversammlung." In *In deiner Gnade, Gott, verwandle die Welt. Porto Alegre 2006, Neunte Vollversammlung des Ökumenischen Rates der Kirchen,* Klaus Wilkens, editor. Frankfurt am Main: Verlag Otto Lembeck, 2007. Pp. 13–53.

"Entre elegías y herejías." In *Bajar de la Cruz a los Pobres: Cristología de la Liberación,* José María Vigil, editor. Comisión Teológica Internacional de la

Asociación Ecuménica de Teólogos/as del Tercer Mundo. México: Ediciones Dabar, 2007. Pp. 199–203. Translated as "Entre elegias e heresias." In *Descer da cruz os pobres: Cristologia da Libertaçao*, José María Vigil, editor. Saõ Paulo: Paulinas, 2007. Pp. 244–49. Translated as "Tra elegie ed eresie." In *Deporre i Poveri dalla Croce: Cristologia Della Liberazione*, José María Vigil, editor. Commissione Teologica Internazionale della Associazione Ecumenica di Teologi/ghe del Terzo Mondo. Roma: ADISTA, 2007. Pp. 207–11. Translated as "Between Elegies and Heresies." In *Getting the Poor Down from the Cross: Christology of Liberation*. International Theological Commission of the Ecumenical Association of Third World Theologians, 2007. Pp. 215–19.

"Pastoral Theology in a Post-colonial Context: Some Observations from the Caribbean." *Perspectivas* (Hispanic Theological Initiative, Princeton) (Fall 2007): 11–37.

"Laberintos y desencuentros de la fragmentada identidad cultural mexicana." *Pasos* 131 (Departamento Ecuménico de Investigaciones, San José, Costa Rica), segunda época (mayo–junio 2007): 1–9; *Signos de Vida* (Consejo Latinoamericano de Iglesias, Quito, Ecuador) 44 (junio de 2007): 20–27.

Paul Rorem

"Dionysius the Areopagite." In *The History of Christianity,* by Jonathan Hill. Oxford: Lion, 2007. P. 103.

Lutheran Quarterly and *Lutheran Quarterly Books,* Editor

Katherine Doob Sakenfeld

The New Interpreter's Dictionary of the Bible, vol. 2: D–H and vol. 3: I–Ma, Katherine Doob Sakenfeld, editor. Nashville: Abingdon, 2007.

"Postcolonial Perspectives on Premonarchic Women." In *To Break Every Yoke: Essays in Honor of Marvin L. Chaney*, Robert B. Coote and Norman K. Gottwald, editors. Sheffield: Sheffield Phoenix, 2007. Pp. 188–99.

Review of *Hagar, Sarah, and Their Children: Jewish, Christian, and Muslim Perspectives,* Phyllis Trible and Letty M. Russell, editors. *Theology Today* 63:4 (2007): 502–4.

Max L. Stackhouse

Globalization and Grace: God and Globalization, vol. 4, with forward by Justo González. New York: Continuum International, 2007.

News of Boundless Riches: Interrogating, Comparing, and Reconstructing Mission in a Global Era, 2 vols., with introduction by Max L. Stackhouse. Max L. Stackhouse and Lalsangkima Pachuau, editors. Delhi: ISPCK with UTC & CTI, 2007.

What is Public Theology?: Selected Essays with Responses and Comments by Korean Scholars (sponsored by the New Institute for Christian Ethics). Sang Hoon Lee et al., editors and translators. Seoul: Sunhaksa, 2007.

"Civil Religion, Political Theology, and Public Theology." In *The Christian in Public: Aims, Methodologies, and Issues in Public Theology*: Beyers Naudé Centre Series on Public Theology, vol. 3, L. Hansen, editor. (Revised and expanded from 2004 version). Stellenbosch: Sun, 2007. Pp. 79–96.

"Eschatology and Ethics." In *The Oxford Handbook of Eschatology,* Jerry L. Walls, editor. New York: Oxford University Press, 2007. Pp. 548–62.

"Globalization and Christian Ethics." In *The Globalization of Ethics: Religious and Secular Perspectives,* William M. Sullivan and Will Kymlicka, editors. New York: Cambridge University Press, 2007. Pp. 53–74.

"Globalization and Missions" and "Human Rights and Missions." In *The Encyclopedia of Missions and Missionaries*. New York: Routledge On Line and E-Books, 2007.

"A Preface." In *Public Theology and Globalization: A Study in Max L. Stackhouse's Christian Ethics,* by Zhibin Xie (in Chinese). Beijing: CIP, 2007. Pp. 11–14.

"The Sources of Human Rights Ideas: A Christian Perspective." In *Christianity and Human Rights: Influences & Issues,* Frances Adeney and Arvind Sharma, editors. Albany: State University of New York Press, 2007. Pp. 41–54.

"The Tasks of Theological Ethics." In *Interweaving Methodology and Praxis: Exploring Disciplinary Options in Today's World,* I. J. Mohan Razu and John Indukuri, editors. Bangalore: BTESSC/SATRI, 2007. Pp. 47–62.

"The Christian Ethic of Love: A Dialogical Response." In "Two Responses to 'On a Paradox in Christian Love' by Professor Liu," *The Journal of Religious Ethics* 35:4 (December, 2007): 700–11.

"On 'Public Theology': An Interview." *Ministry and Theology*, vol. 11 (November 2007) (in Korean): 42–51.

"Reflections on How and Why We Go Public." *International Journal of Public Theology* 1:3–4 (2007): 421–30.

"Religion, Public Life and Globalization." *Social Sciences Abroad* (Beijing, Academy of Social Science) 2nd issue (2007): 73–77.

"Signs of Hope for the World of Business." *Comment Magazine* (Canada), (October 12, 2007), http://www.wrf.ca/comment/authors2.cfm?ID=138 (accessed September 2, 2008).

"Social Graces: Christianity and Globalization." *Review of Faith & International Affairs,* 5:3 (Fall 2007): 41–49.

"A Tribute to CISRS." *Religion and Society* (Bangalore, India) 52:2 (2007): 35–42.

Iain Torrance

The Oxford Handbook of Systematic Theology, Iain Torrance, John Webster, and Kathryn Tanner, editors. New York: Oxford University Press, 2007.

"A Long Tradition of Engagement: A Tribute to Trinity College, Glasgow, on Its 150th Anniversary." In *The God of Love and Human Dignity: Festschrift for George Newlands,* Paul Middleton, editor. London: T&T Clark/Continuum, 2007. Pp. 5–18.

"Peacemaking and Humanitarian Intervention: The Contribution of the Reformed Tradition to the Morality of Conflict after the Cold War." In *Reformed Theology: Identity and Ecumenicity II: Biblical Interpretation in the Reformed Tradition*, Michael Welker and William M. Alston Jr., editors. Grand Rapids: Eerdmans, 2007. Pp. 419–29.

"The Torture Argument." *The Journal of the Royal Army Chaplains Department*, vol. 46, 2007: 31–35.

Scottish Journal of Theology, Editor (with Bryan Spinks).

J. Wentzel van Huyssteen

Ashgate Science and Religion Series: *Reconstructing a Christian Theology of Nature: Down to Earth,* by Anna Case-Winters. J. Wentzel van Huyssteen and Roger Trigg, series editors. Aldershot: Ashgate, 2007.

"Building Effective Bridges to Culture: God and Redemption in the Work of Richard Wagner." In *The God of Love and Human Dignity: Festschrift for George Newlands,* Paul Middleton, editor. London: T&T Clark/Continuum, 2007. Pp. 85–106.

"A Reply to My Critics: A Response to Six Presentations at the Annual Conference of the Highlands Institute on American Religious and Philosophical Thought (HIARPT) on *Alone in the World? Human Uniqueness in Science and Theology: The Gifford Lectures,* by J. Wentzel van Huyssteen." *American Journal of Theology and Philosophy* 28:3 (2007).

Ross Wagner

"Working Out Salvation: Community and Holiness in Philippians." In *Holiness and Ecclesiology in the New Testament,* Kent E. Brower and Andy Johnson, editors. Grand Rapids: Eerdmans, 2007. Pp. 257–74.

"Identifying 'Updated' Prophecies in OG Isaiah: Isaiah 8:11–16 as a Test Case." *Journal of Biblical Literature* 126 (2007): 251–69.

Resources for Biblical Studies (New Testament), Society of Biblical Literature, Editor